# Life Relaunch Warrior

## Fighting the Unseen Cosmic Battle

Mel and Annie Goebel

An Indie Christian Book

Copyright © 2025 by Mel and Annie Goebel

ISBN (Paperback): 978-1-967120-06-2

ISBN (eBook): 978-1-967120-05-5

All Scripture quotations, unless otherwise indicated, are taken from the Holy Bible, New International Version®, NIV®. Copyright ©1973, 1978, 1984, 2011 by Biblica, Inc.™ Used by permission of Zondervan. All rights reserved worldwide. www.zondervan.com. The "NIV" and "New International Version" are trademarks registered in the United States Patent and Trademark Office by Biblica, Inc.™

Scripture quotations marked (NKJV) are taken from the New King James Version®. Copyright © 1982 by Thomas Nelson. Used by permission. All rights reserved.

Scripture quotations marked (ESV) are from the ESV® Bible (The Holy Bible, English Standard Version®), copyright© 2001 by Crossway Bibles, a publishing ministry of Good News Publishers. Used by permission. All rights reserved.

Scripture quotations marked (NLT) are taken from the Holy Bible, New Living Translation, copyright ©1996, 2004, 2015 by Tyndale House Foundation. Used by permission of Tyndale House Publishers, Carol Stream, Illinois 60188. All rights reserved.

All rights reserved. No part of this book may be reproduced or used in any manner without the prior written permission of the copyright owner, except for the use of brief quotations in a book review. To request permissions, contact info@liferelaunch.org.

Published by Indie Christian Book in Bloomington, Illinois, U.S.A.

www.liferelaunch.org

# Contents

Foreword — v
Introduction — vii

## Part One
## UNDERSTANDING THE BATTLE

1. The Creation of All Things — 3
2. The Unseen Cosmic Battle — 9
3. The Silent Guardian — 17
   *Adam's Absence in Eve's Life*
4. The Origin and Nature of Demons — 29

## Part Two
## THE ENEMY'S TACTICS

5. The Father of Lies — 39
6. Derailing the Kingdom Adventure — 65
7. Subtle Poison — 83
   *Misguided Ideas*

## Part Three
## THE WARRIOR'S EQUIPMENT

8. Warriors Battle in the Light — 97
9. Kingdom Warriors Stand for Truth — 105
10. The Power of Prayer — 133
11. The Warrior's Deepest Secret — 145
    *Presence Before Power*
12. Developing the Kingdom Warrior Mindset — 157
    *The Internal Revolution*
13. Kingdom Warriors — 169
    *Alert to Angelic Encounters*

## Part Four
## THE WARRIOR'S CALL

14. The Awakening . . . . . . . . . . . . . . . . . . . . . . . . . 181
    *Beyond Routine Faith*
15. The Divine Screening . . . . . . . . . . . . . . . . . . . . 193
16. A Call to Kingdom Warriors . . . . . . . . . . . . . . . 207

Epilogue . . . . . . . . . . . . . . . . . . . . . . . . . . . . . . . . 213

APPENDIX A . . . . . . . . . . . . . . . . . . . . . . . . . . . . 215
Study 1 . . . . . . . . . . . . . . . . . . . . . . . . . . . . . . . . . 217
Study 2 . . . . . . . . . . . . . . . . . . . . . . . . . . . . . . . . . 219
Study 3 . . . . . . . . . . . . . . . . . . . . . . . . . . . . . . . . . 221
Study 4 . . . . . . . . . . . . . . . . . . . . . . . . . . . . . . . . . 223
Study 5 . . . . . . . . . . . . . . . . . . . . . . . . . . . . . . . . . 225
Study 6 . . . . . . . . . . . . . . . . . . . . . . . . . . . . . . . . . 227
Study 7 . . . . . . . . . . . . . . . . . . . . . . . . . . . . . . . . . 229
Study 8 . . . . . . . . . . . . . . . . . . . . . . . . . . . . . . . . . 231
Study 9 . . . . . . . . . . . . . . . . . . . . . . . . . . . . . . . . . 233
Study 10 . . . . . . . . . . . . . . . . . . . . . . . . . . . . . . . . 235
Study 11 . . . . . . . . . . . . . . . . . . . . . . . . . . . . . . . . 237
Study 12 . . . . . . . . . . . . . . . . . . . . . . . . . . . . . . . . 239
Study 13 . . . . . . . . . . . . . . . . . . . . . . . . . . . . . . . . 241
Study 14 . . . . . . . . . . . . . . . . . . . . . . . . . . . . . . . . 243
Study 15 . . . . . . . . . . . . . . . . . . . . . . . . . . . . . . . . 245
Study 16 . . . . . . . . . . . . . . . . . . . . . . . . . . . . . . . . 247
APPENDIX B . . . . . . . . . . . . . . . . . . . . . . . . . . . . 249
APPENDIX C . . . . . . . . . . . . . . . . . . . . . . . . . . . . 251
Notes . . . . . . . . . . . . . . . . . . . . . . . . . . . . . . . . . . 289
Bibliography . . . . . . . . . . . . . . . . . . . . . . . . . . . . . 293
About the Authors . . . . . . . . . . . . . . . . . . . . . . . . 295

# Foreword

Some friendships are forged in unlikely places yet stand the test of time. My journey with Mel Goebel began in 1975 within the stark confines of prison walls. I had volunteered to lead a Bible study, never imagining that among those men seeking spiritual guidance would be someone who would become a lifelong brother in Christ.

When I first met Mel, I saw something in his eyes that transcended his circumstances—a genuine hunger for transformation and an authenticity that couldn't be manufactured. Week after week, as we explored Scripture together, I witnessed a remarkable metamorphosis. Mel wasn't just going through the motions; he was encountering Jesus in profound ways that were changing him from the inside out.

After his release, our connection didn't fade as so often happens. Instead, it deepened. For five decades now, our weekly conversations have continued without interruption—a testament to the bond that forms when two people journey together in authentic pursuit of Jesus. When Mel introduced me to Annie, I immediately recognized the same genuine spirit in her. Together, they form a partnership rooted in unshakable faith and genuine love for others.

What distinguishes Mel and Annie is their remarkable absence of pretense. In a world where many present carefully curated versions of themselves, especially in ministry circles, they remain refreshingly real. Their transparency about their own struggles and continued growth makes their message of heart restoration all the more powerful. They don't merely preach transformation—they embody it daily.

*Life Relaunch Warrior: Fighting the Unseen Cosmic Battle* is the culmination of decades spent in the trenches, walking alongside the broken, the addicted, the imprisoned, and the lost. Mel and Annie have taken their own journey of restoration and crafted it into a pathway others can follow toward healing and purpose.

I've had the privilege of watching what God has done through this ministry expand from a simple idea to a movement touching thousands across the nation. What began in small gatherings has multiplied because the fundamental truth at its core resonates with everyone who encounters it: authentic heart change is possible when we create space for Jesus to do His healing work.

The warrior spirit that Mel and Annie bring to their calling inspires everyone around them. They understand that the battle for hearts and minds is real, and they approach it with both strategic wisdom and compassionate grace.

May this book inspire you not only to experience personal restoration but to become a catalyst for revival in your own sphere of influence. The world desperately needs more authentic followers of Jesus who, like Mel and Annie, dedicate themselves fully to reaching those who need hope and a fresh start.

May the Lord bless you and strengthen your faith as you read,
*Dallen Peterson*
Founder, Merry Maids

# Introduction
## The Call to Battle

> For our struggle is not against flesh and blood, but against the rulers, against the authorities, against the powers of this dark world and against the spiritual forces of evil in the heavenly realms.
>
> — Ephesians 6:12

### The Unseen Cosmic Battle: A Reality We Cannot Ignore

There is a battle raging all around us, unseen yet undeniably real. It's a cosmic conflict that transcends the boundaries of time and space, an eternal war fought for the hearts, minds, and souls of humanity. This is no ordinary war—it's a spiritual battle of unimaginable stakes. The outcome of this conflict isn't measured in temporary victories or fleeting losses. It's a battle for your soul and the souls of everyone you love. Whether we acknowledge it or not, every one of us is part of this battle.

Picture the unseen realm for a moment. Imagine a clash of kingdoms—a radiant kingdom of light advancing with the glory of God, opposed by a kingdom of darkness, relentless in its mission to steal, kill, and destroy. On one side stands the Almighty, Creator of the universe, and His heavenly armies, clothed in righteousness and armed with eternal truth. On the other side is Satan, the adversary, and his legion of fallen angels, spreading lies, chaos, and despair. Every moment of your life is contested in this cosmic arena. Every decision, every thought, every word spoken is influenced by forces far greater than we can comprehend.

The Bible brings this reality into sharp focus. "The LORD is a warrior; the LORD is His name" (Exodus 15:3). From the dawn of creation, God has fought for His people, His beloved creation. He stood against the darkness that sought to destroy His plans, waging war on behalf of humanity. This is no distant God, uninvolved and indifferent. This is a God who steps onto the battlefield Himself and is fighting for your love.

And in Revelation 19, we see the ultimate fulfillment of His victory: Jesus Christ, the Warrior King, leading the armies of heaven. He rides a white horse, His robe dipped in blood, His name inscribed as King of Kings and Lord of Lords. With justice and power, He declares final judgment on the forces of evil. The battle belongs to Him, and the victory is assured.

This is the God we serve—a God who doesn't abandon His people to the darkness, but who fights for us with unmatched love and power. And this same God calls us to join Him in the fight as Kingdom Warriors.

## An Invitation to Awaken

This book is your invitation to awaken to that kingdom reality. It's a call to pull back the curtain on the unseen, to step out of unbelief and complacency, and to engage in this unseen cosmic battle as a Kingdom Warrior with courage and kingdom purpose. Far too many of us are sleepwalking through life, unaware of the forces shaping our world and our eternal destiny. Whether you're struggling with faith, stuck in the routines of religion, or longing for deeper meaning, the truth is the same: Jesus has designed you for more.

You weren't created to live in fear, confusion, or mediocrity. You were made to thrive in this unseen cosmic battle, to live with boldness, and to advance God's kingdom on earth. The struggles you face—the doubts that creep into your mind, the wounds that linger in your heart, the temptations that pull at your soul—are not random. They are part of a larger, unseen cosmic conflict that has raged since the beginning of time.

God didn't create you to fight alone. He equips you with His Spirit, His Word, and His presence, giving you everything you need to overcome. But first, you must open your eyes and heart to the spiritual realm.

## Awakening to the Spiritual Realm

*Every Christian is either a missionary or an imposter.*[1]

— Charles Spurgeon

For too long, many of us have lived blind to the spiritual realm. We focus on what we can see, touch, and control, unaware of the forces shaping our thoughts, decisions, and destinies. We explain away struggles as bad luck or coincidence, never pausing to consider that something far greater might be at work. The Bible paints a different picture of reality.

There is an unseen kingdom actively at work, one that exists alongside the physical world we know. God and His angels are advancing His purposes, fighting for redemption, truth, and love. At the same time, Satan and his demons are tirelessly working to deceive, manipulate, and destroy. Every moment, they whisper lies into our minds, planting seeds of doubt, fear, and hopelessness.

Their goal is clear: to separate us from the love and truth of God.

This isn't just a battle happening somewhere "out there" in the world. It's a battle happening in you. It's waged in your thoughts, in your heart, in the choices you make every day. It's a battle for your soul and your eternal destiny. Think about the moments of fear and doubt you've experienced. The lies that tell you you're not enough. The temptations that seem impossible to resist. The shame and guilt that keeps you trapped in the past. These are not just random struggles—they are spiritual attacks. And recognizing this truth changes everything.

When you understand that your life is part of an unseen cosmic battle, your perspective shifts. Your struggles are no longer isolated events. They are part of a larger story—a story where Jesus has already secured the ultimate victory but invites you to take your place in the fight.

## A Call to See Clearly

We know this battle all too well. We've lived it, fought through it, and come out scarred but victorious. And now, we're here to tell you: the unseen realm is real, and the stakes are too high to ignore. The question is, will you choose to see it? Will you open your eyes to the unseen spiritual reality around you and take your place as a warrior in God's kingdom? Or will you remain on the sidelines, blind to the spiritual battle raging for your soul?

## Mel's Story: From Failure to Freedom

Mel's life was a mess from the beginning. He wasn't the kid anyone expected great things from. He was the one who dropped out of school, got mixed up in drugs, and drifted aimlessly, always running from one bad choice to the next. By the time he landed in prison the first time, he wasn't even surprised. The truth was, his entire life had been on a collision course with failure.

When he got out, he planned to get his life in order. Do better. Be a better person. Follow the law and work hard. He was never going back to prison. But because he still believed the lies, he continued to make destructive choices. Before he knew it, he was back to the same lifestyle that had sent him to prison the first time.

And then, he came back.

The second time those iron gates slammed shut behind him, he felt it deeper than before. He wasn't just another inmate returning to the Nebraska State Penitentiary—he was a two-time loser, a dropout from life itself. The other prisoners mocked him as he shuffled past in his shackles. "Welcome back, Goebel! Didn't think we'd see you so soon!" He told himself he didn't care, but the truth was, he felt it: he was a failure. And this time, it wasn't just failure; it was hopelessness.

He slipped back into the routine quickly: lifting weights, running the yard, and figuring out how to smuggle drugs back into circulation. The only way he knew how to survive was to numb himself, and drugs were his escape from the shame that haunted him.

One day, he spotted a new prisoner stepping off the bus. He wasn't like the rest of them. Across the back of his khaki jacket, someone had scrawled in bold black marker: "Smile, Jesus is your friend."

Mel rolled his eyes. "This guy's going to get eaten alive," he thought. But something about it got under his skin. He knew who Jesus was—or at least, he thought he did. Growing up, he'd gone through the motions of religion, but God had never felt real to him. Still, he couldn't shake those words.

## Angel in My Cell

Months passed. Mel was trying to make sense of the Bible after a prisoner named Fred told him, "Jesus is your friend, whether you like Him or not." He'd challenged Mel to open a Bible and see for himself. He started reading, even though he didn't understand it. The other inmates mocked him relentlessly, and one of them even burned his Bible. He wanted to give up. But he couldn't shake the thought that maybe, just maybe, there was something to this Jesus Fred kept talking about.

Then one morning, everything changed.

In the depths of his prison cell, where he was serving time for theft and drugs, heaven reached down to touch Mel on earth. That morning began like any other, until rays of sunlight pierced through the window with an otherworldly brilliance. As he awakened, he became aware of a presence beside him—not threatening, but radiating a power and warmth that defied description.

He froze, unable to move, his heart pounding in his chest. He tried to tell himself he was imagining it, but he couldn't. The light wasn't just around him—it was in him, filling every corner of his soul with a joy and peace he had never known. It was as if every lie he'd ever believed about himself was being burned away.

There was no doubt in his mind: an angel stood in his cell, and the cold concrete floor had become holy ground. The warmth of divine love enveloped him, melting away years of hardness and rebellion. Tears flowed freely as his heart, so long imprisoned by more than just steel bars, finally broke open. There, in the presence of heaven's messenger, he surrendered everything to Jesus—his past, his pain, his future.

In that transformative moment, though he remained within prison walls, Mel's soul found true freedom. What began as a sentence for his crimes became the very place where mercy found him, where divine intervention turned his cage into a sanctuary, and where an angel's visit marked the beginning of a completely new life.

A single, clear message filled his mind, like a banner scrolling across his thoughts: "Today is the day. Today is the day to give your heart to Jesus."

Exploding with emotion, Mel bolted from his bed and ran to the one place he could be alone: a small bathroom with a shower curtain for privacy. He fell to his knees, tears streaming down his face.

And then he prayed. Mel said, "God, if You're real, I need you to take my life and do something with it. I can't do this anymore. And, God, I also need you to move me to a place where I can read my Bible in peace."

## THE TURNING POINT

The angel's presence stayed with Mel as he got up from his knees. He walked back to his cell, straight to the hiding place where he had stashed drugs, and flushed them down the toilet. The old Mel would have clung to those drugs like a lifeline, but in that moment, he didn't need them anymore.

He sat in his cell contemplating all that had happened and wondering if he would notice God moving in his life. And then he heard it: the familiar jingle-jangle of keys as a prison guard came walking down the hall. He was surprised when the guard stopped at his cell. He said, "Prisoner 28138, roll it up! You're getting moved."

What? Could this really be happening?

God heard his prayer! And He'd answered him. He was getting moved. The prison guard, seeing his excitement, said, "What are you so excited about, Goebel? You're just moving across the prison yard; you're not getting released."

Suddenly, a thought came to Mel's mind. "Wow! Asking God for help really works. I should have just asked Him to send me home." How quickly selfishness comes into our mind if we don't guard against it.

That moment changed everything. He walked out of that cell a new man, no longer bound by the lies of the enemy.

Once he was settled in his new, quiet unit, he ran to the chapel, bursting with excitement, and told the chaplain what had happened: "Jesus answered my prayer!"

He told him that for the first time, he understood that God wasn't distant or uninterested. He had been fighting for him all along.

## Annie's Story: From Isolation to Purpose

For Annie, the battle started when she was just a little girl. She was born on the shores of the North Atlantic Sea, which seemed to define her childhood: cold, violent, and isolated.

Annie's Dad was in the Air Force. He did his job well during the week, but on the weekends, he would party. When he partied, he would come home very late at night, usually in one of two ways. Either he came in jolly, pulled out his guitar, and got the kids up to sing songs with him, or he came home angry. More often than not, it was the latter of the two.

Many a night Annie woke up to the sounds of screaming, then saw the red and blue flashing lights. One night her brother came running into the girls' room with their little brother in tow. He slammed the door shut and began pushing the dresser against it. "Get up and help me," he yelled. "Dad is loading his .45 to kill us!"

Then there were Saturday and Sunday mornings to deal with. Dad did not like to be disturbed when sleeping off his hangovers. Unfortunately, five little kids in a crackerbox house make noise. This would infuriate Annie's dad, and he'd come in yelling and swinging his belt.

"You damn kids, keep quiet!"

As the kids grew, they learned to keep quiet on their own.

Annie spent as much time as she could outside. As she explored the land, she dreamed of a safe place to call her own, someone to love, and adventure.

Annie's mom was a Christian and did her best to keep the peace in the house. On Sunday mornings, she got the kids all quietly out of the house to go to church. Church was Annie's safe haven. It was where she learned about Jesus.

Annie believed everything she learned about Jesus. But when she left that church, she felt He didn't come home with her. Instead, because of the turmoil in her home, she started believing lies.

INTRODUCTION

*You're not enough. You're not loved. You'll always be alone.*
Those lies took root in Annie's heart and became her identity.

Being born into a military family definitely had both advantages and disadvantages. On the one hand, Annie lived in faraway lands that most kids only dreamed of and had exciting adventures. On the other hand, friends were hard to keep, and dark family secrets were easy to hide.

Because of her love for adventure, Annie was thrilled when her dad was stationed for two years in the Middle East, in Izmir, Turkey. As young teens, she and her brother would take off and explore the city, the mountains, and the Aegean Sea. It was at this time in her life that she began to believe there was more to life than what she was experiencing in her home. Now, with a broader perspective, she was ready to take charge of her life.

### Running on Empty

When Annie's family returned stateside to their house in Texas and her dad came home drunk wielding his .45 once again, she decided it was time. She escaped through her window to find the life she'd dreamed of.

But she quickly learned that life on the streets for a teenage girl is no fairytale. No prince charming rode in on a white horse to carry her away.

She soon found herself begging for spare change so she could eat, sleeping in alleys or abandoned buildings with other street kids, and even stealing just to survive. Still, it was better than going home. At least she was free. Or so she told herself.

After two years on and off the streets, spending time in jail and juvenile detention, Annie decided she needed a better plan. She turned herself in to the authorities and went home.

That's when she found out she was going to be a teenage mom. Her mom had her accepted into an unwed mothers' home, where she placed her son up for adoption at birth. Shortly thereafter, her dad was discharged from the military. He dumped all his hard liquor down the toilet, and Annie's parents left Texas. He promised to never drink hard liquor again, only beer. He kept that promise to the end of his life.

But for Annie, the damage was already done. She stayed in Texas, determined to take care of herself. She was sixteen and still believing those lies.

*You're not enough. You're not loved. You'll always be alone.*

"I'm going to be my own adult, and I'm going to take care of myself. I don't need them," Annie told herself. And so, she dropped out of school, got a job, and started living her life her way.

## Under the Stars

But those lies she believed about herself infected every decision she made. Over the years, she had some great jobs and some not-so-good jobs. Through it all, she tried very hard to find her prince charming, her hero. On the outside, she wore the mask of someone living a life filled with adventure and fun. On the inside, she still felt alone, unloved, and without value.

Self-medicating was Annie's remedy for how she really felt. Drugs and alcohol were her medicines of choice to cover her pain. Her substance use went on for ten years, during which her life spiraled down further and further.

Then one night in the Black Hills of South Dakota, she knew she couldn't go on any longer. She realized she was at the bottom of her pit.

She was now a statistic. She was using, living with a drug dealer, and had dropped out of school at sixteen. According to society, she was now a "throwaway." She would never amount to anything. Everything she had done to take care of herself, to do things her own way, had led to destruction. She felt hopeless.

And then, the tiniest flame of hope sparked in her darkness. Memories of those Sunday services with her mom and siblings came to her, and she remembered Jesus.

Annie had always believed in Him. But she had never truly given her life to Him.

It was time.

She went outside, into the night. Under the starry sky, she cried out, "Jesus, please save me. I can't do it anymore. I just keep making it worse. Save me. I need You."

There was no heavenly angel chorus, no voice from heaven. The world was as it always had been. Nothing had changed, and yet everything changed.

Annie had no idea what was going to happen; she just knew something was going to happen. Jesus was going to save her. She didn't know for sure what that meant, but she knew He could do it.

## The Adventure Begins

That night marked the beginning of Annie's kingdom adventure. It wasn't easy—she had years of pain and bad habits to unravel—but for the first time, she had hope. Jesus met her in her darkest moment and gave her a reason to keep going. He didn't just save her life; He gave her a new one.

Jesus gave Annie a thirst to get an education and to read the Bible. As she read God's Word, she replaced the lies she had believed with the truth and started learning what it meant to follow Jesus. Slowly but surely, He began to heal the wounds in her heart and show her that her past didn't define her. She wasn't the unloved, broken woman she had believed she was. She was His child, and He had a plan for her life.

## Your Invitation to the Unseen Battle

Just like we had to awaken to the spiritual realm, so do you. This isn't just our story—it's yours too. Whether you realize it or not, you are part of this unseen cosmic battle. The enemy is fighting for your heart, mind, and soul, but Jesus is calling you to rise up as a warrior in His kingdom. There are lives Jesus desires you to reach with Him.

This is your call to the battle.

When we talk about Kingdom Warriors, we're referring to men, women, and young adults who have committed themselves to fighting in this unseen cosmic battle alongside Jesus, their warrior King. They see themselves as part of something bigger than just everyday life—they're participants in a spiritual reality that shapes how they view their purpose and actions.

This book will guide you through that adventure. Together, we'll uncover truths about the spiritual realm, expose the enemy's tactics, and equip you to walk in victory as a Kingdom Warrior. We will be called to powerful faith, accepting wisdom for our adventure in the unseen cosmic battle.

Kingdom Warriors operate with an unwavering faith that serves as both their foundation and the driving force in their relationship with Jesus. They approach challenges with the conviction that the Holy Spirit's supernatural power transcends physical limitations, allowing them to persevere when faced with adversity. Kingdom Warriors view setbacks not as permanent obstacles but as opportunities for spiritual growth, believing that their faith provides the necessary resilience to overcome any challenge in their path toward fulfilling their kingdom purpose.

This growing faith in a relationship with Jesus is truly something special for many Kingdom Warriors. It's not just a religious idea—it becomes the real backbone that gives strength, direction, and meaning when life gets tough.

While many of us go through our daily lives focused on what we can see and touch, these Kingdom Warriors are tuned into a spiritual reality that shapes everything they do. They understand there are forces of good and evil at work in our world, and they've chosen to actively engage in this struggle with Jesus leading the way.

What's so powerful about this perspective is that it gives everyday choices and challenges a deeper meaning. When you see yourself as a warrior in Jesus' kingdom, suddenly those small acts of kindness, standing up for what's right, or persevering through difficulty become part of a greater purpose. It's not just about getting through the day—it's about advancing something eternal.

And the beautiful thing is that the call to participate in this spiritual battle isn't limited to certain types of people. Whether you're young or old, man or woman, anyone can embrace this calling to fight alongside Jesus in transforming our world from the inside out.

# Part One

## Understanding the Battle

## Chapter 1

## The Creation of All Things

In the beginning God created the heavens and the earth.

— Genesis 1:1

In the beginning, before time itself existed, there was God: eternal, all-powerful, and perfect in wisdom. The universe as we know it was still unformed, a canvas awaiting the Master Artist's touch. The heavens and the earth did not yet exist; there was only the voice of God, poised to speak life into being.

### The Beginning of Creation

And then, in an act of pure love and creative power, God spoke. "Let there be light," He commanded, and instantly, radiant light burst forth into the darkness, separating day from night. God saw that the light was good, marking the completion of the first day of creation.

On the second day, God created the expanse called sky, separating the waters above from the waters below. With divine precision, He established the atmosphere that would sustain all life.

The third day witnessed the emergence of dry land from the waters below. God commanded, "Let the land produce vegetation," and immediately, the earth sprouted with every kind of seed-bearing plant and fruit-bearing tree. The barren ground transformed into a lush garden of life, each plant designed to reproduce after its kind.

## The Heavenly Bodies

On the fourth day, God's attention turned to the heavens. He created the sun, moon, and stars—not as deities to be worshipped, as other nations would later believe, but as luminaries to mark seasons, days, and years. The sun would govern the day, the moon would rule the night, and the stars would guide travelers and inspire wonder in the hearts of humanity for generations to come.

> For nothing will be impossible with God.
>
> — Luke 1:37

## Life in the Waters and Sky

The fifth day dawned with God's command for the waters to teem with living creatures and for birds to fill the skies. The oceans, once empty, now pulsed with life, from tiny fish to great sea creatures. The air became alive with the beating of wings and songs of birds. God blessed these creatures, commanding them to multiply and fill their domains.

## Land Animals and Humankind

On the sixth day, God created land animals of every kind—livestock, creatures that move along the ground, and wild animals.

Each was perfectly designed for its habitat and purpose in the created order.

But the crown of God's creation was yet to come. In a profound act that revealed His very nature, God said, "Let us make mankind in our image, in our likeness." Unlike any other creature, humans were fashioned to reflect God's character and to have relationship with Him. From the dust of the ground, God formed man and breathed into his nostrils the breath of life. From the man's side, God created woman—different yet equal, both bearing the divine image.

God blessed the humans and gave them responsibility over all creation—to care for it, cultivate it, and exercise wise dominion. They were placed in a garden of perfect beauty and abundance, with freedom to enjoy what God had created.

## COMPLETION AND REST

Looking over all He had made—from the vastness of galaxies to the intricacy of a butterfly's wing—God declared it "very good." His creation was complete, perfect in design and purpose.

On the seventh day, God rested. Not from exhaustion, but to establish a pattern for humanity and to declare the completeness of His work. He blessed this day and made it holy, setting it apart as a reminder of His creative power and provision.

> To believe in the things you can see and touch is no belief at all
> —but to believe in the unseen is a triumph and a blessing.[1]
>
> — ABRAHAM LINCOLN

## THE ONGOING WORK OF CREATION

Though the initial work of creation was complete, God's creative power continues to sustain all things. Every sunrise, every birth, every changing season speaks of His ongoing care for what He has made. The stars remain in their courses by His command, and every creature draws breath by His provision.

In heaven, God created the spiritual realm with the same attention to detail and purpose. He formed angelic beings to serve and worship Him, powerful spirits who would act as His messengers and ministers. The heavenly realm became a place of perfect worship, where created beings continually praise the Creator.

## Creation's Purpose

All of creation—heaven and earth—exists for God's glory. The psalmist would later write, "The heavens declare the glory of God; the skies proclaim the work of his hands" (Psalm 19:1) Every mountain and valley, every star and planet, every creature from the smallest insect to the largest whale, and every human being bears witness to the wisdom, power, and love of their Creator.

> Now faith is confidence in what we hope for and assurance about what we do not see.
>
> — Hebrews 11:1

In creating all things, God revealed Himself to be a God of order, beauty, diversity, and provision. His creation reflects His character—His attention to detail, His delight in beauty, His wisdom in design, and most importantly, His desire for relationship with humans who bear His image.

The story of creation is not merely an account of how things began; it is the foundation of our understanding of who God is, who we are, and why we exist. It reminds us that we live in a created universe that points beyond itself to its Creator, who made all things for His glory and our good.

In the next chapter, we will explore the cosmic battle that emerged within this perfect creation—a spiritual conflict that continues to this day and forms the backdrop for our adventure as Kingdom Warriors.

> *Your life relaunch begins with this truth: you were created for more than survival—you were created for Kingdom impact.*

## Chapter 2

# The Unseen Cosmic Battle

> We do not wrestle against flesh and blood, but against principalities, against powers, against the rulers of the darkness of this age, against spiritual hosts of wickedness in the heavenly places.
>
> — Ephesians 6:12 NKJV

## The Perfect Beginning

In the beginning, before our clocks and calendars even made sense, there was incredible perfection throughout the cosmos. Can you imagine a place where absolutely everything just...works? That's what heaven was like—an amazing realm just pulsing with harmony and light.

Picture the most beautiful symphony you've ever heard, but it's not just music—it's the very fabric of creation itself. Countless beings all serving together in perfect unity, no conflict, no misunderstanding, just harmony. At the very heart of all this stood the Creator's throne, and from it came pure light and love that touched absolutely everything in existence.

And right there, in a position of incredible honor, was Lucifer, the Morning Star. He wasn't just any angel; he was the highest of them all. As heaven's chief musician and worship leader, he had the incredible responsibility of directing that heavenly harmony.

It's fascinating to think about this time before time, isn't it? A perfect existence where everything and everyone knew exactly their purpose and fulfilled it completely. There's something both awe-inspiring and humbling about contemplating those earliest moments of spiritual reality, the perfect beginning point from which everything else would eventually unfold.

## The Birth of Sin

Yet in this perfect environment, something unprecedented happened: the birth of sin.

In this flawless reality, the very first discordant note in that universal harmony didn't come from some outside force or enemy. It emerged from within Lucifer himself.

Picture this beautiful being, looking at his own reflection, his own magnificence, and slowly beginning to think, "Maybe this glory is mine, not just a reflection of my Creator." Pride—something that had never existed before in all of creation—took root in his heart. Ezekiel could have been describing Lucifer when he wrote the powerful verse, "Your heart became proud on account of your beauty, and you corrupted your wisdom because of your splendor" (Ezekiel 28:17).

This subtle shift changed everything. It marked the beginning of the first cosmic rebellion. Lucifer's focus turned inward, admiring his own excellence instead of reflecting his Creator's glory. What started as just self-admiration grew into ambition and eventually exploded into full-blown rebellion. His words in Isaiah are chilling: "I will ascend above the tops of the clouds; I will make myself like the Most High" (Isaiah 14:14).

> There are two equal and opposite errors into which our race can fall about the devils. One is to disbelieve in their existence. The

other is to believe, and to feel an excessive and unhealthy interest in them.[1]

— C.S. Lewis

## The First Cosmic Rebellion

Lucifer was no fool, though. As a master of wisdom, he didn't just lash out. He launched a careful campaign of subtle manipulation. He began questioning the Creator's authority, planting tiny seeds of doubt among the other angels. His approach was cunning—not outright rejecting the divine order, but making subtle suggestions about greater freedom, higher positions, and potential they hadn't realized yet.

Using his position of influence, he spread these revolutionary ideas throughout the heavenly hosts. Scripture tells us he actually succeeded in convincing a third of the angels to join his cause (Revelation 12:4). When Lucifer fell, those angels were cast down to earth with him and became what we now know as demons.

This rebellion resulted in an incredibly significant demonic presence throughout creation. We see glimpses of this in the New Testament accounts, where Jesus confronts and casts out many demons.

But despite their power, those of us who follow Jesus don't need to live in fear of these fallen angels. God maintains ultimate authority over them and will judge them in the end. It's incredible to think that we're empowered by the Holy Spirit to resist evil and overcome both the temptations and attacks of these demonic forces.

What's particularly profound is that these beings were created perfect and free, yet they chose to align themselves with Lucifer's rebellion. This massive defection represents the first divided loyalty in the entire history of creation. It's a powerful reminder of how precious our freedom to choose is, and how significant our daily decisions to align with God's kingdom really are in this ongoing cosmic story.

## The Open Conflict

After Lucifer and his followers fell, the tension finally broke into open conflict with explosive force. Lucifer—now transformed into Satan, literally "the Adversary"—led his followers in an audacious attempt to usurp the throne of heaven itself. The scale of this conflict goes way beyond what our human minds can fully grasp—these mighty beings wielding powers we can barely comprehend, clashing in a war that would determine the fate of everything. We love how the Bible captures it in Revelation, so succinct but incredibly powerful: "Then war broke out in heaven. Michael and his angels fought against the dragon, and the dragon and his angels fought back. But he was not strong enough, and they lost their place in heaven" (Revelation 12:7-8).

> The Christian life is not a playground; it is a battleground.[2]
>
> — Warren Wiersbe

## The Fall and Its Consequences

The Fall that followed was absolutely devastating. The rebels' defeat was total and catastrophic. Lucifer and all his followers were cast out of heaven, falling from their incredibly exalted positions to become enemies of everything good. The Morning Star's beauty became corrupted, his wisdom twisted, his light transformed into darkness. This heavenly musician became the prince of darkness, and those who followed him became demons.

But the consequences of this rebellion went far beyond just those involved. The introduction of sin into creation created a cosmic rift that would affect everything that was to come. When God later created Earth and placed us humans here, this battle extended into our realm, making our world a key battlefield in this ongoing cosmic conflict.

And here's something that always amazes us—ironically, Satan is still instrumental in God's ultimate plan. Even in rebellion, he can't escape being part of the greater story God is telling.

## The Battle Continues

The battle that began in heaven continues to this day, playing out across the cosmos but especially on Earth. This planet—seemingly insignificant in the vast expanse of space—has become the central battleground in this cosmic conflict. Why? Because it is here that God has placed His image-bearers, humans created to reflect His character and extend His kingdom.

Satan's rebellion fundamentally changed his relationship with humanity. Rather than serving alongside us as fellow worshippers of the Creator, he became our adversary. His mission shifted from leading worship to leading rebellion, and humans became both his targets and potential recruits in his ongoing war against God.

Scripture reveals that Satan has established a complex hierarchy of spiritual forces aligned against humanity. Ephesians 6:12 speaks of "rulers," "authorities," "powers of this dark world," and "spiritual forces of evil in the heavenly realms." This is not poetic language but a description of actual spiritual entities organized in ranks and roles, all aimed at opposing God's purposes and destroying His image-bearers.

These spiritual forces wage war primarily through deception. Just as Satan questioned God's character and commands in the Garden of Eden ("Did God really say...?"), his forces continue to plant doubts about God's goodness, His Word, and His plans. This deception targets every area of human existence—our minds, emotions, relationships, culture, and social structures.

*In the spiritual battlefield, your greatest victory often follows your deepest surrender.*

But the war for humanity's soul is a seemingly hidden one, the battlefield not one of flesh and blood but of truth and lies. Our spiritual adversaries strike with whispers rather than weapons, planting seeds of doubt that grow into forests of confusion. Like master illusionists, they distort reality, questioning divine goodness while presenting falsehood draped in attractive garments. Their deception spreads like a virus through minds, hearts, and earth's institutions—transforming culture, corrupting leadership, and infiltrating systems of power in government. Those who believe themselves immune often become unwitting agents, advancing dark designs while claiming independence. The greatest triumph of these spiritual forces is convincing many they don't exist at all. Yet warriors of light and darkness fight in the pinnacles of power on earth.

When bitterness takes root in the human heart, it can create fractures through which darkness seeps. Those who nurture their grievances often find themselves gradually transformed by them, their vision narrowing until vengeance feels like justice. In these shadowed moments, ordinary people can commit extraordinary acts of cruelty, as if possessed by forces beyond themselves.

We see it in the media every day: the most terrifying violence often emerges from calculated evil and emotional pain that has fermented into rage. We witness this in communities ravaged by addiction, where substances promising escape become chains of bondage and death. We see it in the eyes of those who once swore they could never harm another, yet find themselves standing in the aftermath of actions they cannot comprehend.

This struggle between light and darkness plays out not just in dramatic headlines but in quiet decisions made every day—to forgive or resent, to heal or harm, to build or destroy. The battlefield isn't distant; it's within the human heart, where our deepest wounds can either be transformed into wisdom or weaponized into destruction.

*Kingdom Warriors understand that
the greatest battlefield isn't external, but within—
where flesh wages war against spirit.*

Yet even as this battle rages, we must remember a crucial truth: this is a conflict with a predetermined outcome. Satan's defeat is not in question, only the timing of its final manifestation. At the cross, Jesus delivered the death blow to the enemy's kingdom: "Having disarmed the powers and authorities, he made a public spectacle of them, triumphing over them by the cross" (Colossians 2:15).

What we're experiencing now is not a war whose outcome is uncertain, but the final campaigns of a defeated enemy who refuses to surrender. Like pockets of resistance after a decisive battle, demonic forces continue to fight even though their ultimate defeat is assured.

This understanding transforms how we approach spiritual warfare. We don't fight for victory—we fight from victory. We don't battle with desperation but with confidence, knowing that our Champion has already won the decisive engagement. Our role is not to secure the victory but to implement it, pushing back darkness and establishing Jesus' kingdom in every sphere of influence.

As Kingdom Warriors, we've been drafted into this cosmic conflict not as victims or even mere soldiers, but as representatives of the victorious King. We've been given both authority and responsibility to engage in this battle, equipped with spiritual weapons that "have divine power to demolish strongholds" (2 Corinthians 10:4).

In the chapters that follow, we'll explore how this unseen cosmic battle affects your daily life, how to recognize the enemy's strategies, and how to walk in the victory Jesus has already secured. The conflict is real, but so is our Commission—and so is our triumph in Christ.

## Chapter 3

# The Silent Guardian

## Adam's Absence in Eve's Life

> Then the LORD God said, "It is not good for the man to be alone. I will make a helper suitable for him."
>
> — Genesis 2:18

### The Original Command

You know, there's something profoundly interesting about that perfect garden of Eden. Can you imagine walking in perfect harmony with God, where communion was unhindered and all of creation existed in perfect balance? In this paradise, God established just one boundary: "You are free to eat from any tree in the garden; but you must not eat from the tree of the knowledge of good and evil, for when you eat from it you will certainly die."

What's really fascinating is the timing of this command. God gave these words directly to Adam before Eve was even created from his side. Think about what that means for a moment. Adam received this divine instruction personally, making him the primary bearer of this knowledge. When Eve appears later in the story, the Bible doesn't actually record God repeating this command to her directly. Yet when she's tempted by the serpent, she clearly knows about the prohibition, which suggests Adam had shared God's command with her.

This creates such an interesting dynamic in their relationship, doesn't it? Adam held the responsibility to be both recipient and transmitter of God's word. This position came with an implicit responsibility of spiritual protection and guidance—a responsibility that would soon be profoundly tested.

## The Silent Presence

One of the most striking aspects of the temptation story in Genesis 3 is revealed in a detail that's so easy to miss if you're not paying close attention: "She also gave some to her husband, who was with her, and he ate it" (verse 6). This single phrase—"who was with her"—carries enormous implications that should stop us in our tracks. Adam wasn't somewhere else in the garden when the serpent approached Eve. He wasn't called over after she had already fallen. The Biblical text strongly suggests he was present throughout the entire exchange.

Can you picture this scene? Adam stood by as the serpent questioned God's word: "Did God really say...?" He remained silent as the enemy suggested God was withholding something good from them. He offered no correction when Eve slightly misquoted God's command, adding "and you must not touch it"—words God had never actually spoken according to the recorded command.

Most critically, Adam watched as Eve reached for the fruit, took it, and ate it—yet he made no move to intervene. Then, without any recorded protest or hesitation, he accepted the fruit from her hand and participated in the same disobedience.

This silence and passivity represent one of history's most consequential moments of inaction. But what explains it?

> The first to plead his case seems right, until another comes and examines him.
>
> — Proverbs 18:17

## The Psychology Behind Adam's Silence

Adam's silence during Eve's temptation reveals several potential psychological and spiritual dynamics that might resonate with our own experiences:

### The Desire for Validation

One possibility is that Adam harbored his own doubts about God's command. Perhaps he was curious about the forbidden fruit but hesitant to act on this curiosity directly. Eve's engagement with the serpent and her eventual decision to eat may have provided the validation he secretly sought.

The text tells us the fruit was "pleasing to the eye, and also desirable for gaining wisdom" (Genesis 3:6). Adam may have shared this desire but needed external confirmation that acting on it was acceptable. In this interpretation, Eve's transgression became the permission Adam sought for his own latent rebellion.

Doesn't this reflect a timeless pattern in human psychology? We often look to others to validate choices we already wish to make but fear to initiate. When we see others cross boundaries we've contemplated crossing, their actions can seem to legitimize our own desires.

### Conflict Avoidance and Passive Agreement

Adam may have remained silent to avoid confrontation—both with the serpent and potentially with Eve. Rather than asserting God's clear command and creating tension, he chose the path of passive agreement.

*True Warriors know that isolation is a sign not of strength but of vulnerability; fellowship is where battles are won before they're fought.*

This pattern of conflict avoidance resonates through human relationships across time. When someone we care about moves toward a harmful decision, speaking up requires courage. It's often easier to remain silent, especially when intervention might be interpreted as controlling or judgmental.

Adam's silence might reflect this deeply human tendency to avoid difficult conversations, even when the stakes are extraordinarily high. His failure wasn't just in eating the fruit himself, but in failing to lovingly protect Eve by reminding her of God's word when it mattered most.

## Abdication of Responsibility

The narrative may also reveal Adam's willingness to abdicate his responsibility. Having received God's command directly, he held a special obligation to uphold and protect it. Yet in the critical moment, he surrendered this responsibility.

Like conflict avoidance, this abdication pattern continues throughout human history. Those entrusted with protecting others often fail at crucial moments, not through active malice but through passive neglect of their responsibilities. Adam's silence represents the first instance of a leader failing to lead when leadership was most needed.

Later, when confronted by God, Adam's response further solidifies his abdication: "The woman you put here with me—she gave me some fruit from the tree, and I ate it" (Genesis 3:12). Not only does he blame Eve, but he implicitly blames God for providing Eve in the first place. This deflection compounds his earlier failure to take responsibility.

## The Spiritual Dimension

Beyond psychological explanations, Adam's silence carries profound spiritual implications that speak to our own spiritual battles:

## The First Spiritual Protection Failure

Adam's silence represents the first failure of spiritual protection in human history. Having received God's word directly, he had both the knowledge and the responsibility to recognize the serpent's deception. His presence during Eve's temptation provided the opportunity to intervene with truth.

This established a tragic pattern that would repeat throughout biblical history—those who know God's truth failing to speak it when others are vulnerable to deception. The prophet Ezekiel would later describe this as the failure of watchmen who do not sound the alarm when danger approaches.

> *Kingdom Warriors know that every person*
> *they encounter is either a brother or sister in Christ,*
> *or one who has yet to come home.*

## The Inversion of Divine Order

Some theological traditions see in this narrative an inversion of the created order God had established. Rather than fulfilling his responsibility to lovingly speak truth in a moment of deception, Adam passively followed Eve into disobedience.

The apostle Paul references this aspect when writing to Timothy: "And Adam was not the one deceived; it was the woman who was deceived and became a sinner" (1 Timothy 2:14). This verse suggests Adam wasn't deceived in the same way Eve was—he transgressed with eyes more fully open to the nature of his choice, making his silent complicity even more significant.

## The Failure of Spiritual Authority

Adam's silence also represents a failure to exercise appropriate spiritual authority. He was charged not with domination or control, but with lovingly guiding according to God's word. Authority, in its divine design, exists to protect and serve—yet Adam failed to use his position as bearer of God's direct command to protect Eve from deception.

## The Eternal Consequences

Adam's silence in this pivotal moment had consequences that extended far beyond the garden:

## Shared Responsibility, Distinctive Roles in the Fall

While both Adam and Eve participated in the fall, they played different roles. Eve was actively deceived by the serpent's arguments, while Adam's transgression centered more on passive acquiescence followed by active participation.

This distinction appears in how God addresses them afterward. To the woman, God says: "With painful labor you will give birth to children" (Genesis 3:16), while to Adam, He says: "Because you listened to your wife and ate fruit from the tree about which I commanded you..." (Genesis 3:17). God specifically notes Adam's failure to fulfill his responsibility regarding the command he had personally received.

## The Curse and Its Connection to Adam's Silence

The curse pronounced upon Adam directly connects to his failure: "Cursed is the ground because of you...By the sweat of your brow, you will eat your food" (Genesis 3:17-19). The very creation over which Adam had been given authority would now resist him. His work, which was originally meant to be fulfilling stewardship, would become toilsome labor.

This consequence bears a poetic connection to his failure. Having failed to exercise appropriate spiritual authority in the garden, his authority over the earth would now be compromised. The ground would resist his leadership just as he had failed to assert spiritual leadership in the critical moment.

*The wisdom of Kingdom Warriors: when the battle intensifies, draw closer to your fellow soldiers, not further away.*

## The Theological Impact on Humanity

Paul's letter to the Romans draws a direct connection between Adam's transgression and the fallen human condition: "Sin entered the world through one man, and death through sin, and in this way death came to all people, because all sinned" (Romans 5:12).

Theologically, Adam's silence and subsequent eating of the fruit represents the moment when humanity's fellowship with God was broken. His failure to speak truth in the face of deception allowed the first seeds of doubt about God's character to take root in human consciousness.

## Lessons for Our Unseen Spiritual Battles

Adam's silence during Eve's temptation provides powerful lessons for our own spiritual battles:

## The Danger of Passive Agreement

The most dangerous form of alignment with sin isn't active participation—it's silent presence that fails to challenge deception. When we witness others being drawn toward spiritual danger and remain silent, we participate in their vulnerability.

This calls us to courageous truth-speaking, especially when those we care about are vulnerable to deception. Speaking truth in love becomes not just an option but a spiritual responsibility.

## The Call to Spiritual Protection

Adam's failure reminds us of our responsibility to protect others spiritually. This isn't about control or spiritual superiority, but about lovingly sharing the truth we've received when others face deception.

In our own spiritual communities, we're called to be watchmen for one another—alerting each other to dangers, reminding each other of God's truth, and standing firm together against deception.

## The Need for Proactive Engagement

Had Adam proactively engaged with the serpent's deception rather than remaining passively present, the outcome might have been different. This teaches us to approach spiritual challenges with intentionality rather than hoping they will resolve themselves.

When we see spiritual deception approaching those we love, waiting until after they've fallen to offer wisdom is waiting until it's too late. Spiritual protection requires watchfulness and timely intervention.

## The Importance of Taking Responsibility

After the fall, Adam's attempt to shift blame—to Eve and indirectly to God—compounded his original failure. This pattern of avoiding responsibility continues to plague humanity.

True spiritual growth requires us to take responsibility for our actions and inactions, refuse to blame others for our failures, and acknowledge where we've fallen short.

## Redemption Beyond the Garden

The story of Adam's silence doesn't end with judgment. Through the narrative of Scripture, we see God's redemptive plan unfold—a plan that would ultimately address Adam's failure through the perfect obedience of Jesus Christ.

Where Adam remained silent before deception, Jesus spoke truth with authority. Where Adam failed to protect Eve from the serpent's lies, Jesus confronted Satan directly with God's word. Where Adam passively accepted temptation, Jesus actively rejected it.

Paul draws this contrast explicitly: "For as in Adam all die, so in Christ all will be made alive" (1 Corinthians 15:22). Christ becomes the "last Adam"—the one who succeeds where the first Adam failed.

This redemptive arc reminds us that God's story doesn't end with human failure but moves toward divine restoration. While Adam's silence contributed to humanity's fall, Jesus' obedient voice opened the path to our redemption.

## The Call to Holy Courage

Adam's silence in Eden's pivotal moment challenges us to examine our own moments of spiritual passivity. Where have we remained silent when truth needed to be spoken? Where have we witnessed deception approaching loved ones yet failed to intervene with loving wisdom?

The garden narrative calls us to holy courage—to a willingness to speak truth lovingly, to protect others spiritually, and to take responsibility for our unique role in Jesus' kingdom. It reminds us that in spiritual warfare, silence often represents not neutrality but surrender.

As Kingdom Warriors, we're called to learn from Adam's failure by speaking God's truth boldly in a world filled with the same serpentine deceptions. Unlike Adam, we now have the indwelling Holy Spirit of God empowering us for this very purpose.

The question Adam faced in the garden—whether to speak God's truth in the face of deception—is one we continue to face daily. May we choose courage where he chose silence, protection where he chose passivity, and responsibility where he chose blame. In doing so, we participate not in the legacy of the first Adam's fall but in the redemptive work of the last Adam, Jesus Christ.

## The Unseen Battle Continues

While the first battle ended decisively, it initiated an ongoing conflict that would span the ages. Satan, though defeated, was not destroyed. His fall from heaven marked the beginning of a new phase in the unseen cosmic conflict—one that would eventually encompass Earth and humanity through Adam and Eve's sin.

As we face our own spiritual battles, we can draw strength from knowing that the war's outcome is already determined. Though Satan's initial rebellion shattered the original harmony of creation, his defeat is certain, and a new creation awaits—one where harmony will be restored, never to be broken again.

Throughout this book, we will explore the unseen cosmic spiritual battle, shedding light on how this conflict shapes our world and affects our very souls. The heart of this war lies not in the visible world of politics or military conflict, but in the hidden territories of our thoughts, desires, and beliefs. By understanding this battle, we can begin to recognize the forces at play in our lives, equipping ourselves with the spiritual awareness and tools necessary for a Kingdom Warrior to overcome.

But before we can understand the unseen cosmic battle, we must first explore its nature. Spiritual warfare is the contest between two opposing forces: God and His truth, and the forces of darkness that seek to deceive, destroy, and lead people away from the truth. At the center of this battle is the mind and heart of every human being. These are the territories the enemy seeks to occupy and influence.

The enemy's tactics are subtle, working through temptations, distractions, and false beliefs. The battle is fought not with physical weapons but with thoughts, ideas, ideologies, and ideations. This unseen cosmic battle is about shaping worldviews, altering perceptions, and capturing imaginations. It is a war for the mind and heart—a deep, spiritual war that determines who or what we will serve.

The human mind is the battlefield where many spiritual battles are fought. It is here that the seeds of unbelief, doubt, confusion, isolation, compromise and deception are planted. Thoughts are powerful forces that shape beliefs, values, and ultimately, actions.

Throughout history, the mind has been the prime target of those seeking to manipulate and control. The enemy seeks to fill the mind with lies, distractions, and misguided ideas.

In the next chapter, we will discuss the origin and nature of demons, what makes them dangerous, and how we can fight them.

## Chapter 4

# The Origin and Nature of Demons

> And the angels who did not keep their positions of authority but abandoned their proper dwelling—these he has kept in darkness, bound with everlasting chains for judgment on the great Day.
>
> — Jude 1:6

As Kingdom Warriors, understanding our enemy is crucial to winning the battle we're engaged in. Let me share something fascinating about demons that will equip you for this spiritual warfare.

In Chapter 2, we shared the Bible's account of the origin of these beings. As you may remember, they weren't created as demons—they were originally angels who followed Satan in his rebellion against God. Isn't that remarkable? These beings made a choice to rebel against their Creator, and that decision transformed them from glorious angels into the dark forces we now call demons.

> Demons are like obedient dogs; they come when they are called.[1]
>
> — REMY DE GOURMONT

Unlike us, these are spiritual beings without physical bodies. Paul reminds us in Ephesians 6:12, "For our struggle is not against flesh and blood, but against the rulers, against the authorities, against the powers of this dark world and against the spiritual forces of evil in the heavenly realms." This is why our physical efforts alone can never win this battle—we're dealing with a spiritual reality that requires spiritual weapons.

What makes demons particularly dangerous is that they're not mindless forces—they possess intelligence and knowledge. James 2:19 tells us, "You believe that there is one God. Good! Even the demons believe that—and shudder." They know who Jesus is, and they recognize His power. Remember in Acts 19:15 when a demon said, "Jesus I know, and Paul I know about, but who are you?" These beings have awareness and can recognize spiritual authority.

Throughout Scripture, we see them described as evil spirits. In Luke 8:2, we read about "Mary (called Magdalene) from whom seven demons had come out," and in Matthew 12:45, Jesus describes how an evil spirit "goes and takes with it seven other spirits more wicked than itself." This hierarchy of wickedness suggests that not all demons are identical in their evil nature—some are actually worse than others!

Their organization doesn't stop there. They operate within a hierarchical structure, and at the top is Satan, who's called the "prince of this world" (John 12:31), the "god of this age" (2 Corinthians 4:4), and the "ruler of the kingdom of the air" (Ephesians 2:2). This isn't a chaotic rabble—it's an organized opposition with leadership and strategy in the unseen cosmic spiritual realm.

One of the most sobering realities about demons is their ability to possess or influence humans. The dramatic encounter in

Mark 5:1-20 shows us what this can look like at its most extreme. A demon-possessed man living in a graveyard was so strong that chains couldn't hold him, crying out day and night, cutting himself with stones. When Jesus confronted the demons, they identified themselves as "Legion...for we are many" (Mark 5:9). This single man was inhabited by multiple demonic entities that had completely overwhelmed his life.

*When darkness seems to have the final word,
Kingdom Warriors stand firm on the promise that
Jesus' light always breaks through.*

But possession isn't their only tactic. They can influence human behavior in more subtle ways. In Matthew 9:32-33, we see a man who couldn't speak because of demonic oppression. In Luke 13, Jesus healed a woman who had been bent over for eighteen years because she had been "crippled by a spirit" (verse 11). Her physical condition had a spiritual cause! When Jesus released her, saying, "Woman, you are set free from your infirmity" (verse 12), she stood straight and tall for the first time in nearly two decades! Now that is Jesus' love.

Something else that makes these enemies particularly dangerous is their deceptive nature. In 2 Corinthians 11:14, we learn that "even Satan masquerades as an angel of light." They don't always appear as obviously evil—sometimes they present themselves as messengers of truth and light. They work through false teachers and prophets, as Peter warns us in 2 Peter 2:1-3, bringing in "destructive heresies" that can lead many astray.

They're experts at planting doubt about God's word—this was their very first tactic used in the Garden of Eden, when the serpent asked Eve, "Did God actually say...?" They're counterfeiters, able to demonstrate what appear to be miracles and signs, as Paul warns in 2 Thessalonians 2:9, using "displays of power through signs and wonders" to deceive.

Their arsenal includes psychological warfare, constantly accusing believers day and night (Revelation 12:10). They specialize in creating fear and anxiety—that's why Paul reminds us in 2 Timothy 1:7 that "the Spirit God gave us does not make us timid, but gives us power, love and self-discipline." They cause confusion and discord, because as 1 Corinthians 14:33 reminds us, "God is not a God of disorder but of peace."

One of their most effective strategies is planting thoughts of condemnation in our minds, making us feel guilty and separated from Jesus, despite the powerful truth of Romans 8:1: "There is now no condemnation for those who are in Christ Jesus."

> Dear friends, do not believe every spirit, but test the spirits to see whether they are from God, because many false prophets have gone out into the world.
>
> — 1 JOHN 4:1

These spiritual enemies are strategic in their attacks. They seek vulnerable moments—remember how Satan tempted Jesus when He was hungry after forty days of fasting? They use pride as an entry point (1 Timothy 3:6) and exploit anger, which is why Paul warns us not to "let the sun go down while you are still angry" in Ephesians 4:26-27. They work to create division in relationships and set traps and snares.

Peter describes Satan as one who "prowls around like a roaring lion looking for someone to devour" (1 Peter 5:8). This isn't a passive enemy but an active predator looking for weaknesses and opportunities. They work through worldly systems (1 John 5:19) and have assigned territories, as we see in Daniel 10:13 with the "prince of Persia" who opposed God's messenger. They influence world systems and can control specific geographical areas.

Perhaps most dangerous of all, 2 Corinthians 4:4 tells us that "the god of this age has blinded the minds of unbelievers, so that

# Chapter 5

# The Father of Lies

You belong to your father, the devil, and you want to carry out your father's desires. He was a murderer from the beginning, not holding to the truth, for there is no truth in him. When he lies, he speaks his native language, for he is a liar and the father of lies.

— John 8:44

## The Origin of Deception

You know those piercing words where Jesus really cuts to the heart of the matter? John 8:44 is one of those moments. Jesus is showing us that deception isn't just something Satan does; it's who he is at his core. It's his fundamental character. From the very beginning in the Garden of Eden, his strategy has been to distort truth, plant doubt, and entice through falsehood. Remember his first recorded words to humanity? "Did God actually say...?" He immediately started questioning the clarity and goodness of God's instruction. And that pattern of deception has continued uninterrupted throughout human history, constantly adapting and refining for each generation, culture, and individual.

Here's the thing for us as Kingdom Warriors engaged in spiritual battle: understanding the enemy's deceptive strategies isn't optional—it's essential. Paul warned that "we are not unaware of his schemes" (2 Corinthians 2:11). If we remain naïve about Satan's deceptive tactics, we're fighting at a severe disadvantage, vulnerable to attacks we neither recognize nor understand.

> Never forget that the devil's cleverest trick is to persuade you that he does not exist![1]
>
> — CHARLES BAUDELAIRE

## The Strategic Target: A Warrior's Identity

What's fascinating—and honestly, quite revealing—about Satan's approach is where he aims his most persistent and devastating lies. He targets a Kingdom Warrior's identity. He understands something crucial: when your sense of who you are in Jesus becomes distorted, every other aspect of your spiritual life becomes compromised.

## The Identity Assault: "You Are What You Do"

One of Satan's primary deceptions is convincing you that your identity is based on your performance rather than your position in Jesus. Have you noticed these kinds of thoughts creeping in?

"Your past failures define you."

"God's love for you is proportional to your spiritual productivity."

"You must earn God's approval through your service."

"Your worth is measured by your spiritual achievements."

"Your value is based on what other people think of you."

This performance-based identity creates a destructive spiral in our lives. When we succeed spiritually, or in public opinion, pride

What kingdom assignment is Jesus calling you to? Ask and you will receive!

In the next chapter, we'll explore how the enemy uses misguided ideas to further his purposes, and how we can stand firm against these attacks, acknowledging that our thought patterns literally shape our spiritual reality. And that's precisely why Satan targets this domain with such strategic precision.

emerges. When we fail, despair takes over. Both reactions separate us from the grace that is our true strength.

Jesus faced this exact temptation in the wilderness when Satan challenged, "If you are the Son of God..." (Matthew 4:6). This wasn't merely a temptation to perform a miracle but an attack on Jesus' identity. Satan was suggesting that Jesus needed to prove His divine sonship through performance, rather than resting in the Father's declaration, "This is my beloved Son, with whom I am well pleased" (Matthew 3:17, ESV).

You and I face this same deceptive attack. The truth that counteracts this lie is found in Ephesians 2:8-9: "For by grace you have been saved through faith. And this is not your own doing; it is the gift of God, not a result of works, so that no one may boast." Our identity is established by God's gracious declaration that we are His sons and daughters, not by our spiritual performance.

## The Disqualification Lie: "Your Failures Have Disqualified You"

Have you ever noticed how quickly Satan leverages our failures? When we stumble in our spiritual adventure, he immediately whispers that devastating lie: "You're disqualified from effective service. Your failure has rendered you useless to Jesus' kingdom."

This lie is particularly effective because it contains a partial truth—sin does have consequences and can temporarily disrupt our fellowship with Jesus and the Holy Spirit. But Satan distorts this truth into the falsehood that failure permanently disqualifies us. *"I'm not good enough to be used by Jesus."*

Peter experienced this deceptive attack after denying Jesus three times. His failure was real and significant, but Jesus specifically restored him to ministry, commanding him to "Feed my sheep" (John 21:17). The restorative truth that counters Satan's disqualifying lie is found in 1 John 1:9: "If we confess our sins, he is faithful and just to forgive us our sins and to cleanse us from all unrighteousness." God's restoration is always available to the repentant warrior.

> The devil's greatest trick wasn't convincing the world he didn't exist, but convincing Kingdom Warriors they fight alone.
>
> — Anonymous

## The Orphan Lie: "You're On Your Own"

Satan works relentlessly to make us feel isolated in our spiritual battle. Have you felt this? This deception manifests in thoughts like:

"No one understands what you're going through."
"You have to fight these battles alone."
"God is distant and uninvolved in your struggles."
"You can't be honest about your weaknesses with other believers."

This lie of isolation is devastating because it separates us from both divine and human sources of strength and encouragement. We begin to hide our struggles, fight our battles in isolation, and eventually become overwhelmed by the enemy's focused attacks.

Jesus counteracted this deception by promising, "I will not leave you as orphans; I will come to you" (John 14:18). You are never alone in the battle. The truth that dispels this lie is found in Hebrews 13:5: "I will never leave you nor forsake you" (ESV). God's presence remains constant, regardless of our emotional perception, and He has placed us in the body of Christ for mutual support and protection.

## The Battlefield of the Mind

The primary arena where Satan's deceptive attacks take place is the battlefield of the mind. Paul recognized this when he wrote about "tak[ing] every thought captive to make it obedient to Christ" and warned about Satan's ability to blind minds: "And even if our gospel is veiled, it is veiled to those who are perishing. The god of this age has blinded the minds of unbelievers, so that they cannot see the light of the gospel that displays the glory of Christ, who is the image of God" (2 Corinthians 4:3-4).

As Kingdom Warriors, we must understand how the enemy plants and nurtures lies within our thought processes. The battle for your mind is fought in the trenches of your soul.

## Planting Seeds of Doubt

Satan's deception often begins subtly, with small seeds of doubt about God's character, His Word, or His purposes. Like his approach in Eden, he asks, "Did God really say...?" or "Did God really mean...?" These questions aren't seeking clarification but are designed to introduce uncertainty about what God has clearly communicated.

We counter this tactic by following Jesus' example in the wilderness. When faced with Satan's deceptive use of Scripture, Jesus responded with "It is written..." providing the full context and meaning of God's Word (Matthew 4). We must know Scripture well enough to recognize when it's being distorted or misapplied. This is discernment.

> The devil trembles when he sees the weakest Christian on his knees.[2]
>
> — William Cowper

## False Reasoning and Twisted Logic

Satan doesn't just plant doubts; he provides seemingly reasonable arguments to nurture those doubts into full-grown deception. He constructs logical-sounding but faulty deductions in our minds:

"If God loved you, He would have answered that prayer."

"If that person were truly spiritual, they wouldn't have treated you that way."

"If Christianity were true, Christians wouldn't struggle with these problems."

"If God were good, He wouldn't allow this suffering."

These arguments appear rational but are built on false premises or incomplete information. They create internal cognitive conflict that can weaken faith and distort spiritual perception.

Paul warned about this process: "See to it that no one takes you captive through hollow and deceptive philosophy, which depends on human tradition and the elemental spiritual forces of this world rather than on Christ" (Colossians 2:8). We must learn to recognize and reject reasoning that, while plausible-sounding, contradicts the truth of God's Word.

## Emotion-Based Deception

Satan is adept at using emotional states to introduce and reinforce deception. When we experience fear, disappointment, shame, or anger, our cognitive defenses are weakened, making us more susceptible to believing lies that we would normally recognize and reject.

You know what's fascinating about how Satan works? He's incredibly clever at validating lies through our emotions. He knows that when we're feeling deeply—whether it's fear, disappointment, or even excitement—our discernment filters get weaker.

Have you ever noticed how a thought that would seem obviously false when you're calm suddenly feels completely true when you're anxious or upset? That's no accident! Satan waits for those emotional high tides to plant his most convincing deceptions.

Think about it—when you're feeling rejected, a thought like "No one really cares about you" doesn't just seem plausible; it feels absolutely confirmed by your emotions. That's because Satan knows our emotions create a powerful sense of validation that can override what we intellectually know to be true.

What's empowering, though, is recognizing this pattern. When you can step back and say, "Wait, I'm feeling intensely right now, so I need to be extra careful about what thoughts I accept as truth," you're already disrupting his strategy.

The beautiful truth is that while our emotions are real and valid experiences, they make terrible truth-validators. God gave us emotions for connection and expression, not for discernment of reality. That's why Scripture keeps pointing us back to God's unchanging truth rather than our shifting emotional landscape.

Isn't it amazing that once you understand this tactic, what used to trip you up can actually become a trigger for greater discernment? The very moment Satan tries to use your emotions against you can become your signal to lean more deeply into God's truth!

After Elijah's great victory at Mount Carmel, a death threat from Jezebel sent him into fear and depression, where he became vulnerable to the lie that he was alone and his ministry had failed. God countered this emotion-based deception with truth: there were still seven thousand who had not bowed to Baal.

We must recognize that emotional distress creates vulnerability to deception. In such states, decisions and theological conclusions should be held lightly until emotional stability returns. Scripture reminds us: "The heart is deceitful above all things, and desperately sick; who can understand it?" (Jeremiah 17:9, ESV). Our emotions, while God-given, can be unreliable guides to truth, especially when we're under spiritual attack.

> *Kingdom Warriors understand that freedom from*
> *flesh isn't found in denying its existence, but in*
> *daily dying to its demands.*

You know what is amazing when you think about it? When we talk about following Jesus, we're not just talking about adopting a new set of beliefs or trying harder to be good people. We're talking about something far more radical and miraculous—our hearts literally becoming new creations!

Think about the power in that truth. Paul writes that "if anyone is in Christ, the new creation has come: The old has gone, the new is here!" (2 Corinthians 5:17). This isn't just poetic language or a nice metaphor—it's a spiritual reality that changes everything about how we navigate life's battles.

We've seen people struggle for years trying to overcome destructive patterns through sheer willpower, only to find themselves back in the same cycles of defeat. But that's because transformation doesn't happen from the outside in—it happens from the inside out, beginning with this supernatural heart transplant that God performs.

God made an incredible promise through Ezekiel: "I will give you a new heart and put a new spirit in you; I will remove from you your heart of stone and give you a heart of flesh" (Ezekiel (36:26). That's not behavior modification–that's identity transformation at the deepest level!

The beautiful thing about this new heart is that it naturally desires what God desires. The things that used to have such a powerful pull begin to lose their grip, not because we're gritting our teeth harder, but because our very desires are being realigned with God's heart.

Isn't it freeing to know that in this spiritual battle, we're not fighting to become something we're not? We're fighting from the position of who we already are in Jesus—new creations with new hearts that beat in rhythm with kingdom purposes. The struggle is real, but it's not about becoming something different—it's about living from the reality of who Jesus has already made us to be!

## Warfare Deception

With particular cunning, Satan spreads specific lies about spiritual warfare itself, creating confusion about the very unseen cosmic battle in which we're engaged.

## The Extremes of Warfare Deception

Satan promotes two opposite but equally deceptive extremes regarding spiritual warfare:

1. **"Everything is a direct demonic attack."** This deception leads us to see demons behind every struggle, failing to recognize the role of our own sinful nature, the fallen world system, or God's sanctifying work through trials. This creates paranoia, misperception of responsibility, and ineffective battle strategies.
2. **"Nothing is spiritual warfare."** The opposite deception dismisses the reality of spiritual opposition entirely, attributing all problems to psychological, social, or physical causes. This leaves us unprepared for actual spiritual attacks and blind to the enemy's involvement in our struggles.

The balanced truth is found in Scripture's multifaceted view of life's challenges, which can stem from our own sinful nature, the fallen world system, direct spiritual attack, or God's loving discipline. Discernment, rather than simplistic formulas, is required to navigate these spiritual complexities.

## The Lie of Enemy Power

Satan exaggerates his own power and reach, creating the false impression that he possesses attributes that belong only to God:

- **The lie of omnipresence**—creating the impression that he can be everywhere at once, monitoring all believers simultaneously.
- **The lie of omniscience**—suggesting he can read minds and know the future, rather than being limited to observation and prediction based on patterns.
- **The lie of sovereignty**—implying he can control circumstances and force believers to sin, rather than being limited to temptation and influence.

The truth that counters these deceptions is found in verses like 1 John 4:4: "the one who is in you is greater than the one who is in the world." Satan is a created being with significant but limited power, always subject to God's sovereign constraints. We need neither underestimate nor overestimate our adversary.

## Technological Deception

In our digital age, Satan has adapted his deceptive strategies to leverage technology. We now face:

- Information overload that drowns out biblical truth with a flood of competing voices and perspectives.
- Sophisticated propaganda using artificial intelligence, deepfakes, and psychological manipulation techniques that make discerning truth increasingly difficult.
- Echo chambers that reinforce existing beliefs without challenge, creating ideological bubbles that can harbor and nurture deception.
- Digital relationships that lack the full-spectrum discernment provided by in-person interaction, making it easier for those disguising themselves as apostles of Jesus to deceive believers online.

While technology itself is morally neutral, we must recognize how Satan leverages it for deception. We need heightened discernment when consuming digital content and forming online relationships. Jesus warned, "See that no one leads you astray" (Matthew 24:4, ESV)—a caution particularly relevant in our information-saturated age.

## Deception Through False Spirituality

One of Satan's most effective deceptive strategies is counterfeiting genuine spiritual experiences and practices.

### Counterfeit Spiritual Experiences

Scripture warns that "Satan himself masquerades as an angel of light" (2 Corinthians 11:14). He can produce counterfeit spiritual experiences that mimic authentic encounters with Jesus but lead us away from biblical truth.

These counterfeit experiences often feature:

- Spiritual "revelations" that contradict or even subtly change Scripture
- Mystical encounters that inflate our spiritual pride
- Supernatural signs that create dependency on experiences rather than faith
- Manifestations that draw attention to the individual rather than glorifying Jesus

The test for authentic spiritual experiences is always alignment with Scripture. John advised, "Dear friends, do not believe every spirit, but test the spirits to see whether they are from God, because many false prophets have gone out into the world" (1 John 4:1). We must evaluate all spiritual experiences by their fidelity to God's Word and their fruit in producing Christlikeness.

## Deceptive Religious Practices

Satan doesn't just oppose spiritual disciplines; he offers corrupted alternatives that appear spiritual but lead away from genuine communion with Jesus:

- **Legalism**—transforming spiritual disciplines from means of grace into measurements of worth, creating pride or despair rather than intimacy with Jesus.
- **Ritualism**—emptying spiritual practices of their heart engagement while preserving their outward form, creating the appearance of godliness without its power.
- **Mysticism detached from Scripture**—promoting spiritual experiences and insights that are disconnected from biblical revelation, prioritizing subjective impressions over objective truth.
- **Performance-based worship**—turning worship from genuine adoration of God into a performance that feeds human pride and seeks human approval.

Jesus confronted these deceptive religious practices when He condemned the Pharisees: "These people honor me with their lips, but their hearts are far from me. They worship me in vain; their teachings are merely human rules" (Matthew 15:8-9). We must constantly examine our spiritual practices to ensure they're fostering genuine communion with Jesus and the Holy Spirit rather than religious counterfeits.

## Weapons Against Deception

Though Satan's deceptive arsenal is sophisticated and relentless, we've been provided with divine weapons specifically designed to counter these attacks.

## The Sword of Truth

*[Handwritten at top: SWORD OF THE SPIRIT, which is THE WORD OF GOD.]*
*[Handwritten: JESUS SAYS HE IS THE TRUTH. THY WORD IS TRUTH]*

The primary weapon against deception is truth itself. Jesus declared, "You will know the truth, and the truth will set you free" (John 8:32). We must immerse ourselves in God's Word, developing a deeply <u>biblical</u> <u>worldview</u> that can recognize and reject Satan's lies. *[Handwritten: IF YOU HOLD TO MY TEACHINGS.]*

This sword of truth functions in several ways:

*[Handwritten: PAGE 260 VERSES]*

- **Exposing lies through contrast**—The more we know God's truth, the more easily we recognize what contradicts it. Like bank tellers trained to identify counterfeit currency by studying genuine bills, we identify spiritual counterfeits by knowing authentic truth.

- **Providing corrective lenses**—Scripture gives us the correct interpretation of our experiences, circumstances, and internal thoughts, preventing Satan from supplying his deceptive narrative. *[Handwritten margin: Holy Spirit]*

- **Establishing boundaries for revelation**—God's Word creates parameters for evaluating claimed revelations, promptings, or spiritual insights, allowing us to "test everything; hold fast what is good" (1 Thessalonians 5:21, ESV). *[Handwritten margin: think NOT beyond what is written]*

- **Renewing the mind**—Regular engagement with Scripture literally rewires thought patterns, making us less susceptible to deceptive thinking. As Paul writes, "Be transformed by the renewing of your mind" (Romans 12:2). *[Handwritten margin: OLD FRIENDS / immature words]*

*[Handwritten: HOW HAVE YOU CHANGED?]*

*[Handwritten right margin: I DEFINE TRUTH AS A PERSON (CHRIST) AND WHAT HE SAYS. HIS WORD IS TRUTH.]*

## The Shield of Faith

Faith serves as a protective shield against Satan's deceptive arrows. This isn't blind faith or wishful thinking, ==but confident trust in Jesus' character and promises as revealed in Scripture.==

Ephesians 6:16 instructs us to "take up the shield of faith, with which you can extinguish all the flaming arrows of the evil one." These flaming arrows often take the form of thoughts that contradict God's character or promises—precisely the kinds of deceptions Satan specializes in.

The shield of faith operates as:

- **Active trust in God's character**—When Satan suggests God is unloving, unfaithful, or unkind, faith holds firmly to the truth of who Jesus has revealed Himself to be.
- **Confidence in God's promises**—When circumstances seem to contradict God's promises, faith continues to trust in what Jesus has said rather than what appearances suggest.
- **Spiritual protection during doubt**—Even when we experience intellectual questions or emotional doubt, faith continues to function as a protective barrier until clarity returns.

Faith grows stronger as it is exercised in the unseen cosmic battle. Each time we choose to believe God's Word over Satan's deception, our faith becomes more resilient against future attacks.

You know, there's something beautiful about how Jesus works in our lives when we're willing to listen. Our story about moving from Colorado to Florida is such a powerful example of the gentle but unmistakable way Jesus guides us!

It all started with what seemed like just a casual question from Annie during our stay at our friend Dallen's guest house.

"Do you think we could ever live in Florida?"

Mel, looking through his own time lens, said, "Maybe in five years." But Jesus had different plans.

Just two years later while sitting at home on our beautiful deck, gazing out at Pikes Peak, this thought came to Mel's mind: "Now is the time. Put your house on the market." That's exactly how the Holy Spirit often speaks! Not with thunder and lightning, but with that quiet impression that carries surprising authority. And how beautiful it felt when the powerful presence of the Holy Spirit encouraged us to go forward.

What stands out is how we moved together in unity. When Mel shared what he believed the Holy Spirit was saying, Annie's response wasn't doubt or questioning—it was, "I sense peace about this decision." That kind of spiritual alignment between spouses is such a beautiful gift—peace given to each by the Holy Spirit.

And then those confirmations! The offer coming in while we were at a board meeting in Florida, less than a year later—talk about divine timing! The realtor said, "Mel, you are not going to believe this! I have a firm offer on your home, but there is one stipulation. He wants you to leave the stencil scriptures on the walls."

We had gotten so used to the scriptures on our walls we didn't even consider the effect they may have on a potential buyer. But God knew. The perfect buyer wanted our home because of the presence of His Word.

That's the kind of personal touch that lets you know it's truly Jesus orchestrating things. He doesn't just move us geographically; He even uses the scriptures on our walls to continue ministering to others after we're gone.

The way the exact price we asked Jesus for came back—that's not coincidence. That was Him showing us, "I've got every detail covered." He loves to be that involved in our lives, guiding not just the big decisions but arranging all the small details that confirm we're on the right path. Defend against the arrows of the enemy by recognizing and remembering Jesus' loving involvement in your life. We promise He's there—you just have to look.

## The Gift of Discernment

To combat deception effectively, we need spiritual discernment—the ability to distinguish truth from error, especially when the difference is subtle. Scripture speaks of "distinguishing between spirits" (1 Corinthians 12:10) and calls us to have our "powers of discernment trained by constant practice to distinguish good from evil" through the power of the Holy Spirit (Hebrews 5:14, ESV)

Spiritual discernment is developed through:

- **Prayer for wisdom**—James 1:5 promises, "If any of you lacks wisdom, you should ask God, who gives generously to all without finding fault, and it will be given to you." We should regularly pray for increased discernment.
- **Scripture study**—Thorough knowledge of biblical theology creates a framework for evaluating all claims and experiences with God's Word.
- **Fellowship confirmation**—God often provides discernment through the collective wisdom of mature Kingdom Warriors, which is why important decisions and spiritual insights should be confirmed within a trusted warrior community.
- **Spirit-led sensitivity**—As we walk closely with the Holy Spirit, we develop increasing sensitivity to His warnings and confirmations regarding various teachings and practices.

Discernment functions as a spiritual immune system, identifying and rejecting falsehood before it can take root and cause damage. And like any immune system, it becomes stronger through exposure and exercise.

## Humble Accountability

Pride makes us particularly vulnerable to deception. Scripture warns, "God opposes the proud but shows favor to the humble" (James 4:6). Satan strategically targets those who isolate themselves from accountability or consider themselves above correction.

We counter this vulnerability through:

- **Intentional accountability relationships** with mature Kingdom Warriors who have permission to ask hard questions and offer correction when needed.
- **Teachable hearts** that remain open to instruction and correction, recognizing that "the way of a fool is right in his own eyes, but a wise man listens to advice" (Proverbs 12:15, ESV).
- **Transparent Warrior Fellowships** where we can share struggles, doubts, and temptations without fear of judgment, creating environments where deception cannot thrive in secrecy.
- **Regular self-examination** following Paul's instruction to "Examine yourselves to see whether you are in the faith; test yourselves" (2 Corinthians 13:5).

Pride blinds us to our own deception, while humility opens our eyes to see where we've been misled. The humble Kingdom Warrior who remains accountable to Scripture and community has significant protection against Satan's deceptive attacks.

## Recognizing and Rejecting Lies

Practical wisdom for Kingdom Warriors requires not just understanding Satan's strategies but developing specific skills to recognize and reject his lies in daily battle.

### Interrogating Thoughts

Not every thought that enters your mind originates from your own thinking. Peter asked Ananias, "How is it that Satan has so filled your heart that you have lied to the Holy Spirit?" (Acts 5:3).

This demonstrates that the enemy can plant thoughts directly. We must develop the habit of interrogating thoughts, especially those that produce confusion, condemnation, or fear.

Effective thought interrogation includes questions like:

- "Does this thought align with what Scripture teaches about Jesus' character?"
- "Would the Holy Spirit speak to me in this tone or with this message?"
- "Does this thought lead me toward or away from trust in Jesus?"
- "Is this voice condemning me (Satan) or convicting me toward restoration (Holy Spirit)?"

By developing the habit of examining thoughts rather than passively accepting them, we catch deception before it takes root.

You know, one of the most powerful skills we can develop as Kingdom Warriors is examining our thoughts rather than just letting them flow through our minds unchallenged. It's like setting up a spiritual checkpoint, where each thought has to show its ID before you let it influence your mind and heart!

How many times have you caught yourself spiraling downward because of a single thought that snuck in unexamined? Maybe something like "I'll never be good enough" or "God's probably disappointed in me again." Those thoughts can take root so quickly if we don't stop them at the door! You'll never be able to stay on course with Jesus if you let them settle in and make themselves at home.

We've found that asking simple questions can be incredibly powerful. When a thought like "Nobody really cares about what I'm going through" shows up, instead of accepting it, first ask, "Is this actually true? Does this align with what God says about my value and His care for me?" Usually, the lie falls apart under that kind of scrutiny!

Or how about when you're facing a challenge and the thought comes, "You're going to fail at this just like last time"? That's when you can stop and say, "Wait a minute—does this thought build faith or fear? Is this the voice of the Holy Spirit encouraging me forward, or the enemy trying to hold me back?" When you examine it that way, it's so much easier to reject it with confidence and boldness.

A friend of Annie's once told her she used to constantly battle the thought, "You're not a good mother." Instead of letting it torment her, she started examining it: "Would Jesus, who entrusted these children to me, speak to me this way? Or is this condemnation rather than loving conviction?" Once she recognized it wasn't from Jesus, she could replace it with truth: "I am growing as a mother, learning each day, and deeply loved by Jesus in the process."

Isn't it amazing how different life feels when you stop letting every thought that enters your mind set up residence there? When you develop this habit of examining thoughts, suddenly you're no longer at the mercy of random mental traffic—you're actively partnering with the Holy Spirit to guard your heart and mind.

What thought has been trying to take root in your mind lately that might need some examining?

## Breaking Toxic Thinking Patterns

Satan's lies are most effective when they integrate into established neural pathways and thinking patterns, causing us to make an Agreement. We must identify and interrupt these deceptive thought loops through practices like:

- **Thought-stopping techniques**—consciously halting negative thought spirals by saying "stop" or "I rebuke this thought in the name of Jesus" (even out loud), followed by replacing the lie with biblical truth.

- **Scripture memorization targeted to specific vulnerabilities**—identifying personal areas of vulnerability to deception and memorizing specific verses that directly counter those lies in our lives.
- **Praise as spiritual warfare**—using worship and thanksgiving to break deceptive thinking, as it's difficult to simultaneously believe a lie about Jesus while actively praising His character.
- **Speaking truth audibly**—literally speaking Jesus' truth out loud, engaging multiple senses to reinforce truth against internal lies.

The apostle Paul described this process: "We demolish arguments and every pretension that sets itself up against the knowledge of God, and we take captive every thought to make it obedient to Christ" (2 Corinthians 10:4-6). This is active warfare, not passive experience.

### The Power of Declaration

Kingdom Warriors must move beyond defensive recognition of lies to offensive declaration of truth. Throughout Scripture, verbal declaration of Jesus' truth carries spiritual power: Jesus countered Satan's temptations by declaring "It is written…" David faced Goliath with declared confidence in God's power. Paul instructed believers to "put on" spiritual armor, including "the sword of the Spirit, which is the word of God" (Ephesians 6:17).

Effective truth declarations are specifically targeted to counter specific lies.

You know what's powerful about countering the enemy's lies? It's like having the perfect antidote for each specific poison he tries to use against you.

When that voice whispers, "You're too broken for God to use," you can declare with confidence, "But God chose the foolish things of the world to shame the wise; God chose the weak things of the world to shame the strong" (1 Corinthians 1:27). That targeted truth doesn't just silence the lie—it transforms it into an opportunity for Jesus' power to shine even brighter through your weakness.

Or when the enemy tries the classic "You're all alone in this battle" deception, there's something so powerful about responding with, "Even though I walk through the valley of the shadow of death, I will fear no evil, for you are with me" (Psalm 23:4, ESV). It's not just denying the lie; it's replacing it with a vivid picture of Jesus walking right beside you through your darkest moments.

We've found that when anxiety tries to convince us that "everything is falling apart," specifically countering it with "He who began a good work in you will carry it on to completion" (Philippians 1:6) reminds us that Jesus never starts something He doesn't finish. The specificity of that promise directly neutralizes the particular fear that's trying to take hold.

Isn't it amazing how God's Word contains the perfect counterpunch for every deceptive jab the enemy throws our way? What specific lie have you been hearing lately that might need a precisely targeted truth to disarm it in the authority of Jesus?

## More Than Positive Thinking

You know, there's such a profound difference between positive thinking and anchoring our lives in Scripture, though they might look similar on the surface.

Positive thinking says, "I believe things will work out," which can be helpful in some situations, but it's really just us trying to convince ourselves of something we hope is true. It's like building a house on sand—it might stand for a while, but when the real storms come, there's nothing solid holding it up.

Scripture, on the other hand, gives us statements like, "We know that in all things God works for the good of those who love him" (Romans 8:28). That's not just positive thinking—that's standing on a promise from the Creator of the universe! It's truth that exists whether we feel positive about it or not.

You may notice that positive thinking tends to collapse when circumstances get tough enough, because it's ultimately anchored in our own mental efforts. But when we base our thoughts on Scripture, we're connecting to something outside ourselves, something that remains true even when our emotions or circumstances are screaming the opposite.

Think about it: positive thinking might help you feel better temporarily, but Scripture actually transforms how you see reality itself. Positive thinking says, "I can handle this." Scripture says, "I can do all things through him who strengthens me" (Philippians 4:13). One relies on your limited resources; the other connects you to an infinite source of power and wisdom.

You know what we have come to realize about speaking truth in Jesus' authority? It's about relationship, not ritual. When we declare, "Greater is He who is in [us] than he who is in the world" (1 John 4:4), we are not reciting some magical incantation that forces Jesus' hand. We are standing in the faith and confidence of who Jesus is and what He's already accomplished.

Keep in mind: we don't always remember to stand on truth. Just like everyone else, sometimes we mistakenly rely on our own strength. Learning to follow Jesus is an adventure we are on until the day we meet Him face to face.

Sometimes we can fall into treating Scripture declarations like spiritual vending machines—insert the right verse, get the desired outcome. But that misses the heart of what's happening when we speak with Jesus' authority. It's more like a child confidently invoking their father's name because they know intimately who He is and how He feels about them.

When facing something that seems overwhelming, there's such a difference between desperately repeating "I can do all things through Christ" like a good luck charm versus speaking it with quiet confidence and respect because you've experienced His faithfulness in your life. One is trying to manipulate circumstances; the other is resting in a relationship. Remember, the enemy knows how to use truth against us.

What's beautiful about speaking with Jesus' authority is that it flows from trust, not technique. It's not about getting the words exactly right or saying them with enough force. It's about knowing whose name you're invoking and having experienced Jesus' character enough to be certain He'll be true to who He is.

Isn't there something powerful about approaching spiritual warfare not as mastering formulas but as deepening fellowship with Jesus, whose authority we're standing in?

When you're facing the heat of your unique battle, there's something incredibly powerful about personalizing Jesus' truth to your specific situation. It's like the difference between wearing someone else's armor and having armor custom-fitted just for you! *INSERT YOUR NAME I AM WITH YOU*

We've found that when we are facing our own particular struggles with fear about the future, simply repeating "Fear not" doesn't quite reach the depths of our hearts. But when we personalize it to "Even as we face this uncertain medical diagnosis, You have not given us a spirit of fear, but of power, love, and a sound mind"—that truth cuts right through to our specific circumstance.

Think about David when he faced Goliath—he didn't just quote general truths about God's power. He personalized it: "The Lord who rescued me from the paw of the lion and the paw of the bear will rescue me from the hand of this Philistine." He connected God's faithfulness in his past to the exact giant standing before him in that moment.

That's what makes Scripture so incredibly powerful in our lives. It's not a book of distant, abstract truths—it's living and active, designed to be applied with surgical precision to your unique battlefield. When you're struggling with rejection, the promise that "nothing can ever separate us from God's love" (Romans 8:38, NLT) becomes your specific shield. When you're battling addiction, "I can do all things through Christ who strengthens me" becomes your personal battle cry.

When we verbally declare Jesus' truth against Satan's lies, we actively participate in spiritual warfare rather than passively receiving deceptive attacks. These declarations reinforce faith, focus attention on truth, and exercise spiritual authority against the father of lies.

## The Ultimate Truth-Teller

Ultimately, victory over Satan's deception comes not through techniques alone but through relationship with Jesus Christ, who declared, "I am the way and the truth and the life" (John 14:6). Jesus is not merely a truth-teller, but Truth incarnate, the living antithesis to Satan's deceptive nature.

Kingdom Warriors overcome deception most effectively by:

- **Maintaining continuous communion with Jesus**—Regular, intimate fellowship with Jesus develops spiritual sensitivity that intuitively recognizes what aligns with His character and what doesn't.
- **Seeing all truth claims through the lens of Jesus**—Evaluating every teaching, impression, or experience by asking, "Does this reflect the Jesus revealed in Scripture?"
- **Walking in daily dependence on the Holy Spirit**—Jesus promised that the Holy Spirit "will guide you into all the truth" (John 16:13). Moment-by-moment reliance on His guidance provides real-time protection against deception.
- **Living in the warrior fellowship of faith**—Jesus established His church as a community of truth where believers sharpen and protect one another against deception. Isolated warriors are vulnerable warriors.

While Satan is indeed the father of lies, his deceptive power pales in comparison to Jesus, who is Truth itself. "The reason the Son of God appeared was to destroy the devil's work" (1 John 3:8). And in this unseen cosmic battle against deception, that's exactly what Jesus does in and through us.

In the next two chapters, we will explore the subtle poison of misguided ideas and how they can derail our spiritual adventure if left unchecked.

## Chapter 6

# Derailing the Kingdom Adventure

> Enter through the narrow gate. For wide is the gate and broad is the road that leads to destruction, and many enter through it. But small is the gate and narrow the road that leads to life, and only a few find it.
>
> — Matthew 7:13-14

### The Subtle Strategy of Distraction

You know what's fascinating about this unseen cosmic battle we're in? Satan has all these tactics he uses against us—from those obvious temptations to those intense spiritual attacks. But we have come to realize that one of his most effective strategies is something much more subtle: distraction.

Think about it—when we face direct temptation to sin, our spiritual alarm bells usually start ringing, right? But distractions? They operate under our radar, gradually shifting our focus away from Jesus' presence and purposes without triggering those internal warning systems.

Peter warns us, "Be alert and of sober mind. Your enemy the devil prowls around like a roaring lion looking for someone to devour" (1 Peter 5:8). But here's what's interesting—this watchfulness isn't just about the obvious attacks. It's about those subtle maneuvers, too. When a lion hunts, it doesn't always announce itself with a roar. Often, it stalks silently, counting on a distraction to separate its prey from the safety of the herd. In the same way, Satan uses distractions to isolate us from our spiritual community and from divine protection.

What makes this strategy so devastating is that it doesn't require us to overtly reject God or consciously choose sin. We simply become gradually preoccupied with other concerns until our spiritual focus dissolves almost imperceptibly. Jesus warned about this when He said, "the worries of this life and the deceitfulness of wealth choke the word, making it unfruitful" (Matthew 13:22). These "worries" aren't necessarily sinful in themselves—and that's precisely what makes them such ideal vehicles for distraction.

> The Christian life is not a constant high. I have my moments of deep discouragement. I have to go to God in prayer with tears in my eyes, and say, "O God, forgive me," or "Help me."[1]
>
> — Billy Graham

## The Anatomy of Spiritual Distraction

Have you noticed how Satan's distractions follow distinct patterns? They target specific vulnerabilities in our spiritual life:

## Busyness: The Thief of Spiritual Depth

Remember that moment when Jesus said, "Martha, Martha, you are anxious and troubled about many things, but one thing is necessary" (Luke 10:41-42, ESV)? He was highlighting one of Satan's primary distraction tactics: overwhelming us with excessive activity. Even legitimate responsibilities—important ones!—

can become spiritual liabilities when they consume so much of our time and energy that prayer, scripture, and communion with Jesus get squeezed out.

In our productivity-obsessed culture, busyness carries a badge of honor, doesn't it? The enemy leverages this cultural value, keeping us running from task to task, meeting to meeting, activity to activity. We become spiritually exhausted, operating on autopilot, too depleted to engage meaningfully with Jesus' presence. Our prayer lives become shallow, our worship perfunctory, and our spiritual discernment dulled—not because we've rejected these disciplines, but because we've allowed ourselves to be distracted from them.

The dangerous thing is that this busyness creates an illusion of spiritual productivity. We can mistake religious activity for spiritual depth, becoming like the church at Ephesus who was commended for their works but had abandoned their first love (Revelation 2:2-4). The enemy is perfectly content to see us busy with Christian activities if it keeps us from growing in intimate communion with Jesus Himself.

## Digital Distractions: The Fragmentation of Attention

Paul charges us, "Whatever is true, whatever is noble, whatever is right, whatever is pure, whatever is lovely, whatever is admirable—if anything is excellent or praiseworthy—think about such things" (Philippians 4:8). But doesn't that command seem increasingly challenging in our hyper-connected age, where digital technologies fragment our attention into smaller and smaller pieces?

The unprecedented access to information, entertainment, and social connection through our devices presents the enemy with powerful new avenues for distraction. Our smartphones ping with notifications, our social media feeds scroll endlessly, and our entertainment options multiply, each designed to capture and hold our attention. Did you know the average person checks their phone 96 times daily? That's approximately once every 10 minutes of waking life—creating this state of continuous partial attention.

This digital fragmentation affects us spiritually in profound ways. Prayer requires sustained attention and focus—precisely what our technology-saturated environment erodes. Scripture meditation needs mental space and silence to allow God's word to penetrate deeply—conditions increasingly rare in our notification-filled lives. The enemy doesn't need to make us reject prayer or Scripture; he simply needs to keep us constantly distracted by the next digital stimulus.

Even our consumption of spiritual content can become a distraction when it replaces direct engagement with Jesus. Listening to messages, reading Christian blogs, or participating in online religious discussions can create an illusion of spiritual growth while actually keeping us in a passive, consumer mindset rather than active devoted communion with Jesus.

> *The path of least resistance often leads to the battle of most regret. Kingdom Warriors choose the narrow way.*

## Comfort and Pleasure: The Anesthesia of the Soul

Paul warned that "people will be lovers of themselves, lovers of money...lovers of pleasure rather than lovers of God" (2 Timothy 3:2-4). The pursuit of comfort and pleasure represents another prime avenue for distraction. The enemy knows that a soul anesthetized by comfort becomes dull to spiritual realities.

Our culture's obsession with comfort and entertainment provides fertile ground for this distraction strategy. Did you realize the average American spends over four hours daily watching television, not counting other forms of entertainment? This immersion in entertainment subtly shapes our expectations about life, training us to expect constant stimulation, immediate gratification, and freedom from discomfort.

The spiritual life, by contrast, often involves waiting, self-denial, and perseverance through difficulty. Let's be honest—prayer can feel boring compared to entertainment designed by experts to trigger dopamine release. Scripture study requires mental effort, while social media offers effortless scrolling. Fasting means embracing discomfort, while our culture tells us to indulge every appetite.

By keeping us addicted to comfort and amusement, the enemy ensures that spiritual disciplines feel increasingly foreign and unappealing. We don't explicitly choose against God; we simply drift toward what feels immediately rewarding and away from practices that require spiritual exertion.

## Noise and Information Overload: Drowning Out Jesus' Voice

"Be still, and know that I am God" (Psalm 46:10). This command has never been more countercultural than in our information-saturated age. The enemy exploits our culture's noise and constant information flow to drown out the still, small voice of Jesus and the Holy Spirit.

It's staggering to think about—the average person now consumes approximately 34 gigabytes of information daily, equivalent to reading 174 newspapers from cover to cover. This information tsunami overwhelms our mental processing capacities, leaving little space for contemplation, reflection, or spiritual listening. We become so accustomed to external input that internal silence becomes uncomfortable, even anxiety-producing.

This constant noise creates ideal conditions for spiritual distraction. Remember when Elijah didn't hear God in the earthquake, wind, or fire, but in a gentle whisper (1 Kings 19:11-12)? Similarly, Jesus often speaks not through spiritual spectacles but through quiet impressions, subtle promptings, and the gentle conviction of His Spirit. When our lives are filled with constant noise—whether literal audio, information input, or mental stimulation—we become less able to discern these quieter Holy Spirit communications.

The enemy doesn't need to silence Jesus' voice entirely; he simply needs to ensure we're too distracted by other voices to notice it.

## The Four Competing Voices

Speaking of voices, did you know there are always four voices competing for attention in our minds? It's quite a revelation when you start to recognize them!

There's **the world** and its desires constantly bombarding us with messages about what we should have, who we should be, and what success looks like. That voice is relentless in our culture, isn't it? Always whispering that we need more, deserve more, should want more.

Then there's the voice of the **flesh and its temptations**—that internal pull toward comfort, pleasure, and self-gratification. It's that voice that says, "Just this once won't hurt" or "You've earned this" when we know something isn't aligned with Jesus' best for us.

The **devil comes in with his accusations**—perhaps the most insidious voice of all. He's the one reminding you of past failures, planting seeds of doubt about your worth, and questioning your identity in Christ. That voice specializes in "You're not enough" and "God couldn't possibly love someone who's done what you've done."

But here's the amazing truth that changes everything—Kingdom Warriors don't have to remain passive listeners to these competing voices! They take authority over their thoughts in the powerful name of their King Jesus!

When you recognize whose voice you're hearing, you can choose which one gets your attention. You can actively dismiss the voices that pull you away from your true identity and kingdom purpose. Just like a commander on a battlefield directing troops, you can command your thoughts to align with the truth of God's word and who He says you are.

We can choose to listen only to the fourth voice, the **voice of Jesus** through His Word and His Spirit who dwells within us.

Isn't it incredible that we have this authority? That you don't have to be victim to every thought that passes through your mind? Kingdom Warriors understand this battlefield of the mind and face each day equipped with the sword of the Spirit, which is the Word of God, ready to counter lies with truth.

What voice has been loudest in your life lately? And how might your day change if you consciously chose to listen most attentively to the voice of your King?

*The adventure of a Kingdom Warrior is marked not by absence of struggle, but by presence of purpose.*

## Worry and Anxiety: The Redirection of Faith

"Do not be anxious about anything" (Philippians 4:6). This command recognizes that anxiety represents a profound distraction from faith and trust in God. Worry effectively redirects our faith from Jesus to our problems, drawing mental and emotional energy away from spiritual focus.

Satan strategically uses the legitimate challenges of life—health concerns, financial pressures, relationship difficulties, work stress—to capture our attention and redirect it from Jesus' promises to our problems. Remember how Peter, when walking on water, began to sink when he fixed his gaze on the waves instead of Jesus (Matthew 14:30)? The same happens to us.

Anxiety creates a particularly effective distraction because it masquerades as responsibility. We mistake our worried rumination for problem-solving, not recognizing that it actually diminishes our spiritual effectiveness. As Jesus taught, worry adds nothing to our lives but consumes the mental and emotional energy that could be directed toward prayer, worship, and kingdom service (Matthew 6:27).

The enemy knows that anxious thoughts create a mental environment inhospitable to the peace of God that surpasses understanding (Philippians 4:7). By keeping us fixated on potential negative futures, he prevents us from experiencing Jesus' and the Holy Spirit's presence in the present moment.

## Success and Achievement: The Idolatry of Accomplishment

Jesus asked, "What good is it for someone to gain the whole world, yet forfeit their soul?" (Mark 8:36). He recognized the tremendous distracting power of success and achievement. The enemy exploits our desire for accomplishment, recognition, and advancement, knowing these pursuits can gradually displace Jesus as our ultimate concern.

Even ministry success can become a spiritual distraction when it focuses our attention on visible results rather than faithful obedience. The drive for achievement infiltrates our spiritual motivation, subtly shifting our kingdom purpose from glorifying Jesus to building our own reputation or influence.

This distraction operates with particular effectiveness among capable, driven followers of Jesus. Satan doesn't tempt them to abandon their faith but to pursue success with such single-minded determination that spiritual depth becomes collateral damage. Their identity gradually shifts from being "in Christ" to being defined by accomplishments, titles, recognition, and worldly desires.

The enemy whispers that we can attend to deeper spiritual matters after reaching the next goal, knowing that there's always another achievement on the horizon. Like the rich fool in Jesus' parable who focused on building bigger barns rather than his spiritual condition (Luke 12:16-21), we can become distracted by success and worldly pleasures until time runs out.

> Therefore do not worry about tomorrow, for tomorrow will worry about itself. Each day has enough trouble of its own.
>
> — Jesus (Matthew 6:34)

## Cultivating Jesus Focus in a Distracted World

While Satan's distraction strategies are powerful, they aren't irresistible. As Kingdom Warriors of light, we can cultivate practices that counter these diversionary tactics and maintain Jesus' focus:

## Intentional Presence Through Spiritual Rhythms

"Seven times a day I praise you for your righteous laws" (Psalm 119:164). The practice of fixed-hour prayer—stopping at designated times for communion with Jesus—creates regular interruptions to distraction's flow. These intentional pauses throughout the day bring us back to kingdom awareness, preventing the drift into extended periods of godless consciousness.

Establishing regular rhythms of Scripture reading, prayer, worship, Sabbath, and other spiritual practices creates a framework that resists the fragmenting effect of distractions. These aren't rigid religious rituals but lifelines that repeatedly pull us back to a Jesus and Holy Spirit reality amid distraction's current.

Jesus modeled this practice of intentional spiritual rhythm, regularly withdrawing from activity to pray even when pressing needs surrounded him (Luke 5:16). He recognized that maintaining communion with the Father took precedence over the urgent demands that could have consumed His attention.

## Simplification: Creating Space for Jesus

"But seek first his kingdom and his righteousness, and all these things will be given to you as well" (Matthew 6:33). This principle calls us to a radical simplification—placing Jesus' kingdom above the accumulating distractions that fragment our lives. Practical simplification might mean:

- Reducing digital consumption and creating tech-free zones and times
- Evaluating activities and commitments against kingdom priorities
- Decluttering physical spaces to reduce visual distractions during solitude
- Practicing silence and solitude to counteract information overload
- Learning to say "no" to good opportunities that divert focus from Jesus' best
- Focusing attention on eternal concerns while others fixate on the temporary
- Choosing simplicity amid constant pressure toward more acquisition
- Creating space for silence when noise is everywhere

This simplification isn't about rigid self-discipline but about creating space where deep communion with Jesus becomes possible. As we systematically remove distractions, we discover the truth of Jesus' promise that only one thing is truly necessary.

## Mindful Awareness: Recognizing Distraction's Patterns

"Search me, God, and know my heart...See if there is any offensive way in me, and lead me in the way everlasting" (Psalm 139:23-24). This prayer invites God to reveal the specific distractions that most effectively pull us away from spiritual focus in developing our relationship with Jesus.

Warriors of light develop awareness of their personal vulnerability to particular distractions. Some of us are most easily distracted by busyness, others by entertainment, still others by worry or achievement. By recognizing our individual patterns, we can establish targeted countermeasures against our specific vulnerabilities.

This awareness extends to noticing when distraction is occurring. With practice, we can catch ourselves earlier in distraction's cycle, learning to recognize the subtle shift in focus before it carries us far from Jesus' presence. Mindfulness of Jesus' and the Holy Spirit's presence helps us detect when that awareness begins to fade.

Regular practice can help deepen your relationship with Jesus while cultivating peace, compassion, and spiritual awareness in your daily life.

You know, keeping Jesus and the Holy Spirit in a conscious state of mind isn't just a nice spiritual practice—it's absolutely transformative! It's like having the wisest mentor and closest friend walking with you through every situation, every decision, every challenge you face.

You may find that when you deliberately maintain that awareness of Jesus' presence throughout your day, even the most ordinary moments take on extraordinary meaning. That quick prayer while waiting in traffic, that moment of gratitude while washing dishes—these become sacred spaces of connection. Think about how different your reactions might be when someone frustrates you if you're consciously aware that the Holy Spirit is right there, ready to guide your response! It changes everything, doesn't it?

And here's what's amazing—this conscious awareness isn't about perfection or spiritual performance. It's about relationship. It's about walking through life with the comforting knowledge that you're never alone, never without guidance, never without divine perspective on whatever you're facing.

When Kingdom Warriors live with this constant connection to Jesus and the Holy Spirit, they move from merely surviving each day to experiencing the adventure of kingdom living! Every conversation, every challenge becomes an opportunity to see God at work. Isn't that the kind of vibrant, powerful life we're all longing for?

## Sacred Resistance: Standing Against Culture's Current

"Do not conform to the pattern of this world, but be transformed by the renewing of your mind" (Romans 12:2). Countering distraction requires deliberate resistance against cultural norms that facilitate spiritual drift.

This resistance might involve: Establishing technology boundaries when others remain constantly connected Practicing Sabbath in a culture that never stops producing and consuming

This counter-cultural stance isn't about rigid rule-following but about creating conditions where deep spiritual life can flourish. By resisting the normalized distractions of our age, we create space where Jesus' presence can be experienced more fully in hearing the Holy Spirit. This practice helps warriors keep a kingdom mindset as we journey on this earthly adventure!

## Accountability in Community: Guarding Each Other

"But encourage one another daily...so that none of you may be hardened by sin's deceitfulness" (Hebrews 3:13). The subtle nature of distraction makes community accountability essential. Others often notice our spiritual drift before we recognize it ourselves.

Spiritual friends can ask penetrating questions: Where is your spiritual attention focused lately? What's occupying your thoughts during free moments? How is your prayer life and Scripture engagement? What distractions are you struggling with most? How is your sense of Jesus' and the Holy Spirit's presence in daily life? Or simply, like our friend Michael Barry likes to ask, "How's your heart today?"

This loving accountability creates an early warning system against distraction, helping us course-correct before major spiritual drift occurs. The enemy prefers isolated believers, knowing they're more vulnerable to his distraction strategies when separated from the discernment of a spiritual warrior community.

## The Spiritual Battle for Attention

Understanding distraction as spiritual warfare changes how we respond to it. What seems like a simple attention management problem is actually a battlefront in cosmic conflict. The enemy targets our focus because he knows that what captures our attention ultimately captures our mind and heart.

This perspective elevates seemingly small daily choices to their true spiritual significance: Choosing prayer over social media scrolling becomes an act of spiritual warfare Maintaining Sabbath despite pressure to remain productive becomes resistance against enemy strategy Creating tech-free family time becomes reclaiming territory from the distraction of the enemy Intentional silence becomes a weapon against Satan's noise campaign

Jesus taught that our eye (what we focus on) determines whether our whole body is full of light or darkness (Matthew 6:22-23). What we give our attention to shapes our spiritual condition. Satan understands this principle, which is why distraction forms a central part of his strategy against warriors. Did you get that? Distraction is his strategy against Kingdom Warriors!

This battle for attention cannot be fought through willpower alone. Like all spiritual warfare, victory comes through dependence on Jesus' strength rather than our own efforts. "'Not by might nor by power, but by my Spirit,' says the Lord Almighty" (Zechariah 4:6). The same Holy Spirit who raised Christ from the dead empowers us to overcome the enemy's distractions and fix our eyes on Jesus where we never leave His presence on this kingdom adventure.

## Reclaiming Attention as Worship

Ultimately, what we pay attention to becomes our worship. Satan's distraction strategy aims to fragment our worship, diverting it from the Creator to countless created things. Resisting distraction, then, becomes an act of focused worship—offering our undivided attention to the One who alone deserves it, Jesus.

The spiritual heroes throughout biblical history were people of remarkable focus. Noah remained focused on building the ark amid universal distraction. Abraham kept his focus on God's promise despite decades of waiting. Jesus Himself stayed perfectly focused on His mission despite constant opportunity for diversion.

Listening to Jesus and the Holy Spirit moment by moment forms the essential heartbeat of an effective Kingdom Warrior's life. This continuous divine communion transforms ordinary believers into spiritually attuned Kingdom Warriors who can respond instantly to heaven's strategic promptings. When warriors cultivate this heightened spiritual awareness, they avoid wasted energy on self-directed efforts and instead align perfectly with Jesus and the Holy Spirit's precise timing and methods.

The practice of moment-by-moment listening shifts believers from operating through religious formulas to experiencing the exhilarating adventure of Spirit-led living. In critical spiritual battles, this attentiveness becomes the difference between victory and defeat, as warriors receive real-time tactical guidance that the enemy cannot anticipate. Like special forces operators maintaining constant radio contact with headquarters, Kingdom Warriors who remain in unbroken communion with Jesus and listening to the Holy Spirit position themselves to receive divine intelligence, unexpected course corrections, and supernatural provision exactly when needed.

An example of this connection is revealed in an amazing supernatural experience Mel had at the Denver International Airport. You won't believe how God showed up in such an unexpected place!

On a ministry business trip a few years back he was just strolling along the moving walkway on concourse A, nothing special about the moment. He and his friend George were chatting, and he casually mentioned, "The Library of Hope is doing really well." Just normal conversation between us.

The surprising part? This woman walking right in front of them—a complete stranger—suddenly turned around and asked, "What is the Library of Hope?" Mel thought, what are the chances? He was thrilled to share and responded with excitement, "We send libraries of hope to prisons across the country!"

But here's where it gets interesting. Instead of sharing my enthusiasm, she gave him this look of complete disgust. It was so stark, so unexpected. As they approached the TSA checkpoint, Mel felt prompted by the Spirit to say out loud, "To some we are the fragrance of death, to others the fragrance of life."

He wasn't trying to make a scene, and just handed his ID to the security agent and went about putting his shoes in those plastic trays like everyone else. But then something extraordinary happened! That same security guy actually left his position at the checkpoint and ran over to Mel.

"Sir," he said with genuine hunger in his eyes, "tell me more about the fragrance of life!"

Can you imagine? In that brief moment, in one of the busiest airports in America, Mel quickly handed him a book, wrote a Scripture in it, and he hurried back to his post. The presence of the Holy Spirit was so tangible in that moment.

George turned to Mel, completely amazed, and asked, "What just happened?"

Mel simply repeated, "To some we are the fragrance of death, to others the fragrance of life."

Isn't it incredible how God works? In the middle of an airport, with hundreds of people rushing past, two hearts responded in completely opposite ways to the same message. One turned away in disgust, while another was so drawn to the message of life that he literally left his post to find out more!

This is why we need to remain conscious of Jesus and the Holy Spirit in every moment. You never know when an ordinary comment on a moving walkway might become a divine appointment that changes someone's life forever!

This intimate dialogue with heaven isn't reserved for spiritual elites but represents the birthright of every Kingdom Warrior willing to quiet competing voices and train their spiritual senses to recognize the Shepherd's voice above all others.

These examples remind us that spiritual focus isn't a modern challenge created by digital technology. Throughout human history, the enemy has employed age-appropriate distraction strategies to divert human attention from Jesus. What's changed is not the strategy but its intensity and the sophistication of its tools in our hyperconnected age.

As Kingdom Warriors, we're called to reclaim our attention as sacred territory in this unseen cosmic battle. With Jesus' help, we can recognize distraction for what it is—not merely an inconvenience but a strategic enemy assault. And armed with this awareness, we can cultivate spiritual disciplines that keep our focus where it belongs: on the Author and Perfecter of our faith, Jesus, who invites us into undistracted communion with Himself.

"Let us...[fix] our eyes on Jesus, the pioneer and perfecter of faith" (Hebrews 12:2). This simple command stands as both our greatest challenge and our surest path to victory in a world engineered for distraction. As we learn to keep our focus on Jesus amid countless diversions, we experience the freedom and power of the Holy Spirit that comes from undivided spiritual attention. And in that focused gaze, we find not only protection from the enemy's schemes but the transforming presence of the One who deserves our complete attention, Jesus.

In the next chapter, we'll continue to explore how the enemy uses misguided ideas to further his purposes, and how we can stand firm against these attacks, acknowledging that our thought patterns literally shape our spiritual reality. And that's precisely why Satan targets this domain with such strategic precision.

## Chapter 7

# Subtle Poison

## Misguided Ideas

> See to it that no one takes you captive through hollow and deceptive philosophy, which depends on human tradition and the elemental spiritual forces of this world rather than on Christ.
>
> — Colossians 2:8

### Beyond Deception: The Power of Misguided Ideas

As we've explored in our discussion of the Father of Lies, Satan employs various deceptive tactics in the battlefield of our minds. Building on this understanding, we now turn our attention to a specific and particularly dangerous form of deception: misguided ideas.

Misguided ideas go beyond simple deception—they represent entire systems of thought that can redirect a warrior's path away from kingdom purposes. As Paul warns in Colossians 2:8: "See to it that no one takes you captive through hollow and deceptive philosophy, which depends on human tradition and the elemental spiritual forces of this world rather than on Christ."

What makes misguided ideas especially dangerous is that they often contain significant elements of truth mixed with subtle distortions. Unlike obvious temptations that trigger our spiritual alarm systems, these ideas can infiltrate our thinking without detection, gradually reshaping our understanding of God, ourselves, and our purpose in this world.

> *Kingdom Warriors know that what you feed grows stronger. Starve your flesh; nourish your spirit.*

## Common Patterns of Misguided Ideas

Several patterns emerge when we examine how these dangerous concepts gain traction in believers' lives:

## Half-truths: The Most Dangerous Distortions

While Chapter 5 addressed how Satan uses half-truths in general deception, let's explore how these operate specifically within philosophical and theological systems.

Misguided ideas often begin with legitimate biblical concepts but subtly shift their emphasis or application. For example, the biblical truth that God blesses obedience can be distorted into a prosperity gospel that promises material wealth for spiritual faithfulness. While God does bless his people in a variety ways than just material wealth. The truth element makes the distortion more difficult to identify.

Another example is how the biblical concept of grace can be distorted into antinomianism—the idea that since we're saved by grace, moral obedience doesn't matter. This takes a precious truth and twists its application in ways that lead to spiritual harm.

These half-truths are particularly effective because they allow believers to feel they're embracing biblical concepts while actually adopting perspectives that gradually lead them away from the fullness of kingdom truth.

## Complex Systems That Overemphasize Single Truths

Many misguided ideas develop when a single biblical truth is elevated above others, creating an imbalanced theological system.

For instance, emphasizing God's sovereignty to the exclusion of human responsibility can lead to fatalism. Conversely, overemphasizing human choice while minimizing God's sovereignty can lead to a works-based understanding of relationship with God.

Similarly, focusing exclusively on God's love without acknowledging His holiness creates a distorted picture, as does emphasizing judgment without mercy. Biblical truth exists in balanced tension, and misguided ideas often result from breaking that tension by elevating one aspect at the expense of others.

The danger isn't that these ideas contain no truth—it's that they take genuine truth and place it in a framework that ultimately distorts the whole.

## Cultural Adaptation That Compromises Truth

Another pattern emerges when legitimate efforts to make faith relevant to contemporary culture go beyond contextualization to compromise.

The desire to connect with culture is appropriate—Paul himself became "all things to all people" (1 Corinthians 9:22). However, misguided ideas often form when cultural values subtly become the lens through which Scripture is interpreted, rather than Scripture being the lens through which we evaluate culture.

For example, individualism might lead to reading Scripture with an excessive focus on personal blessing rather than community responsibility. Materialism might influence us to interpret promises of blessing primarily in financial terms. Political ideologies might color how we understand biblical concepts of justice, freedom, or authority.

These cultural adaptations often begin with good intentions—making faith accessible and relevant—but can gradually lead to misguided ideas that more closely reflect cultural values than kingdom truths.

## Intellectual Appeals That Bypass the Heart

Some of the most persuasive misguided ideas appeal strongly to the intellect while bypassing spiritual discernment. They offer complex systems that seem to explain everything, providing intellectual satisfaction while potentially leading away from authentic relationship with Jesus.

These approaches often reduce the mystery of faith to formulaic systems, promising comprehensive understanding and control. They appeal particularly to those who value intellectual mastery, offering the false security of having everything figured out.

The danger lies not in intellectual engagement itself—God created our minds for His glory—but in systems that elevate human reasoning above divine revelation and spiritual discernment, or that promise a level of comprehensive understanding that Scripture itself doesn't claim to provide.

## Identifying Vulnerable Seasons

Certain seasons of life leave us particularly vulnerable to misguided ideas. Recognizing these periods can help us maintain heightened vigilance when we most need it:

## Times of Suffering and Disillusionment

When facing unexpected suffering or disappointment, especially within the church or spiritual community, we naturally seek explanations and solutions. This search makes us receptive to ideas that promise to make sense of our pain or offer a path forward.

During such seasons, misguided ideas that offer simple explanations or quick solutions can be especially appealing. Prosperity theology often gains traction with those experiencing financial hardship. Legalistic systems appeal to those hurt by moral failures in the church. Hyper-grace teachings can attract those wounded by legalism.

Our vulnerability during suffering isn't a weakness of character but a reality of the human experience. Jesus Himself recognized that sheep without a shepherd are particularly vulnerable to being led astray. Awareness of this vulnerability during difficult seasons can help us approach new ideas with appropriate caution.

> A lie doesn't become truth, wrong doesn't become right, and evil doesn't become good just because it's accepted by a majority.[1]
>
> — Booker T. Washington

## Transitions and Identity Formation

Major life transitions—whether educational, vocational, relational, or geographical—often involve questioning and reforming aspects of our identity. During these periods of reevaluation, we're naturally more open to new ideas that help us make sense of our changing circumstances.

Young adults leaving home, people changing careers, those experiencing major relationship changes, or believers finding new church communities are all navigating identity questions that create openness to new perspectives. This openness, while potentially healthy, also creates vulnerability to misguided ideas.

These transition periods require both grace and vigilance—allowing space for growth and reconsideration while maintaining connection to the anchoring truths of Scripture and community discernment.

## Reaction to Extremes

Perhaps the most common pathway into misguided ideas is reacting against perceived or real extremes we've experienced. When we've been hurt by the misapplication of a truth, we're prone to embrace an opposite error rather than finding the balanced center.

Those wounded by legalistic environments may swing toward antinomianism. Those disappointed by charismatic excesses might reject all aspects of spiritual gifts and supernatural ministry. Those hurt by authoritarian leadership might reject all authority structures.

This pendulum swing is natural but dangerous. The path to truth rarely lies in reaction but in the balanced center that Scripture presents. Recognizing our tendency to react against past hurts can help us pause and seek God's wisdom rather than simply embracing an opposite extreme.

## Overcoming Misguided Ideas

Building on the foundations of spiritual discernment discussed in Chapter 5, here are specific strategies for identifying and overcoming misguided ideas:

## Balanced Biblical Engagement

While we've already established Scripture as our foundation for truth, overcoming misguided ideas requires a particular approach to biblical study that emphasizes comprehensiveness and context.

Rather than selective reading that focuses only on favorite passages or themes, we need engagement with the full counsel of Scripture. This means studying entire books rather than isolated verses, understanding historical and literary context, and recognizing how individual passages fit within the broader biblical narrative.

This comprehensive approach provides protection against misguided ideas that selectively emphasize certain biblical themes while ignoring others. When we encounter a teaching that seems to elevate one scriptural theme, we can evaluate it against the whole counsel of God's Word.

*True transformation happens when we stop fighting against our calling and start fighting for it.*

## Theological Humility

One of the most effective protections against misguided ideas is maintaining theological humility—recognizing that our understanding is limited and always growing. This doesn't mean abandoning conviction, but holding our interpretations with appropriate humility.

Phrases like "I could be wrong about this," or "I'm still growing in my understanding," aren't signs of weak faith but of theological maturity. They reflect the recognition that while Scripture itself is infallible, our interpretations are not.

This humility creates space for ongoing growth and correction, allowing the Holy Spirit to continue refining our understanding rather than becoming locked into rigid perspectives that might contain elements of error.

## Historical Awareness

Many seemingly "new" misguided ideas are actually recycled errors the church has already addressed throughout its history. Familiarity with historical theology provides valuable perspective on contemporary teachings.

When encountering an exciting "new revelation," it's worth asking whether the church has encountered similar ideas before and how they were evaluated. Many modern movements present as innovative what are actually variations of Gnosticism, Pelagianism, Docetism, or other historical departures from orthodox understanding.

This historical awareness doesn't mean that all traditional interpretations are automatically correct, but it does provide the wisdom of centuries of Spirit-led reflection on Scripture. As the saying goes, those who don't learn from history are doomed to repeat it.

## Practical Fruit Assessment

Jesus taught that we would recognize false prophets by their fruits, and this principle applies equally to identifying misguided ideas. While incorrect teaching might initially energize or inspire, its long-term fruit reveals its true nature.

We should ask: Where does this teaching ultimately lead in terms of character formation and kingdom mission? Does it produce people who increasingly reflect the character of Christ—His love, humility, holiness, and self-sacrifice? Does it advance or hinder the Great Commission and Great Commandment?

Sometimes teachings that seem exciting initially later reveal their problematic nature through their practical results in communities and individual lives. Patience in evaluation allows these fruits to become evident.

## Helping Others Navigate Misguided Ideas

As Kingdom Warriors, we're called not only to avoid deception ourselves but to help others navigate these challenges as well. This requires wisdom and grace:

## Creating Safe Spaces for Questions

When people are processing potentially misguided ideas, they need environments where they can express questions and doubts without judgment. Shutting down conversation often drives exploration underground rather than providing guidance.

By creating safe spaces for honest questions, we allow people to process their thinking out loud where community discernment can help guide them. This doesn't mean endorsing every idea but providing a relational context where truth can be pursued together.

This approach requires patience and respect, recognizing that spiritual growth often involves seasons of questioning and exploration. Jesus Himself demonstrated remarkable patience with His disciples' misunderstandings, gently guiding them toward truth rather than shutting down their questions.

## Modeling Discernment in Process

Rather than simply telling others what to believe, we can have greater impact by transparently sharing our own discernment processes. By making visible how we evaluate ideas against Scripture, seek counsel, and pray for wisdom, we provide a model others can follow.

This might sound like: "When I encountered that teaching, I initially found it appealing because…But when I examined it more closely, I realized…Here's how I worked through that process…" This approach is more empowering than simply pronouncing judgment on ideas.

## Addressing Heart Needs Behind Attraction to Misguided Ideas

When someone is drawn to a misguided idea, there's often a legitimate need or desire that makes the teaching attractive. By identifying and addressing that underlying need, we can help them find satisfaction in truth rather than distortion.

For instance, someone attracted to prosperity teaching might have legitimate needs for provision and assurance of God's care. Someone drawn to legalism might be seeking security and clear boundaries. Someone exploring universalism might be wrestling with questions about God's justice and love.

By acknowledging these legitimate concerns and showing how Scripture addresses them in truthful ways, we can help redirect the search for answers toward solid ground.

## Truth as Our Pathway to Freedom

As we navigate the complex landscape of ideas in our pluralistic world, let's remember Jesus' promise: "You will know the truth, and the truth will set you free" (John 8:32). Misguided ideas, despite their partial truths, ultimately lead to various forms of bondage—intellectual, emotional, relational, and spiritual.

The adventure toward freedom involves growing discernment that can distinguish life-giving truth from subtle poison. This discernment doesn't develop overnight but through consistent spiritual practices, community accountability, and humble dependence on the Holy Spirit's guidance and God's word.

As Kingdom Warriors, we're called to be people of truth—not in an arrogant or rigid sense, but with humble confidence in God's revelation and ongoing openness to deeper understanding. When we commit ourselves to this path, we not only protect our own hearts and minds but become guides who can help others navigate safely through the complex terrain of ideas toward the freedom Jesus' promises.

In the next chapter, we'll explore how warriors fight their battles in the light.

# Part Three
# THE WARRIOR'S EQUIPMENT

## Chapter 8

## Warriors Battle in the Light

> But if we walk in the light, as he is in the light, we have fellowship with one another, and the blood of Jesus, his Son, purifies us from all sin.
>
> — 1 John 1:7

You want to know something powerful? You are meant to be a light-bearer—not just someone who occasionally shines, but someone who absolutely blazes with transformative purpose.

Imagine walking into any room and bringing something different. Not through force or manipulation, but through an authentic, radiant presence that cuts through darkness like a laser. That's what it means to be a true Kingdom Warrior—someone who doesn't just talk about light but actually embodies it.

Let's get real for a moment. Walking in light isn't about being perfect. It's about being honest—brutally, beautifully honest. With yourself, with others, with God. It means having the courage to look at your own stuff—your struggles, your wounds, your messy parts—and instead of hiding them, bringing them into the light. Because here's the secret: darkness loses its power when you refuse to let it hide.

> Light itself is a great corrective. It brings autonomy out of hiding.
>
> — JAMES HAWKINS

## Truth as a Rescue Mission

Your life is like a lighthouse. Think about that for a second. In the midst of cultural chaos, personal storms, and spiritual battles, you have the ability to provide clear direction. Not through arguing or forcing your views, but by simply being authentically aligned with truth. Your very presence becomes a beacon that helps others find their way.

Truth isn't a weapon—it's a warrior rescue mission. When you speak truth, you're not trying to wound; you're trying to set people free. It's like cutting through a thick fog, revealing a path that was always there but couldn't be seen. Your words, when rooted in love and wisdom, can slice through deception faster than any argument.

*True warriors understand that temptation loses its power in the light of Jesus' presence.*

## The Warrior's Equipment

Righteousness isn't about being religious. It's about carrying Jesus' actual presence. Imagine having a power so pure that darkness actually has to retreat when you show up. That's not arrogance—that's understanding the authority you've been given. You're not fighting in your own strength, but with the power of Jesus that has already conquered every darkness.

Wisdom is your superpower. But not the kind of wisdom that makes you sound smart—the kind that helps you navigate life's most complex moments with supernatural clarity. It's about knowing when to speak, when to be silent, when to move forward, and when to wait. This wisdom doesn't come from books—it comes from intimate connection with Jesus and the Holy Spirit.

Holiness isn't a restrictive set of rules. It's a transformative fire that burns away everything that doesn't look like Jesus. You're being constantly refined, not to make you perfect, but to make you powerful. Every compromise that gets burned away creates more space for divine Holy Spirit presence.

> *Kingdom Warriors understand that confession to trusted brothers and sisters breaks the power of darkness that thrives in secrecy.*

## THE WARRIOR'S FEET OF PEACE

Want to know about the most powerful walking shoes you'll ever wear? They are not the kind you can buy in a store. Although sketchers are nice footwear.

Imagine having feet that don't just walk through life but literally transform the ground beneath them. Seriously. Your warriors' feet aren't just for moving from point A to point B. They're spiritual game-changers, designed to bring peace into the most chaotic spaces imaginable.

Think about peace for a second. Most people picture peace as just the absence of conflict. But we're talking about something far more explosive—*shalom*. This is peace that doesn't just sit quietly, but actively heals, restores, and rebuilds. When you walk into a room with this kind of peace, broken things start to mend. Walls come down. Hope starts to breathe.

Your kingdom feet are beautiful—not because of how they look, but because of where they're willing to go. They carry good news into dark places. They're ready to declare freedom to those who feel trapped, to bring sight to those who can't see a way forward. This isn't just a metaphor. This is your daily Kingdom Warrior mission.

The world is full of chaos. Conflict. Brokenness. And you? You're walking around with a divine kingdom GPS that can navigate through any spiritual terrain. Fear tries to destabilize you. Your feet are anchored in something deeper. Doubt tries to trip you up. You're standing on kingdom promises that cannot be shaken.

For we live by faith, not by sight.

— 2 Corinthians 5:7

## The Shield of Faith

Let's talk about the most powerful kingdom defense system you'll ever own—it's nothing like any protection you've ever imagined.

Close your eyes for a moment and picture a shield. But this isn't just any shield. This is a living, breathing, dynamic force that moves with you, anticipates attacks before they happen, and does something wild: it can actually turn incoming threats into kingdom opportunities.

Your faith isn't a passive thing. It's not some fragile glass shield that might shatter at the first sign of trouble. This is a massive, curved shield that can cover your entire being—protecting you in ways you can't even comprehend. When doubt tries to throw its fiery darts, your kingdom faith doesn't just block them. It extinguishes them mid-air.

Here's the mind-blowing part: this shield gets stronger the more you use it. Every challenge you face, every moment of uncertainty, is actually a training ground. Those things that are trying to take you out? They're actually making your faith more powerful. It's like spiritual weight training, and you're getting stronger with every rep.

Imagine walking into any situation—no matter how chaotic, how overwhelming—and having an unshakeable confidence. Not because you're some superhuman, but because you're connected to something far greater than yourself. Your kingdom faith isn't about positive thinking. It's about knowing Who stands behind you, Warrior King Jesus.

The enemy loves to launch psychological warfare. Darts of fear. Missiles of condemnation. Arrows of doubt. But here's the truth: These attacks are already defeated before they even reach you. Your faith isn't just defensive—it's an offensive weapon that pushes back darkness.

> *Kingdom Warriors understand that every temptation overcome becomes a testimony of God's transforming power.*

## Warriors Helmet of Salvation

This is one of the most critical pieces of armor you'll ever wear—and it's also something you cannot buy in a store. This is about protecting your mind, and trust me, your mind is your most powerful battlefield.

Imagine having a helmet that does more than just shield you from physical blows. We're talking about protection that guards against every mental attack, every whispered lie, every attempt to mess with your identity. This isn't just defense—this is a complete mental transformation.

Your mind is constantly under siege. Thoughts of doubt, waves of condemnation, identity attacks that try to tell you who you're not—they're coming at you from all directions. But what if I told you that you have an ultimate protection system? A helmet of salvation that doesn't just block these attacks—it completely neutralizes them.

This isn't about trying to think positive. This is about a total kingdom identity reset. Your salvation isn't just a past event—it's a complete, ongoing transformation. It covers everything: who you were, who you are, and who you're becoming. Past, present, future—all secured.

The enemy's favorite weapon is psychological warfare. Those poisonous thoughts that creep in? The moments of self-doubt? The whispers that try to define you by your mistakes? They're rendered powerless. Not because you're some superhuman, but because of Who lives in you.

> In a time of deceit telling the truth is a revolutionary act.
>
> — UNKNOWN

## KINGDOM WARRIOR'S SWORD OF THE SPIRIT

Finally, your Sword. There is no weapon more powerful in the Spiritual Realm. It carries more power than you can ever imagine. It is your Sword of the Spirit.

Your Sword is your weapon for offensive warfare. Though it isn't a weapon of destruction. This is a weapon of liberation. A sword so sharp it can cut through the deepest darkness, so precise it can surgically remove lies, so powerful it can break chains that have held people captive for years.

Forget everything you know about weapons. This sword isn't about violence—it's about truth. And not just any truth. We're talking about a living, breathing truth that has the power to transform entire atmospheres with a single utterance.

Imagine having a weapon that can dismantle lies before they even take root. A sword that doesn't just defend you but actively advances kingdom freedom. When the enemy launches psychological attacks, mental bondages, spiritual oppression—you've got something that cuts right through it all.

This isn't about memorizing Bible verses like some spiritual weapon catalog. This is about intimacy. About knowing the heart behind the words. Every time you dive into Scripture, you're not just reading—you're connecting. You're becoming fluent in a language that literally reshapes reality.

Jesus showed us how to use this sword. When temptation

came, He didn't argue. He simply spoke truth. "It is written." Three simple words that shut down the enemy's entire strategy. That's the power you're carrying.

> The strongest souls fight their hardest battles in silence.
>
> — UNKNOWN

Warriors, every piece of your Armor is crucial to the battle. Each piece, precisely designed by God so you can stand firm. So stand.

In the next chapter we will talk about warriors rising up and operating in kingdom truth.

## Chapter 9

# Kingdom Warriors Stand for Truth

> Stand firm then, with the belt of truth buckled around your waist, with the breastplate of righteousness in place.
>
> — Ephesians 6:14

> Guide me in your truth and teach me, for you are God my Savior, and my hope is in you all day long.
>
> — Psalm 25:5

Truth has become a casualty in our world of shifting opinions and relative values. Yet for Kingdom Warriors, truth isn't merely a concept to defend—it's a Person to follow, a light to guide our path, and a foundation upon which we build our lives.

When Jesus declared, "I am the way and the truth and the life" (John 14:6), He wasn't speaking of truth as an abstract philosophy. He embodied truth in its purest form. In a world drowning in deception, half-truths, and comfortable lies, Kingdom Warriors stand as beacons of authentic truth that transforms rather than condemns.

Have you ever noticed how refreshing it is to be in the presence of someone completely genuine—someone whose words and actions align perfectly? This is the kind of integrity truth demands of us. Truth isn't just about speaking facts—it's about living with such consistency that our very lives proclaim Jesus' reality.

The adventure of standing for truth begins within. We must first allow God's truth to confront the comfortable deceptions we've embraced about ourselves, others, and even God. This inner work requires courage—the courage to ask, "Search me, God, and know my heart" (Psalm 139:23), even when His light exposes areas that need transformation.

*Kingdom Warriors know that sometimes faithfulness looks like taking one more step when you can't see the end of the road.*

Kingdom Warriors know that truth and love must walk hand in hand. Truth without love becomes harsh and judgmental. Love without truth becomes enabling and hollow. But when we speak truth with genuine love as Paul instructs in Ephesians 4:15, we create space for genuine warrior transformation.

In your daily interactions, how might Jesus be calling you to stand for truth? Perhaps it means speaking up when gossip spreads or refusing to participate in dishonest business practices. Maybe it means acknowledging your struggles rather than maintaining a façade of perfection. Or perhaps it means lovingly sharing God's perspective with someone caught in self-destruction.

Standing for truth often comes with a cost. Jesus Himself was crucified for speaking truth with kingdom power. Yet Kingdom Warriors understand that temporary discomfort pales in comparison to the freedom truth brings. As Jesus promised, "You will know the truth, and the truth will set you free" (John 8:32).

In a culture that celebrates deception when it's convenient and condemns truth when it's uncomfortable, your commitment to walk in truth marks you as distinctly different. This difference isn't meant to alienate but to illuminate—to show others a better way.

Today, ask the Holy Spirit to guide you into all truth as Jesus promised in John 16:13. Allow Him to shine His light on any areas where you've compromised with falsehood. Choose to align your words, thoughts, and actions with God's truth, and watch how this alignment transforms not only your life but the lives of those around you.

## Warriors Stand for Truth Unashamedly

*When flesh and spirit battle within, Kingdom Warriors remember they are no longer slaves to sin but sons and daughters of the King.*

I have no greater joy than to hear that my children are walking in the truth.

— 3 John 1:4

Have you ever felt that knot in your stomach when you knew you needed to speak the truth in a difficult situation? That tension between wanting to be liked and needing to stand firm?

I've been thinking about what it truly means to stand unashamedly for truth in today's culture. It's not just about being right—it's about being faithful to Jesus who is Truth itself.

When Paul declared, "I am not ashamed of the gospel, because it is the power of God that brings salvation to everyone who believes" (Romans 1:16), he wasn't boasting about his courage. He was expressing a profound revelation: the message we carry isn't just good advice—it's life-transforming kingdom power!

Think about Daniel for a moment. When faced with the choice between blending in or standing out, he chose to pray openly, even when it meant a trip to the lions' den. What gave him that kind of boldness? I believe it was his unshakable faith and confidence in who God is.

That's the heart of unashamed Kingdom Warriors—they've experienced Jesus' truth so personally that remaining silent feels impossible. When you've been rescued by truth, you can't help but share it with others.

*In authentic fellowship, Kingdom Warriors find both the courage to stand and the humility to kneel.*

But let's be honest—this isn't easy, is it? In a world that celebrates moral relativism, standing firmly on absolute truth often comes with a cost. You might be labeled intolerant, narrow-minded, or worse. The pressure to water down God's Word to make it more palatable is real.

Jackie Hill Perry is a Christian author, poet, and speaker who has shared her personal testimony of coming out of a homosexual lifestyle after encountering God's truth in Scripture. Despite tremendous pressure from both secular culture and even some progressive Christian voices to embrace her former identity, she has stood firmly on her conviction that God's design for sexuality is revealed in Scripture.[1]

Nabeel Qureshi was raised in a loving, devout Pakistani Muslim family. He was deeply committed to Islam and well-versed in its teachings, actively practicing his faith and defending it through college. However, during his university years, he formed a friendship with a Christian named David Wood who challenged him to investigate the historical claims of Christianity.[2]

What makes Nabeel's story remarkable was his commitment to truth above all else. Initially, he sought to disprove Christianity, but as a medical doctor and someone trained in analyzing evidence, he approached his investigation with intellectual honesty. After several years of rigorous study of the historical evidence for the resurrection of Jesus, the reliability of the New Testament, and the claims of Jesus' divinity, Nabeel came to the painful realization that Christianity was true.

His conversion cost him dearly. In his book *Seeking Allah, Finding Jesus*, he poignantly describes how his family initially felt betrayed and heartbroken. His decision to follow Christ essentially meant losing the close relationship he had with his parents and extended family—something that caused him tremendous grief.

Despite these personal costs, Nabeel became one of the most articulate and compassionate Christian apologists of recent times. He traveled extensively, sharing his testimony and defending the truth of Christianity, particularly to Muslim audiences.

Even when diagnosed with advanced stomach cancer at age thirty-three, Nabeel continued to stand for the truth of Jesus Christ. Throughout his painful battle with cancer until his death in 2017, he maintained his faith and continued to share how Jesus had transformed his life, refusing to question God's goodness even in his suffering.

Nabeel's life exemplifies what it means to be a Kingdom Warrior who values truth above comfort, cultural acceptance, or even family ties. His intellectual honesty, willingness to follow evidence wherever it led, and his loving approach to interfaith dialogue have inspired countless others to examine the truth claims of Christianity with similar integrity.

Here's what we have discovered: people are hungry for truth spoken with love. They're tired of shifting opinions and hollow promises. There's something compelling about someone who stands firmly without arrogance, who speaks truth in love without condemnation.

Remember Shadrach, Meshach, and Abednego? When everyone else bowed to the golden image, they remained standing —not out of rebellion, but out of reverence for a higher truth. Their response wasn't angry or defensive: "The God we serve is able to deliver us…But even if he does not…we will not serve your gods" (Daniel 3:17-18). That's the quiet confidence of those who know their Jesus!

This isn't about pointing fingers or imposing rules. It's about walking alongside people, shining light on the path ahead like a friend guiding another through dark woods.

"Your word is a lamp for my feet, a light on my path" (Psalm 119:105). Isn't that a wonderful image? God's truth isn't meant to be a floodlight that blinds—it's a lamp that illuminates just enough of the path for the next step.

What would happen if we approached each conversation asking, "How can I shine just enough light to help this person take their next step toward Jesus?" Sometimes that means boldly proclaiming truth; other times it means patiently answering questions or simply demonstrating righteousness through our actions.

Like Philip with the Ethiopian eunuch, sometimes the most powerful question we can ask is simply, "Do you understand what you are reading?" (Acts 8:30). That open-handed approach invites people into discovery rather than forcing compliance.

Standing unashamedly for truth isn't about winning arguments—it's about winning hearts. It's about loving people enough to offer them the same life-transforming truth that has changed us.

## WARRIORS DIE TO SELF DAILY

> I die daily.
>
> — 1 CORINTHIANS 15:31, NKJV

Have you ever noticed how the most profound spiritual truths often sound completely counterintuitive? The idea of "dying to self" certainly qualifies. In a world obsessed with self-promotion, self-fulfillment, and self-actualization, the concept of daily self-denial seems almost foreign. Yet this is precisely the path to true freedom and power in the Kingdom.

When Paul wrote, "I die daily," he wasn't being dramatic or poetic. He was describing the moment-by-moment unseen cosmic battle every warrior faces—the choice between following our own desires or surrendering to follow Jesus' lead. It's like Jesus said: "Whoever wants to be my disciple must deny themselves and take up their cross daily and follow me" (Luke 9:23).

As we have, you may find in your own kingdom adventures that your greatest battles aren't usually against external forces. The fiercest opponent we face is often the one looking back at us in the mirror—that part of us that wants comfort over calling, recognition over righteousness, and control over surrender.

*In the battle against your flesh, surrender is the path to victory—not to your desires, but to your Deliverer.*

This daily dying isn't about self-hatred or harsh religious duty. It's actually an invitation to something greater. Every time we say "no" to self, we're really saying "yes" to Jesus living through us. As Paul discovered, "I have been crucified with Christ and I no longer live, but Christ lives in me" (Galatians 2:20).

What would happen if we approached each day asking, "Where am I holding onto control that I need to surrender? What desires am I nursing that are hindering the Spirit's work in me?" These questions aren't meant to induce guilt but to create space for greater kingdom power and freedom.

The beautiful truth is that every act of self-denial clears a path for resurrection power to flow. When we choose Jesus' agenda over our own comfort, His purposes over our preferences, something supernatural happens—we become vessels through which His unhindered power and love can flow like rivers of living water to those around us.

This daily dying isn't a one-time commitment but a lifestyle of continual surrender. Some days it might mean giving up your right to be right in a disagreement. Other days it might mean serving when you'd rather be served or speaking truth when silence would be easier.

The world won't understand this kingdom path. It appears weak to those watching from the outside. But Kingdom Warriors know the secret—in this dying, we find true kingdom living. In this surrender, we discover true kingdom power. In this daily cross-bearing, we experience the resurrection kingdom life that nothing in this world can offer.

## Kingdom Warriors Endure Persecution

> In fact, everyone who wants to live a godly life in Christ Jesus will be persecuted.
>
> — 2 Timothy 3:12

Have you ever noticed how we're often caught off guard when opposition comes our way because of our faith? We think, "Wait, I'm doing what's right—why is this happening to me?" Yet Paul's words to Timothy are refreshingly honest: persecution isn't the exception for faithful Kingdom Warriors—it's the rule.

Jesus' didn't beat around the bush about it with His straightforward words to His disciples: "If they persecuted me, they will persecute you also" (John 15:20). It's almost as if He's saying, "Don't be surprised by this—it comes with the territory." There's something strangely comforting about this honesty, isn't there? Jesus doesn't sugarcoat the cost of following Him as a Kingdom Warrior.

What amazes me about Kingdom Warriors throughout history is not that they avoided persecution, but how they endured it. Think about Stephen—stones raining down on him from every direction, yet his face was like that of an angel, and he saw Jesus standing at the right hand of God (Acts 6:15; 7:54-59).

What gave him that supernatural perspective in such a terrible moment?

I believe it's because warriors understand something profound: persecution isn't just something to endure—it's something to embrace as participation in Jesus' sufferings. Remember how the apostles responded after being beaten for preaching Jesus? They left "rejoicing because they had been counted worthy of suffering disgrace for the Name" (Acts 5:41). They didn't just tolerate persecution—they saw it as a kingdom badge of honor!

This perspective completely transforms how we face opposition. When your coworkers mock your faith, when your family misunderstands your commitment, when your devotion to Jesus costs you opportunities or relationships—these aren't interruptions to your spiritual adventure. They're confirmation that you're on the right path.

## Courage in the Yard

We all have opportunities to suffer for the righteousness of God if we are alert to what's going on around us. Mel's prison story of helping a brother living there is a good example. He knew the young man, Rocky, had accidentally accepted a gift from a gang leader, and now they wanted him to pay them back with sexual favors.

Rocky was terrified and ran to Mel and a couple other brothers standing in the yard. In tears, he told them that he was to meet some of the gang members in the empty gym, or else.

Mel was a new believer and on fire in his faith. He felt obligated to help him.

Instead of the young man, Mel showed up in the gym carrying the items Rocky had been gifted, hoping they would accept them as payment and let him off of his debt.

"Who do you think you are, telling us what to do?"

Those words hung in the air like a thundercloud ready to burst. The tension of that moment was so thick, Mel can still feel it—every instinct in his body screaming for him to back down. You see, what he had done had broken one of the cardinal rules of prison life: "Do your own time. Don't mess with my time. Don't tell me what I can do in this prison and what I can't do."

Men got shanked for less than what he'd just done. But something had changed in him. Jesus had rewired his thinking, rearranged his priorities. Even though his heart hammered against his ribs, he stood his ground. "Because of Jesus, Rocky is my brother," he managed to say, his voice betraying his fear. "I have to help him."

The gang leader—Eric—with seven or eight of his crew, all of them looking like they were hungry for blood. Mel's blood. Then a scripture, John 15:20, came to his mind.

"A servant is not greater than his master."

The message was clear: *"If Jesus took a beating for who He was, I should be willing to take one for my faith."* He quickly ran through his options in his head, mentally counting the allies who would fight with him if things went south. But even as he said those words, he realized that was the old Mel talking—the one who survived by intimidation and alliances. Something else was rising up in him now as he felt the powerful presence of Jesus.

As Eric stepped right into Mel's personal space, his chin almost touching Mel's nose, he shouted, "You take me on, Goebel, if you're so bad!"

At the same time, one of his gang members was screaming, "Knife him!"

Mel stood there and looked the gang leader straight in the eye, calling him by name. "Eric, if you were threatened, I would do the same thing for you," he said calmly. "Because of Jesus, he's my brother." He repeated those words three times, each time more confidently than before.

And then the strangest thing happened. Eric just turned and walked away. His whole crew followed, with Mel standing there in stunned silence.

Mel knew he had just witnessed something extraordinary—a moment where love overcame violence and good prevailed over evil. And as he stood there, another scripture bubbled up from somewhere deep inside him: "The one who is in you is greater than the one who is in the world" (1 John 4:4).

For months afterward, Eric avoided Mel entirely—neither threatening nor acknowledging him. But gradually, almost imperceptibly, something shifted. The gang leader began to return Mel's greetings, then eventually stopped to chat when their paths crossed in the yard.

## From Enemy to Guardian

Have you ever witnessed a transformation so profound that it could only be explained as Holy Spirit divine intervention? That's what happened with Eric.

Eric wasn't just any prisoner. He was a lifer—someone with nothing to lose and everything to control within those concrete walls. As the kingpin of the prison, his word was practically law. The guards might have worn the uniforms, but Eric held the real power in that yard.

That's what made what happened next so extraordinary.

After their confrontation, something shifted in Eric. It wasn't immediate—these things rarely are. But gradually, whispers started circulating through the cellblocks. Eric had put out the word: "No one touches the man of God."

Can you imagine that? The very man who had stood nose-to-nose with Mel, threatening violence, had become his unexpected protector. The most feared man in the prison had appointed himself as guardian of the Gospel.

"Did you hear what Eric did yesterday?" a fellow prisoner, named Dave, asked Mel one afternoon as they walked the perimeter of the yard.

"No, what happened?" Mel replied.

"Some new transfer was talking about shutting you up during the next Bible study. Eric overheard him." Dave shook his head in amazement. "He told the guy that if he so much as looked at you wrong, he'd answer to him personally."

This wasn't just about Mel—it was about something much bigger. Jesus had somehow reached into the hardened heart of this prison leader and awakened something long dormant. Eric didn't attend the Bible studies, but he made sure everyone knew they were protected spaces.

Then something happened that can only be described as straight from the throne room of God: revival broke out. Not the quiet, orderly kind you might see in a church. This was raw, powerful, and unstoppable.

Men who had committed unspeakable crimes found themselves weeping as they encountered Jesus' forgiveness. Hardened criminals who had spent decades building walls around their hearts suddenly found those walls crumbling under the weight of divine love.

One evening during a particularly powerful meeting, the door to the gathering space opened. Conversations hushed as Eric himself walked in. Without a word, he took a seat in the back row. He didn't participate, didn't speak—he just watched with those intense eyes that had once promised violence but now held something like curiosity.

Three weeks later, Eric approached Mel in the yard.

"Can we talk?" he asked, his voice lacking its usual edge of command.

They walked in silence for a few minutes before he spoke again.

"My whole life, I've controlled everything and everyone around me through fear," he said finally. "But you—you stood up to me without fear and without hate. I couldn't understand that. I still don't fully understand it, but I want to."

That conversation was the first of many. Eric never had a dramatic conversion moment—his journey to faith was more like a slow thaw after a lifetime of winter. But his protection allowed the Gospel to spread through that prison like wildfire.

By the time Mel was released, over a hundred men were attending those weekly gatherings. Men who had once defined themselves by their crimes were now finding new identities as children of God. The violence in the yard had decreased dramatically. Even some of the guards had noticed the difference.

Thinking back on those days reminds us that Jesus' methods rarely match our expectations. Who would have thought that the unseen kingdom of God would advance in that prison, not through the removal of opposition, but through the transformation of it. The very man who could have been Mel's greatest enemy became the unlikely champion of the Gospel's advance.

That's how God works sometimes. He doesn't just defeat our enemies—He transforms them. He takes what was meant for evil and repurposes it for good. And in doing so, He creates stories so extraordinary that they can only be explained as supernatural encounters.

How fascinating that persecution often intensifies as our light shines brighter. It's almost as if darkness becomes more threatened as the light grows stronger. Yet this is precisely when Kingdom Warriors stand tallest—not in their own strength. but anchored in an unshakable, bold faith in Jesus' kingdom purposes and promises.

What sustains a Kingdom Warrior through persecution? It's that eternal perspective that sees beyond the temporary pain to the eternal weight of glory. It's the deep conviction that Jesus remains faithful, even when the road gets rough. And most importantly, it's that intimate fellowship with Jesus that allows us to say with Paul, "I want to know Christ—yes, to know the power of his resurrection and participation in his sufferings" (Philippians 3:10).

The beautiful thing about Kingdom Warriors who endure persecution without compromise or bitterness is how their kingdom testimony encourages others. Your steadfastness in the face of opposition might be exactly what someone else needs to see to stand firm in their own faith adventure.

So, when persecution comes—whether as subtle ridicule or more serious consequences—remember that you're in good company. Jesus walked this road before you. Countless faithful Kingdom Warriors have followed in His steps. And your endurance today becomes part of that great cloud of witnesses that inspires others to remain faithful, no matter what comes against them.

## Kingdom Warriors Reject Worldly Pleasures

> Do not love the world or anything in the world. If anyone loves the world, love for the Father is not in them.
>
> — 1 John 2:15

Have you ever noticed how a truly captivating love makes everything else fade into the background? That's what happens when Kingdom Warriors fall deeply in love with Jesus—the world's offerings simply lose their sparkle.

Consider John's bold statement in the above verse. It's not a popular message in our culture of "more, bigger, better," is it? But there's something incredibly freeing about it when you look beneath the surface.

This rejection of worldly pleasures isn't about living some joyless, austere existence—quite the opposite! It's about discovering pleasures so profound and lasting that temporary gratifications pale in comparison. It's like an athlete who willingly passes on the late-night party because the joy of victory the next day will be so much sweeter.

Think about the apostle Paul for a moment. Here was a man who had it all by worldly standards—education, religious status, Roman citizenship, influence. Yet he made this remarkable statement: "But whatever were gains to me I now consider loss for the sake of Christ" (Philippians 3:7). He wasn't gritting his teeth through some painful sacrifice—he had discovered something so valuable that everything else seemed like rubbish in comparison!

We have a friend who once described their journey away from materialism this way: "It wasn't that I decided to want less stuff. I just found something I wanted more." That's the heart of a warrior who rejects worldly pleasures—not out of legalistic obligation but out of discovering a far greater delight.

There's a strategic element here too. Kingdom Warriors understand that attachment to comfort, luxury, or temporary pleasures creates vulnerable points in their spiritual armor. Every possession that owns your heart becomes a potential pressure point through which the enemy can attack. That's why Kingdom Warriors maintain such vigilance against these entanglements.

Moses understood this strategic choice when he opted to "be mistreated along with the people of God rather than to enjoy the fleeting pleasures of sin" (Hebrews 11:25). Notice that Scripture acknowledges sin does have pleasures—they're just passing. They don't last. Moses chose the eternal over the temporary, the lasting joy over the fleeting thrill.

This Kingdom Warriors' perspective may seem challenging because it's so countercultural. Our world constantly tells us that more stuff, more experiences, more pleasures will finally satisfy us. Yet Kingdom Warriors demonstrate the opposite truth—that true contentment comes not from adding more but from being satisfied in Jesus alone.

What would happen if we approached each temptation, each opportunity for worldly gain with this question: "Will this draw me closer to Jesus or distract me from Him? Will this strengthen my spiritual authority or compromise it?" These Kingdom Warrior filters help us make decisions based not on immediate gratification and comfort but on eternal kingdom impact.

The beautiful outcome of this kingdom lifestyle is how it impacts others. When people see genuine joy in someone who isn't chasing the same things everyone else is pursuing, it raises questions. Your contentment with less becomes a powerful testimony that points others toward the lasting treasures found in Jesus.

What worldly pleasure might Jesus be asking you to release today? And what greater satisfaction is He offering in its place?

## Kingdom Warriors Persevere in Spiritual Discipline

> All your words are true; all your righteous laws are eternal.
>
> — Psalm 119:160

Have you ever watched Olympic athletes and marveled at their discipline? The early mornings, the strict diets, the relentless training—all for a moment of glory that might last just seconds. There's something both inspiring and challenging about that level of commitment, isn't there?

Paul draws this exact parallel when he tells Timothy, "Train yourself to be godly. For physical training is of some value, but godliness has value for all things" (1 Timothy 4:7-8). I love the athletic imagery here—spiritual disciplines aren't religious obligations; they're training exercises for Kingdom Warriors!

Think about it—no elite warrior becomes battle-ready by chance. Their effectiveness comes from rigorous, consistent training that prepares them for the moments that matter most. The same is true for Kingdom Warriors who understand that spiritual authority isn't bestowed automatically—it's developed through daily disciplines that attune our spirits to the Holy Spirit's voice.

What drives this kind of disciplined devotion? It's not guilt or religious duty. It's passionate pursuit of Jesus' presence and power. It's what Paul described as "press[ing] on toward the goal to win the prize for which God has called me heavenward in Christ Jesus" (Philippians 3:14). When you're captivated by a vision of the prize—intimate fellowship with Jesus and effectiveness in His kingdom—the disciplines become a joy rather than a burden.

You may notice, as we do, that in our own kingdom adventure spiritual muscles can quickly atrophy when these disciplines are neglected. Prayer becomes shallow, discernment dulls, and spiritual authority weakens. The enemy loves nothing more than a warrior who's grown complacent in training!

How about Daniel? Even as a young man in a foreign land with every excuse to compromise, he resolved to maintain his spiritual disciplines despite immense cultural pressure (Daniel 1:8). What gave him that kind of resolve? Perhaps it was his unwavering conviction that these disciplines weren't just religious rituals—they were his lifeline to God's presence and power in a hostile environment.

The wonderful thing about spiritual discipline is how it transforms us from the inside out. Like physical training that reshapes the body, spiritual exercises forge our character, sharpen our discernment, and increase our capacity to carry Jesus' kingdom presence and power. Every prayer, every fast, every hour in Scripture, every worship gathering is another rep in the spiritual gym, building muscles you'll need in kingdom battle.

This disciplined life creates a heightened spiritual awareness—Kingdom Warriors move through the world recognizing that they stand on holy ground wherever their feet take them. Ordinary locations become sacred spaces; everyday encounters become divine appointments. There's an alertness to Jesus' presence in every environment—whether ordinary or challenging.

## When Discipline Becomes Kingdom Adventure

Have you ever noticed how some of the most beautiful words in our language are the ones we initially resist? For many of us, "discipline" has carried that negative weight—it sounds like restriction, like drudgery, like something that holds us back from real joy.

But here's the amazing paradox Kingdom Warriors have discovered: spiritual discipline isn't the enemy of adventure—it's the gateway to the greatest kingdom adventure possible!

Think about mountain climbing for a moment. The climbers who experience the most breathtaking vistas aren't the ones who take shortcuts or climb haphazardly. They're the ones who've disciplined themselves through rigorous training, who've mastered the techniques, who've committed to the preparation that makes the journey impossible, an adventure.

That's exactly what happens when Kingdom Warriors embrace spiritual discipline. Far from being a restrictive set of religious rules, these disciplines become the very pathways through which the power of the Holy Spirit flows. Prayer, fasting, Scripture meditation, worship—these aren't just spiritual chores. They're the kingdom training ground where warriors learn to recognize the voice of their Commander, Jesus, where they become attuned to the powerful movements of the Spirit.

We have seen this transformation in our own adventures—how the very disciplines that once felt like obligation gradually became the most anticipated moments of our day. That time once crammed into our busy schedules slowly transformed into a refreshing drink, eagerly anticipated as we looked forward to the kingdom adventure of meeting with Jesus there.

You see, Kingdom Warriors understand something the world misses: the Holy Spirit makes discipline lovely. When you've experienced the rush of divine power flowing through you in a moment of spiritual battle—when you've seen chains break, hearts heal, or darkness flee because you were spiritually prepared for that moment—discipline takes on an entirely new meaning.

It's like what happens to athletes who fall in love with their sport. The training that once felt like punishment becomes a joy because they've connected it to the thrill of victory. For Kingdom

Warriors, disciplines aren't disconnected from adventure—they're the very preparation that makes adventure possible!

Daniel discovered this secret when his disciplined life of prayer opened windows to divine revelation that changed the course of empires. David found it when his hours meditating on God's word while tending sheep prepared him to face giants. Esther experienced it when her discipline of fasting positioned her to save a nation.

What would happen if we stopped seeing spiritual disciplines as the opposite of excitement and started recognizing them as the pathway to the most thrilling adventure imaginable—intimate friendship with the Living God?

We've noticed something fascinating about Kingdom Warriors who persevere in spiritual discipline—they develop a certain lightness about them, a holy expectancy or, like a friend likes to say, an expectation of "holy moments." They move through their days with an almost childlike anticipation, knowing that their disciplined preparation has positioned them to perceive and participate in divine encounters others might miss entirely.

For Kingdom Warriors, discipline has become one of the most important words in their vocabulary. Not because they love restriction, but because they've discovered that discipline is actually the key that unlocks the door to true freedom—freedom to move in the power of the Holy Spirit, freedom to stand firm in spiritual battles, freedom to experience depths of God's presence that the undisciplined will never know.

So today, Kingdom Warriors, what if we embraced discipline not as a heavy burden but as an invitation to kingdom adventure? What if every prayer, every fast, every hour in Scripture became not just a spiritual duty but a deliberate step into the most exciting kingdom adventure possible—life in the unhindered presence and power of Jesus?

This is why true warriors smile at the word "discipline." They know it's not the end of kingdom adventure—it's only the beginning.

What spiritual discipline might Jesus be inviting you to strengthen today? And how might strengthening that kingdom discipline position you for greater kingdom impact tomorrow?

## Kingdom Warrior's Fighting Strategies: Abiding in Jesus

> I am the way and the truth and the life. No one comes to the Father except through me.
>
> — John 14:6

Have you ever noticed how the most profound spiritual truths are often the simplest? Take this foundational fighting strategy Jesus gave us: "Abide in Me, and I in you. As the branch cannot bear fruit of itself, unless it abides in the vine, neither can you, unless you abide in Me" (John 15:4, ESV).

It's not complicated, is it? Yet this simple instruction—abide in Me—contains the Kingdom Warrior's most powerful fighting strategy. Everything flows from this connection.

Think about that image Jesus uses—the vine and branches. It's not just a nice metaphor. It's a picture of absolute dependence. Have you ever seen a branch try to produce fruit while disconnected from its vine? Of course not—that would be absurd! Yet how often do we attempt spiritual battles disconnected from our Source?

I've learned this lesson the hard way. Those times when I've rushed into spiritual warfare without first securing my connection to Jesus—relying instead on my experience, my knowledge, or my spiritual gifts—have typically ended in exhaustion or defeat. But the battles I've entered while deeply abiding in Him? Those have revealed a power and authority that clearly wasn't my own.

This abiding isn't passive. Kingdom Warriors actively cultivate this communion through intentional practices: rising early to seek His face before the distractions of the day, maintaining constant conversation with Him throughout their activities, meditating on Scripture until His Word becomes living bread, and practicing kingdom awareness of His presence in every situation.

What's interesting is Jesus' stark honesty about this: "Apart from me you can do nothing" (John 15:5, ESV). Not "Apart from Me you'll be less effective" or "Apart from Me things will be harder." No—nothing. Zero. When Jesus says nothing, He means nothing of eternal significance. We might achieve impressive results in our own strength, but they won't last. Only what flows from abiding bears lasting kingdom fruit.

In the intensity of spiritual battle, this deep communion becomes our refuge, our wisdom, and our strength. It's what enables warriors to move with divine precision and authority. When everyone else is panicking, the abiding warrior can remain centered because they're tapped into a perspective beyond their own. When others see only the visible opposition, the abiding warrior discerns the spiritual realities at play.

The enemy knows the power of this connection, which is why he works tirelessly to disrupt it. He doesn't need to defeat you directly if he can simply disconnect you from the Source of your strength. That's why Kingdom Warriors fiercely protect their communion with Jesus against the busyness, distractions, and spiritual attacks that would weaken this vital connection.

What would our spiritual battles look like if we truly grasped that abiding isn't just a nice spiritual discipline but our very lifeline? What if we approached each day not asking, "What must I accomplish?" but rather, "How can I remain connected to Jesus as I move through this day?"

This is the beautiful simplicity of the Kingdom Warrior's primary fighting strategy—not complex techniques or secret knowledge, but moment-by-moment dependence on Jesus and the Holy Spirit. Through consistent surrender, obedience, and passionate pursuit of His presence, we maintain this connection that allows His life to flow through us as channels of His kingdom power.

So, before you rush into today's battles, before you confront that challenging situation or spiritual opposition, pause and ask yourself: "Am I attempting this connected to or disconnected from Jesus?" Because in that honest answer lies the difference between striving in your own strength and flowing in His kingdom purpose.

## Kingdom Warriors Stay Connected Warriors

> How good and pleasant it is when God's people live together in unity!
>
> — Psalm 133:1

Have you ever watched those nature documentaries where a lone animal gets separated from the herd? It rarely ends well, does it? The predators circle, sensing vulnerability in isolation. This principle is just as true in spiritual warfare.

"And let us consider how we may spur one another on toward love and good deeds, not giving up meeting together, as some are in the habit of doing, but encouraging one another" (Hebrews 10:24-25). There's profound wisdom in these words that Kingdom Warriors take to heart. This isn't just about attending church—it's about kingdom survival strategy.

Think about the Roman soldiers who conquered much of the known world. What made them so formidable wasn't just their individual skill—it was their formation. They fought shoulder to shoulder, shields interlocked, moving as one unit. When one soldier tired, the strength of those beside him kept the line strong. That's the picture of warrior fellowship that transforms ordinary believers into an unstoppable kingdom force.

You may have seen this play out in your own journey. We certainly have. Those seasons when you try to fight alone, thinking, "I can handle this on my own." These inevitably end up being our weakest moments. But when surrounded by warriors who know our struggles, celebrate our victories, and reinforce us in the unseen cosmic battle? That's when we are able to experience breakthrough.

Ecclesiastes puts it beautifully: "A cord of three strands is not quickly broken" (4:12). There's something mathematically supernatural about unity. One Kingdom Warrior can put a thousand to flight, but two can put ten thousand to flight. The impact doesn't just add—it multiplies.

True Kingdom Warrior fellowship goes far beyond surface-level church attendance. It forges bonds of trust where we can be transparently real about our battles. It creates spaces where we can share battle strategies, warn of enemy tactics we've encountered, and strengthen those who are weary. It builds relationships where we're genuinely invested in each other's spiritual growth.

It's extremely moving when we see these moments of fellowship in action in the unseen cosmic battle—when one warrior faces intense spiritual warfare, and others immediately rush to reinforce them. Maybe it's through late-night prayer calls, messages of Scripture that arrive at just the right moment, or practical support that lightens their load. These aren't coincidences; they're the intentional response of Kingdom Warriors who understand that we're fighting this kingdom adventure together.

"Make every effort to keep the unity of the Spirit through the bond of peace" (Ephesians 4:3). Notice Paul doesn't say unity happens automatically—it requires effort, intentionality, sacrifice. The enemy works tirelessly to create division because he knows a divided army defeats itself. That's why Kingdom Warriors actively protect unity by quickly addressing conflicts, extending forgiveness, and choosing love even when it's challenging.

What would happen if every Kingdom Warrior truly embraced this fighting strategy of staying connected? What if we approached our spiritual communities not as optional gatherings but as essential war councils and kingdom battle formations?

This is exactly what happens in Bible-believing fellowships where Kingdom Warriors gather under sound teaching and experienced leadership. These kingdom communities become training grounds where theory becomes practice—where we're equipped through biblical teaching, mentorship, and opportunities to exercise our spiritual gifts. They're the places where iron sharpens iron, where our rough edges get smoothed, and where we learn to function as part of something larger than ourselves.

So today, ask yourself: how connected am I to fellow Kingdom Warriors? Have I been trying to fight alone? What relationships do I need to invest in more deeply? Because in the unseen spiritual battles we face, connection isn't just nice—it's necessary. Standing together, shields locked in unity, we become a formidable kingdom force that the enemy cannot easily overcome.

And beyond the strategic kingdom advantage, there's also the simple truth that God designed us for this togetherness, declaring over it: "How good and pleasant it is when God's people live together in unity!" (Psalm 133:1).

## Kingdom Warriors Engage Through Prayer

> And pray in the Spirit on all occasions with all kinds of prayers and requests. With this in mind, be alert and always keep on praying for all the Lord's people.
>
> — Ephesians 6:18

Have you ever noticed how our perspective on prayer dramatically shapes our approach to it? When we see prayer merely as a religious duty or a way to get things from God, it remains shallow. But when we understand it as direct engagement in spiritual kingdom combat—everything changes!

This revelation transformed our prayer life. The moment we grasped that prayer isn't just talking about the unseen cosmic battle—it is the battle—our approach shifted from casual conversation to strategic kingdom engagement. Prayer suddenly became the holy command center of spiritual warfare.

> Prayer is not preparation for the battle; prayer is the battle.[3]
>
> — OSWALD CHAMBERS

Think about what Paul reveals in Ephesians 6:12. The real unseen cosmic battles we face aren't primarily against human opposition or physical circumstances. Those are just the visible manifestations of a deeper conflict happening in the spiritual realm. When we pray, we're engaging directly with these unseen realities!

Kingdom Warriors approach prayer like skilled generals planning battlefield operations. They understand that timing matters, position matters, and coordinated effort matters. They come before the throne of grace with both holy boldness and strategic precision, wielding what Paul calls "weapons we fight with [that] are not the weapons of the world. On the contrary, they have divine power to demolish strongholds" (2 Corinthians 10:4).

We've witnessed the power of this kind of kingdom prayer! Mel was praying with a group of warriors for a community plagued by violence and drug activity. Instead of just asking God to "help the situation," these Kingdom Warriors exercised their delegated authority in Jesus' name. They proclaimed God's Word over specific streets and buildings. They bound spirits of violence and addiction according to Matthew 18:18. They released declarations of God's kingdom coming in power. Within months, that neighborhood began to transform as drug dealers left, community leaders emerged, and a new sense of kingdom hope prevailed.

What makes this kind of prayer different? It moves beyond surface-level petitions to exercise the authority Jesus has delegated to His Kingdom Warriors. These warriors aren't begging an unwilling God to act—they're partnering with a victorious King who has already conquered and is establishing His rule through their prayers!

These prayer warriors maintain vigilant spiritual alertness, discerning the enemy's schemes and responding with targeted prayers that dismantle demonic operations. They've learned that effective warfare prayer often requires persistence—continuing to stand in faith until breakthrough manifests visibly. Like Elijah who kept sending his servant to look for rain clouds, they pray and keep watching until the answer comes.

What I find most remarkable about praying Kingdom Warriors is how their consistent communion with Jesus transforms even how they view opposition. They develop such spiritual sensitivity that they can separate human instruments from the spiritual forces influencing them. This enables them to love even their enemies while standing firmly against the dark powers operating through them.

Imagine what would happen if every Kingdom Warrior fully embraced this understanding of prayer! What if instead of seeing prayer as something we do after we've tried everything else, we recognized it as our primary battlefield kingdom engagement? What if our first response to every challenge was to take our position on the wall as watchmen, discerning and responding to spiritual realities through powerful intercession?

> Remember these three things: I will make a way for you, I'm fighting your battles, Prayer is your powerful weapon. Trust my timing.
>
> — God

This is the invitation before us—to engage as Kingdom Warriors of prayer who understand both our authority in Jesus and the strategic importance of our position. When we pray this way, we're not just talking about circumstances; we're actively participating in establishing Jesus' kingdom "on earth as it is in heaven."

So today, how will you approach your prayer time? As a religious duty, a wish list, or as a Kingdom Warrior taking your position on the front lines of the most important unseen cosmic battle there is?

What opposition are you facing today because of your faith? How might seeing it as suffering with Jesus transform your perspective? What area of your life is the Holy Spirit inviting you to surrender today? Where might your "no" to self become a powerful "yes" to His greater kingdom purpose in and through you? What truth is God calling you to stand for today? And who might be waiting for you to shine just enough light for their next step?

Kingdom Warriors, stand firm in truth. For in doing so, you don't just defend an abstract principle—you reflect the very character of Jesus, who is Truth itself. Next, let's dive further into to the power of prayer in the life of a Kingdom Warrior.

## Chapter 10

## The Power of Prayer

> And pray in the Spirit on all occasions with all kinds of prayers and requests. With this in mind, be alert and always keep on praying for all the Lord's people.
>
> — Ephesians 6:18

Friend, let me ask you something: what do you think is the most powerful weapon in a Kingdom Warrior's arsenal? Is it knowledge of Scripture? Bold faith? Spiritual gifts? While all these are vital, there's one weapon that stands above them all: prayer.

But not just any prayer. I'm not talking about those hurried words before meals or the routine bedtime recitations. I'm talking about the kind of prayer that shakes heaven and earth. The kind that Jesus Himself modeled when He calmed storms with a word, multiplied food with a blessing, and raised the dead with a command.

As E.M. Bounds so powerfully put it: "The goal of prayer is the ear of God, a goal that can only be reached by patient and continued and continuous waiting upon Him, pouring out our heart to Him and permitting Him to speak to us."[1]

Prayer is not preparation for the battle; prayer is the battle.[2]

— OSWALD CHAMBERS

## BEYOND RELIGIOUS RITUAL

Let's be honest; many of us have turned prayer into something it was never meant to be: a religious duty, a spiritual checkbox, a formula to recite. But that's not what prayer looks like in the hands of a Kingdom Warrior.

Think about Jesus for a moment. Did His prayers sound like memorized scripts or formal presentations? Never! They were direct conversations with His Father—authentic, specific, and expectant. Whether He was feeding thousands or facing the cross, His prayers flowed from relationship, not ritual.

The Father isn't looking for polished words or perfect posture. He's seeking those who will "worship the Father in the Spirit and in truth" (John 4:23)—people who come to Him with honest hearts rather than empty formalities. When you approach prayer as direct communication with the sovereign Commander of the universe, understanding that each conversation carries cosmic implications, everything changes.

## AUTHORITY IN PRAYER: YOUR RIGHTFUL POSITION

Here's where many believers miss the mark entirely. They approach prayer like spiritual beggars, hoping that if they plead long enough, God might reluctantly answer. But that's not your position at all!

Jesus made an astounding promise: "Whatever you bind on earth shall be bound in heaven, and whatever you loose on earth shall be loosed in heaven" (Matthew 18:18). Do you understand what He's saying? You've been delegated authority to participate in heaven's government!

You don't pray from a position of need but from a position of authority. Scripture declares you are seated "with [Christ] in the heavenly realms" (Ephesians 2:6). That's your prayer position—not kneeling before a distant deity hoping for a handout but seated with Christ in a position of shared authority.

This understanding transforms how you pray. Instead of "God, please, if it's Your will, maybe consider doing something about this situation," you begin to declare: "In the name of Jesus, I speak peace to this storm," or "By the authority Christ has given me, I declare healing in this body."

Can you feel the difference? One approach begs from weakness; the other declares from delegated strength. One hopes something might happen; the other expects something will happen.

> Courage is fear that has said its prayers.[3]
>
> — ANNE LAMOTT

## STRATEGIC RATHER THAN SCATTERED

We've noticed something interesting about prayer in the life of many believers—it's often random, scattered, and reactive. A crisis emerges, and suddenly we're praying intensely. The crisis passes, and prayer fades until the next emergency.

But Kingdom Warriors approach prayer with strategic intention, like a military operation with clear objectives, accurate intelligence, and coordinated effort. They don't fire "shotgun prayers" (scattered, general petitions) but "laser prayers" (focused, specific declarations).

This strategic approach begins with something counterintuitive—listening. Before launching into prayer, take time to receive divine intelligence through Scripture meditation, prophetic insight, and Holy Spirit guidance. Remember Jesus' own words: "I do nothing on my own authority, but speak just as the Father taught me" (John 8:28, ESV).

Ask yourself: am I praying what I think needs to happen, or am I aligning with what the Father is already doing? Am I focusing on superficial issues, or am I targeting root causes? Am I praying about symptoms, or am I addressing spiritual strongholds?

Strategic prayer means identifying priority targets—cultural influencers, geographic gateways, future generations, and spiritual strongholds. When you focus your prayer energy on these key domains, you create a cascading impact throughout lives and society.

## Persistent and Prevailing Prayer

Let us tell you something that might revolutionize your prayer life: some breakthroughs only come through persistent prayer. Jesus emphasized this through His parables about the persistent widow and the midnight visitor (Luke 18:1-8; 11:5-13). These stories reveal that spiritual victories often require sustained perseverance rather than one-time requests.

Have you ever "prayed through," continuing in intercession until tangible breakthrough manifests? This isn't about wearing God down or convincing Him to act. It's about maintaining your prayer position through all resistance until victory emerges.

Remember Daniel? His prayer was answered instantly in the heavenly realm, but it took twenty-one days to break through demonic resistance and become visible on earth (Daniel 10:12-13). What if he had stopped praying on day twenty? When you encounter delays in seeing answers, don't assume divine reluctance. Instead, recognize you've engaged significant spiritual territory worthy of enemy resistance.

The persistence required isn't a sign of God's unwillingness but of the prayer's importance. The enemy doesn't fight against prayers that don't threaten his domain. If you're facing resistance, you're likely on the right track!

> The prayer of a righteous person has great power as it is working.
>
> — JAMES 5:16B

## WARFARE PRAYER: ENFORCING VICTORY

Let's talk about a dimension of prayer many modern believers have forgotten—warfare prayer. Paul didn't mince words when he wrote, "Our struggle is not against flesh and blood, but against...spiritual forces of evil in the heavenly realms" (Ephesians 6:12). Some situations you're facing aren't just natural circumstances—they're spiritual battlegrounds.

Here's the good news: you're not fighting *for* victory; you're fighting *from* victory! Colossians 2:15 declares that Christ has "disarmed the rulers and authorities and put them to open shame, by triumphing over them" (ESV). Your warfare prayers don't win the victory; they enforce the victory Jesus already secured.

Effective warfare prayer requires discernment. Is the opposition coming from territorial spirits, generational patterns, demonic attachment, or institutional strongholds? Each category requires tailored prayer strategies drawing on appropriate scriptural promises and declarations.

Don't be intimidated by this dimension of prayer. If you're in Jesus, you have both the authority and the backing of heaven to engage in spiritual warfare. The enemy has no legal right to territory that belongs to Jesus—and that includes your family, your mind, your health, your calling, and your community.

## THE WEAPON OF DECLARATION

Have you ever noticed how Jesus prayed? He rarely used the tentative, questioning language we often use. Instead, He declared: "Peace, be still!" to the storm. "Lazarus, come forth!" to the dead. "Be clean!" to the leper.

Kingdom Warriors understand the creative power of declaration—speaking forth God's truth to shape reality. This isn't positive thinking or mind-over-matter; it's aligning your words with God's Word to release His power into situations.

Declaration differs from both petition ("Please do this") and confession ("I have done this") to become proclamation ("This is true"). When you integrate Scripture promises, prophetic insights, and kingdom principles into powerful declarations, you establish divine reality against contrary circumstances.

This is why Kingdom Warrior prayers often sound bold by religious standards. While religious prayer speaks tentatively ("If it be thy will"), warrior prayer declares confidently ("Your kingdom come, your will be done"). This confidence stems not from presumption but from intimate knowledge of Jesus' character and purposes.

What situations in your life need more than polite requests? What circumstances need authoritative declarations of God's truth? Start speaking *to* your mountains rather than just speaking *about* them!

## Fasting: Prayer's Amplifier

Want to supercharge your prayer life? Consider adding fasting to your spiritual arsenal. Jesus both practiced and taught fasting, indicating it would characterize His followers after His departure (Matthew 9:15). Throughout Scripture and church history, fasting consistently precedes significant spiritual breakthroughs.

Fasting works on multiple levels simultaneously. Physically, it subdues bodily demands that often crowd out spiritual sensitivity. Mentally, it breaks unhealthy thought patterns and creates space for divine perspective. Spiritually, it demonstrates practical prioritization of kingdom purposes over personal comfort.

But here's what fasting isn't: it's not a spiritual hunger strike to force God's hand. It's not a religious performance to impress others. It's redirected hunger—deliberately channeling physical appetite into spiritual appetite.

This principle applies whether you undertake traditional food fasts, media fasts, relationship fasts, or other forms of deliberate abstinence. Each approach creates focused spiritual attention directed toward specific breakthrough objectives.

Have you ever experienced the clarity and power that comes through combining prayer with fasting? If not, consider starting with a simple fast—perhaps one meal or one day—specifically focused on a breakthrough you're seeking.

> *In the battle against your flesh, surrender is the path to victory—not to your desires, but to your Deliverer.*

## Prayer That Transforms the Warrior

Here's a powerful truth many miss: effective prayer transforms not just external circumstances but the prayer warrior themselves. As Oswald Chambers wisely noted, "Prayer does not fit us for the greater work; prayer is the greater work."[4]

This is why Scripture repeatedly links prayer effectiveness with character qualities like righteousness (James 5:16), forgiveness (Mark 11:25), marital harmony (1 Peter 3:7), and pure motives (James 4:3). These qualities don't earn God's response but create proper alignment for His power to flow through you without distortion.

The most profound transformation happens in your identity. Through consistent communion with Jesus, you increasingly perceive yourself as God perceives you—as a beloved child with delegated authority rather than as a distant servant seeking occasional favor.

Every time you enter God's presence in prayer, you're being shaped into His image. Your priorities align more closely with His. Your heart breaks for what breaks His. Your capacity to hear

His voice increases. Your authority grows as your submission deepens.

Ask yourself this question: who are you becoming through your prayer life? Is prayer changing not just your circumstances, but your character?

## Corporate Prayer: Multiplied Power

While individual prayer forms the foundation of a warrior's life, there's unique power in praying with others. Jesus promised, "If two of you on earth agree about anything they ask for, it will be done for them by my Father in heaven" (Matthew 18:19).

This creates what we might call "agreement amplitude"—the spiritual principle that aligned voices create greater impact than the sum of individual prayers. It's like separate instruments coming together to form an orchestra, creating harmonies impossible for solo performers.

Corporate prayer also provides essential safeguards against doctrinal distortion, personal deception, and spiritual pride. Even mature intercessors benefit from the discernment, accountability, and perspective adjustment that comes through praying with others.

Where are you experiencing the power of agreement in prayer? Do you have prayer partners who stand with you for breakthrough? Are you part of a community that prays with strategic focus rather than generic repetition?

## Prayer That Shapes History

Friend, when you pray, you're not just affecting your immediate circumstances—you're literally shaping history. Scripture shows this pattern repeatedly: Abraham's intercession affecting nations, Moses' prayers determining battle outcomes, Daniel's prayers triggering angelic intervention, the early church's prayers shifting political realities.

Your prayers can extend beyond immediate concerns to address multi-generational issues. You can pray not merely for current crises but for future generations, recognizing that today's intercession creates tomorrow's inheritance.

Throughout church history, concentrated intercession has consistently preceded historical turning points—from the monastic prayers that preserved Western civilization through the Dark Ages to the Moravian prayer movement that launched modern missions to the Korean prayer revival that transformed a nation.

You stand in this continuing legacy. Your prayers join the historical stream of intercession that shapes human events according to divine purpose. Never underestimate the historical significance of your hidden prayer life!

## Practical Prayer Rhythms

Let's get practical. How do you sustain consistent intercession despite life's demands? Kingdom Warriors develop prayer rhythms that integrate prayer throughout daily life while also maintaining dedicated prayer appointments.

Consider adopting ancient practices like "praying the hours" —pausing at specific times throughout the day for focused communion with Jesus. Or develop "trigger prayers" attached to routine activities—transforming your daily commute, household tasks, or exercise sessions into prayer opportunities.

Many warriors create specific physical spaces reserved exclusively for prayer—whether spare rooms transformed into prayer closets, natural settings that facilitate spiritual focus, or corporate prayer rooms maintained by church communities.

What's your prayer rhythm? When and where do you consistently meet with God? How might you integrate more prayer into the natural flow of your daily life?

## The Ultimate Weapon

In our age of visible platforms and measurable results, prayer represents the ultimate hidden weapon. Its impact often goes undetected by conventional metrics yet fundamentally alters spiritual realities that shape visible outcomes.

Prayer remains simultaneously the most available yet most neglected weapon in the warrior's arsenal. Its power lies precisely in its apparent weakness—operating not through human strength but through humble dependency that accesses divine resources.

As you cultivate a life saturated in transformational prayer, you fulfill Jesus' original vision for His church—"My house will be called a house of prayer for all nations" (Mark 11:17). Your intercession becomes not merely a spiritual discipline but your essential identity as a royal priest who stands between heaven and earth, releasing God's purposes through authoritative communion with King Jesus.

## The Call to Rise

Today, Jesus is beckoning you to emerge from comfortable church routines and embrace a more vibrant spiritual adventure. He calls you to move beyond merely maintaining your relationship with Him and instead join the ranks of Kingdom Warriors who pursue His purposes with passion and dedication.

Do you feel that unexplained stirring in your heart—that holy discontent with spiritual complacency? Jesus is offering you an adventure of faith where mundane religious practice transforms into exhilarating partnership with heaven's purposes.

This transition from spectator to Kingdom Warrior requires courage to step away from predictable faith patterns, but it unlocks a life where divine appointments become regular occurrences and supernatural provision becomes the expected norm rather than the rare exception.

The battle lines are drawn. The trumpet is sounding. The King is calling. And prayer—bold, authoritative, kingdom-advancing prayer—awaits those warriors courageous enough to take up this ultimate weapon.

## Chapter 11

# The Warrior's Deepest Secret
## Presence Before Power

> Remain in me, as I also remain in you. No branch can bear fruit by itself; it must remain in the vine. Neither can you bear fruit unless you remain in me.
>
> — John 15:4

> Be still, and know that I am God.
>
> — Psalm 46:10

Have you ever noticed how our culture celebrates technique, strategy, and skill in almost every domain? We're constantly offered new methods, five-step plans, and innovative approaches. Yet at the heart of every truly effective Kingdom Warrior lies a profound truth that contradicts this obsession with methodology: strength for spiritual battle comes not primarily from techniques or strategies, but from abiding in the presence of Jesus.

We've seen this pattern repeatedly. Kingdom Warriors who transform lives are invariably those who have first been transformed themselves through intentional, consistent communion with their King. Everything flows from this central kingdom reality.

We live in a peculiar time, don't we? Hyperconnected yet spiritually disconnected. Always in touch with everyone, yet rarely fully present with anyone—including God. Kingdom Warriors recognize this cultural current and deliberately swim against it, understanding that presence is not merely a nice spiritual discipline but the very foundation of their effectiveness in the unseen cosmic battle.

> *The true strength of a Kingdom Warrior flows from time spent in the presence of the King.*

Jesus modeled this reality throughout His earthly ministry. It's fascinating to trace His movements in the gospels. Before healing the masses, He withdrew to desolate places to pray (Luke 5:16). Before selecting His disciples—a decision with world-changing implications—He spent the entire night in communion with the Father (Luke 6:12). Before facing the ultimate spiritual battle at the cross, He sought the Father's presence in Gethsemane (Matthew 26:36-44).

The pattern is unmistakable: His power flowed from His presence with the Father. If Jesus Himself—who was one with the Father—prioritized these times of intimate communion, how much more do we need them?

We remember talking with a Kingdom Warrior whose ministry had extraordinary impact in some of the darkest places imaginable. When we asked about his preparation for spiritual battle, he said something I've never forgotten: "I've learned that my effectiveness in any moment is directly proportional to the accumulated time I've spent in Jesus' presence beforehand. Everything else is just technique."

## The Silent Training Ground

Kingdom Warriors understand that training in Jesus' presence often begins with something increasingly rare in modern life: silence. As the psalmist counsels, "Be still, and know that I am God" (Psalm 46:10). This stillness is not passive but profoundly active, requiring disciplined attention and surrender.

True Kingdom Warriors practice what the ancient church called "sacred silence"—regular periods of quieting both external noise and internal chatter to become attuned to Jesus' voice. This might mean rising before dawn when the house is still, finding a secluded spot during lunch breaks, or creating evening disciplines that exclude digital or streaming distractions.

In these sanctified moments, Kingdom Warriors discover that Jesus often speaks not in thunderous proclamations but in "a still small voice" (1 Kings 19:12, NKJV). Like tuning a radio to the right frequency, they learn to distinguish His voice amid competing noise, recognizing its unique tone of truth, love, and holiness.

What makes this practice so powerful is that Jesus is always ready for these encounters. He's not distant or reluctant to communicate but eagerly waiting for Kingdom Warriors who will create space to listen. These sacred moments become a divine training ground where Jesus not only speaks but teaches Kingdom Warriors how to listen more effectively to the Holy Spirit's guidance.

*Before a Kingdom Warrior faces the world,*
*they first face their Savior.*

This is where the kingdom adventure with Jesus moves to deeper intimate relationship. Beyond the initial excitement of enlistment, beyond the fundamental training in spiritual disciplines, Kingdom Warriors discover the profound joy of simply being with their King—sharing hearts, exchanging thoughts, experiencing His delight in their presence.

Rick Warren, the founder of Saddleback Church and author of *The Purpose Driven Life*, has shared many teachings on prayer throughout his ministry. One of his most frequently discussed ideas is the ACTS model of prayer:

- **Adoration:** Beginning with worship and praise
- **Confession:** Acknowledging sins and shortcomings
- **Thanksgiving:** Expressing gratitude for God's blessings
- **Supplication:** Making requests for oneself and others

Warren also frames prayer as a means of aligning our will with God's will, rather than trying to get God to align with our desires. We wholeheartedly agree—prayer is transformative, changing the person praying as much as changing the circumstances.[1]

So today, amid all the spiritual techniques and battle strategies you might be learning, remember the Kingdom Warrior's deepest secret: presence precedes power. What would happen if you carved out space in your day—even just fifteen minutes—for sacred silence? Not to ask for anything. Not to accomplish anything. Simply to be still and know that He is God.

In that presence, you might discover that the most effective preparation for whatever unseen battle awaits isn't another strategy but deeper communion with Jesus, who has already won the war.

## Practicing the Presence

*The secret of Kingdom Warriors: they spend more time with their Warrior King than they do on the battlefield.*

> We should establish ourselves in a sense of God's Presence, by continually conversing with Him.[2]
>
> — Brother Lawrence

Have you ever met someone who seems to carry a certain atmosphere with them? There's something different about their presence—a peace, a focus, a sense of being deeply anchored regardless of circumstances. What you're witnessing is often the fruit of a sacred skill: practicing the presence.

We've always been fascinated by Brother Lawrence, that humble 17th-century Carmelite monk who worked in the monastery kitchen. In the midst of clattering pots and endless chores, he developed what he called "the practice of the presence of God"—training himself to maintain conscious communion with Jesus while performing even the most mundane tasks. His simple approach transformed dishwashing into worship, vegetable chopping into prayer.

What strikes us about Brother Lawrence is how he demolished the false wall we often build between "spiritual activities" and "everything else." Kingdom Warriors adopt this same perspective, refusing to compartmentalize their spiritual lives into Sunday-morning boxes. They recognize that all of life happens in God's presence—the only question is whether we're aware of it.

We talked with a business executive who described how this practice revolutionized her professional life. "I used to see my morning devotions as filling my spiritual tank for the day," she said. "Now I understand that Jesus doesn't stay home when I go to work. During meetings, I silently ask for His wisdom. When facing difficult decisions, I pause for internal guidance. It's transformed not just my spiritual life but my leadership."

This practice isn't complicated, but it does require intentionality. Kingdom Warriors develop what some call "kingdom trigger habits"—using common daily occurrences as reminders to reconnect with Jesus' presence. A phone notification becomes a prompt for a breath prayer. A red light transforms from frustration into opportunity for communion. Walking through doorways serves as a reminder to acknowledge the One who walks with you.

The Psalms repeatedly emphasize this practice of continuous meditation on God's presence and Word. "Blessed is the one...whose delight is in the law of the LORD, and who meditates on his law day and night" (Psalm 1:1-2). This isn't about theological analysis but loving attention—the kind of continuous kingdom awareness that transforms ordinary moments into sacred encounters.

Joshua received similar instruction: "Keep this Book of the Law always on your lips; meditate on it day and night" (Joshua 1:8). Notice the continuous nature of this practice—it's not confined to a morning quiet time but extends throughout each day's activities.

*True warriors know that time in His presence transforms moments of weakness into demonstrations of His power.*

What makes this practice so powerful is how it gradually reshapes our perception of reality. We begin to recognize divine appointments in "coincidental" meetings. We discern spiritual significance in seemingly random events. We experience the truth that the boundary between sacred and secular exists only in our minds, not in Jesus' kingdom.

Annie and I are reminded of a mother who found this practice transformative amid the chaos of raising young children. "I was constantly frustrated that my spiritual life had been reduced to fragmented prayers between diaper changes," she told us. "Then I realized—Jesus was present in those very moments. I began talking with Him while folding laundry, seeking His perspective during discipline challenges, thanking Him while watching my children play. The activities didn't change, but my awareness of His presence in them changed everything."

This continuous communion becomes the Kingdom Warrior's greatest source of strength and discernment in the unseen cosmic spiritual battle. When you've been practicing awareness of Jesus' presence throughout ordinary moments, you're already connected when crisis strikes. You don't have to establish communication in emergency—you simply continue the ongoing conversation.

Perhaps the most beautiful prayer in Scripture regarding this practice comes from Psalm 19:14: "May these words of my mouth and this meditation of my heart be pleasing in your sight, Lord, my Rock and my Redeemer." It acknowledges that both our external communications and internal attention can become offerings of worship when consciously placed in Jesus' presence.

So today, what if you began viewing each activity not as a break from spiritual life but as another context for kingdom communion? What daily kingdom triggers might remind you of His constant presence? How might continuous awareness of Jesus transform your experience of washing dishes, sitting in meetings, or driving through traffic?

This practice doesn't require more time—just more attention to the One who is already with you in every moment, Jesus. In that attention, Kingdom Warriors discover that the division between sacred and secular dissolves, leaving all of life infused with His presence.

## Scripture as Encounter

> Your word is a lamp for my feet, a light on my path.
>
> — Psalm 119:105

Have you ever noticed how strategic the enemy is about one particular aspect of your spiritual life? There's a reason why your Bible reading plan gets interrupted more than almost any other commitment. There's a pattern behind the sudden emergencies that arise during your planned scripture time. There's a calculated purpose to those feelings of inadequacy that whisper, "You won't understand what you're reading anyway."

Satan's primary strategy in spiritual warfare revolves around preventing warriors from engaging with Scripture. He knows what many Kingdom Warriors forget—that unread Bibles leave us vulnerable to his deceptions. It's no accident that "the sword of the Spirit" is identified as "the word of God" in Ephesians 6:17. It's both offensive weapon and protective armor, which is precisely why the enemy works tirelessly to keep this divine arsenal gathering dust while Kingdom Warriors remain unarmed on the unseen cosmic battlefield.

I remember talking with a seasoned spiritual warrior about this battle. "I finally realized," he told us, "that the resistance I felt toward opening my Bible wasn't just laziness—it was warfare. When I recognized it as an attack rather than a personal failure, everything changed. I began to see my Bible reading as an act of spiritual defiance."

*When you remain in Jesus' presence, you fight*
*not for victory, but from victory.*

That's a profound shift in perspective, isn't it? When direct distraction fails, the enemy subtly convinces us that Bible reading is merely an optional spiritual activity rather than vital nourishment necessary for spiritual vitality. He whispers that a quick devotional app or second-hand teaching provides sufficient spiritual sustenance. It's like trying to sustain yourself on spiritual fast food—it might temporarily satisfy, but it cannot sustain a warrior through intense spiritual combat.

The enemy takes special satisfaction when we own multiple Bibles but remain ignorant of their contents, creating the illusion of spirituality without the transformative power that comes only through direct engagement with God's living Word.

For true Kingdom Warriors, Bible reading transcends information gathering to become transformational encounter. They approach scripture not merely to learn about God but to meet with Jesus. Ancient practices like Lectio Divina ("divine reading") train warriors to read slowly, meditatively, allowing the words to penetrate beyond intellect into heart and spirit.

We've watched remarkable transformation occur when believers shift from viewing Bible reading as a religious duty to seeing it as a divine appointment. The businesswoman who begins her day immersed in Scripture, recognizing with the psalmist that God's word is "a lamp to my feet and a light to my path." The student who memorizes key passages not to earn spiritual points but to carry Jesus' presence throughout challenging days, having His truth readily available in moments of temptation or opportunity.

What would happen if we approached Scripture not as a textbook but as a place of encounter? What if we came to the Bible expecting not just to read about God, but to meet with Him personally? What if we viewed resistance to Bible reading not as personal weakness but as enemy opposition to our most powerful weapon?

Prayer follows this same pattern of relationship over ritual. Kingdom Warriors understand prayer not primarily as presenting requests to a distant deity but as intimate dialogue with an ever-present Father. They practice conversational prayer—speaking honestly and listening attentively throughout their day.

Like Jesus, who often rose "very early in the morning, while it was still dark" to pray (Mark 1:35), warriors establish rhythms of dedicated prayer time. As we've discussed previously, many adopt the historic practice of "praying the hours"—pausing at set times throughout the day for reconnection with Jesus, creating a heartbeat of presence that sustains spiritual vitality.

These disciplines of Scripture and prayer become the warrior's primary training ground for recognizing Jesus' presence in all circumstances. The more time spent in deliberate communion, the more naturally they perceive His guidance in ordinary moments. They develop a heightened awareness that transforms mundane routines into sacred adventures, where casual conversations become divine appointments and "chance" encounters reveal divine orchestration.

Warriors who cultivate attentiveness to the Holy Spirit's whispers discover that ordinary moments transform into divine appointments with remarkable frequency. While others see random interactions, these spiritually attuned warriors recognize heavenly orchestration behind "coincidental" meetings at grocery stores, gas stations, and coffee shops.

So today, what if you approached your Bible not as a task to complete but as an encounter to experience? What if you viewed prayer not as religious performance but as genuine conversation with Someone who delights in your company? What if the resistance you feel toward these practices isn't just personal weakness but evidence of their extraordinary power in spiritual warfare?

The enemy wouldn't fight so hard against something that wasn't profoundly transformative. Perhaps the very resistance you feel is the greatest indicator of just how powerful these encounters can be.

## The Integrated Spiritual Life

> And surely I am with you always, to the very end of the age.
>
> — Matthew 28:20

Have you ever noticed how we tend to divide our lives into separate compartments? Work belongs in one box, family in another, recreation in a third, and spirituality often gets relegated to a Sunday morning container that rarely interacts with the rest.

But Kingdom Warriors understand something profound: maintaining awareness of Jesus' presence during the unseen cosmic battle requires breaking down these artificial walls. They train not to compartmentalize their spiritual lives but to integrate awareness of Jesus and the Holy Spirit into every aspect of their existence.

This integrated Kingdom Warrior spiritual life becomes perhaps our most powerful testimony in a fragmented world. When people witness someone moving seamlessly between prayer and problem-solving, between worship and work, between communion and conversation—it confronts the artificial divisions our culture has constructed.

What makes this integration possible is Jesus' extraordinary promise at the end of Matthew's gospel: "And surely I am with you always, to the very end of the age" (Matthew 28:20). Have you ever really let the magnitude of those words sink in? Always. Not occasionally. Not just during designated spiritual activities. Not only when we feel particularly worthy. Always.

This assurance—that Jesus' presence is not occasional but constant, not earned but freely given—transforms spiritual formation from burdensome obligation into joyful response. We're not trying to reach a distant God; we're awakening to the reality of One who is already nearer than our breath.

*In His presence, warriors find the courage to face what seemed impossible in His absence.*

Think about how this changes everything! Prayer becomes not a formal exercise but an ongoing conversation with the Jesus who never leaves. Bible reading shifts from religious duty to eager communication with the Author who walks beside you. Service transforms from charitable activity to direct ministry to the Jesus who promised to be present in "the least of these."

We've watched remarkable shifts occur when Kingdom Warriors truly grasp this promise. The mother who stops seeing childcare as an interruption to her spiritual life and begins recognizing Jesus' presence in each interaction with her children. The tradesman who discovers divine purpose in seemingly mundane tasks, approaching each job as service to the unseen but present Jesus. The student who transforms classroom challenges into opportunities for dependence on the Teacher who accompanies them.

Kingdom Warriors train not to earn Jesus' presence but to become increasingly aware of the presence already promised. Each spiritual discipline becomes a means not of reaching God but of awakening to the Jesus who has already reached us. In this awakening, ordinary people become extraordinary Kingdom Warriors, carrying Jesus' tangible presence into a world desperate for authentic encounter with the living God.

So today, what artificial walls might be dividing your life into spiritual and non-spiritual categories? What activities do you unconsciously approach as if Jesus weren't present? And how might your experience change if you began deliberately practicing awareness of His presence in those very places?

*Kingdom Warriors find their refuge not in retreat,*
*but in the advancing presence of Christ.*

Remember, the promise that fuels our warrior training isn't that Jesus will be with us if we perform the right spiritual exercises. It's that He is with us always—through every unseen battle, every triumph, every ordinary Tuesday afternoon—to the very end of the age. Our kingdom calling is simply to awaken to this extraordinary kingdom reality and allow it to transform every dimension of our lives.

As we move forward to explore a warrior's kingdom mindset in the unseen cosmic battle, let this assurance be your foundation: you never fight alone, you never train alone, you never enter any situation without the presence of the Jesus who has overcome the world.

## Chapter 12

# Developing the Kingdom Warrior Mindset

## The Internal Revolution

> Do not conform to the pattern of this world, but be transformed by the renewing of your mind. Then you will be able to test and approve what God's will is—his good, pleasing and perfect will.
>
> — Romans 12:2

### Faith: The Heartbeat of a Kingdom Warrior

Friend, if there's one thing we've learned on this adventure of following Jesus, it's that faith isn't just a component of becoming a Kingdom Warrior—it's the very foundation, the lifeblood, the oxygen that makes everything else possible.

Think about this for a moment: everything God is calling you to become and everything He's inviting you to do begins with faith. Not just any faith—not a casual, comfortable Sunday morning faith—but a bold, audacious faith that sees the invisible, believes the impossible, and attempts the unthinkable. There's something truly remarkable about how Jesus grows our faith through the Holy Spirit's power. It's not usually the dramatic, mountain-top moments that transform us most deeply—though those certainly happen. It's often in the quiet, everyday moments that the Spirit is at work within us.

Think about how a garden grows. The most important work happens beneath the surface, where we can't see it. Roots stretch deeper, drawing nourishment from hidden places. That's how the Spirit often works in our hearts—in those unseen spaces, strengthening our foundation when we're not even aware of it.

Jesus promised that the Spirit would be our Helper, our Comforter, our Guide. And true to His word, the Spirit meets us exactly where we are. When you're wrestling with doubt, feeling that your prayers are hitting the ceiling, the Spirit is interceding for you with "groanings too deep for words" (Romans 8:26, ESV). When Scripture once felt like distant text but suddenly speaks directly to your situation—that's the Spirit illuminating truth specifically for you.

We've always found it beautiful how the Spirit's work in our lives is both gentle and powerful. Like how water, given enough time, can reshape even the hardest stone. The Spirit's patient persistence transforms areas of our lives we once thought would never change.

And what about those times when you've found courage you didn't know you had? When you've loved someone difficult or forgiven what seemed unforgivable? That's not just willpower—that's the supernatural empowerment faith Jesus promised.

Faith grows not just through our own disciplines and efforts, though those matter, but through this divine partnership. We bring our willingness, our openness, our "yes"—and the Spirit brings the transformation. Little by little, we find ourselves trusting more deeply, loving more authentically, and seeing the world more through Jesus' eyes.

What aspects of your faith journey have you seen the Spirit working in most powerfully?

> You have power over your mind—not outside events. Realize this, and you will find strength.[1]
>
> — MARCUS AURELIUS

## FAITH THAT TRANSFORMS IDENTITY

Before you can fight like a Kingdom Warrior, you must first believe you are one. This is where so many of us get stuck. We see ourselves through the lens of our failures, weaknesses, and limitations rather than through the truth of who God says we are.

But here's the beautiful reality: "I have been crucified with Christ and I no longer live, but Christ lives in me. The life I now live in the body, I live by faith in the Son of God, who loved me and gave himself for me" (Galatians 2:20).

Do you see what Paul is saying? Your old identity has been crucified. The real you—the warrior you—is now defined by Christ living inside you. Faith grabs hold of this truth and refuses to let go, even when feelings and circumstances scream otherwise.

Mel remembers a season when he felt completely inadequate for what God was calling him to do. Every morning, he had to look in the mirror and declare by faith, "I am not who I once was. Jesus lives in me. His power works through me." It felt fake at first—almost dishonest. But day by day, faith was rewiring his internal identity until he began to naturally think, feel, and act from his true identity in Jesus.

## FAITH THAT SEES THE UNSEEN COSMIC BATTLEFIELD

Kingdom Warriors fight differently because they see differently. While the world fixates on what's visible—physical circumstances, material resources, human abilities—Kingdom Warriors of faith perceive the unseen spiritual reality behind it all.

> For our struggle is not against flesh and blood, but against the rulers, against the authorities, against the powers of this dark world and against the spiritual forces of evil in the heavenly realms.
>
> — Ephesians 6:12

Kingdom Faith gives you spiritual vision in a materially blinded world. It's like having special glasses that reveal what's really happening behind the scenes. That difficult person isn't your enemy—they're a soul Jesus died for who's being influenced by darkness. That impossible situation isn't a dead end—it's an opportunity for Jesus' power to manifest in ways you can't yet imagine.

When Joshua stood before Jericho, what did natural eyes see? Impenetrable walls. Hopeless odds. Certain defeat. But faith saw those walls already fallen. Faith heard the victory shout before the first step of the march. Faith enabled Joshua to lead seemingly foolish circles around the city because he was seeing from heaven's perspective rather than earth's.

Can we be honest with you? Sometimes we've walked away from God's greatest opportunities because we lacked the faith to see what He saw. Don't make that mistake. Choose to believe what God says over what your eyes can see.

*Kingdom Warriors understand that their greatest strength lies in recognizing their dependence on God.*

## Faith That Takes Bold Action

Faith isn't just a feeling or a thought—it's a force that propels you into action. "Faith by itself, if it is not accompanied by action, is dead" (James 2:17).

True Kingdom Warriors don't just believe different things; they do different things because of what they believe. Their faith isn't passive—it's explosively active.

Think about David running toward Goliath. Faith didn't just give him courage to face the giant—it gave him the audacity to charge directly at him! While others cowered in fear, faith propelled David forward with a confident declaration: "This day the Lord will deliver you into my hands" (1 Samuel 17:46).

We've seen this truth play out in our own lives. The moments that defined our adventure with God weren't when we had perfect understanding or complete absence of fear—they were simply moments when faith overrode our hesitation and moved our feet forward.

Maybe God is calling you to have that difficult conversation. Perhaps He's nudging you to start that ministry, give that offering, forgive that person, or step into that opportunity. Your mind is calculating all the reasons it won't work. Your emotions are pushing the panic button. But kingdom faith rises up and says, "If God is for us, who can be against us?" (Romans 8:31).

## Faith That Endures Through Warfare

Let's be real—becoming a Kingdom Warrior isn't a one-time decision; it's literally a daily battle, waged against unseen cosmic forces. And this is where faith faces its greatest test. It's relatively easy to believe God for a moment; it's much harder to keep believing when the battle drags on.

> Let us run with perseverance the race marked out for us, fixing our eyes on Jesus, the pioneer and perfecter of faith.
>
> — Hebrews 12:1-2

Faith that makes you a true Kingdom Warrior isn't a sprint—it's a marathon. It's the determination to keep believing when results aren't immediate, to keep obeying when the path gets difficult, to keep worshipping when heaven seems silent.

We think of Abraham, who "against all hope...in hope believed" (Romans 4:18). For twenty-five years, he held onto God's promise, despite all evidence to the contrary. That's the kind of kingdom faith that shapes a warrior—not just faith for a moment, but faith that endures.

There have been seasons in our journey when God's promises seemed more distant than ever. Times when our prayers appeared to bounce off the ceiling. Moments when we were tempted to think, "Maybe we misunderstood God's voice." But something deep within wouldn't let go of what God had spoken. That something was faith—and it's that enduring faith that sustains warriors through the longest battles.

## Faith That Transforms the Impossible

Here's the magnificent truth about faith: it doesn't just help you navigate the impossible—it actively transforms impossible situations into testimonies of Jesus' power.

Jesus said, "If you have faith as small as a mustard seed, you can say to this mountain, 'Move from here to there,' and it will move. Nothing will be impossible for you" (Matthew 17:20).

Kingdom Warriors take Jesus at His word. They don't explain away His promises; they stand on them. They don't accommodate impossibilities; they challenge them with bold faith.

When the disciples faced a crowd of thousands with no food, they saw an impossible problem. But Jesus saw an opportunity for miraculous provision. The difference? Faith. The same faith He's inviting you to exercise in your impossible situations.

We've seen incurable diseases healed, hopeless marriages restored, financial dead ends miraculously opened, and hardened hearts suddenly softened—not because of human effort, but because someone dared to believe God's promise over seemingly impossible odds.

Friend, what "impossible" situation are you facing today? What mountain stands in your path? Instead of trying to find a way around it, what if faith empowered you to speak to it directly? What if the very challenge that threatens to defeat you becomes the platform for God's most dramatic display of power?

*The Kingdom Warrior's path is not about perfection, but resurrection—rising each time we fall.*

## The Daily Choice of Faith

Becoming a Kingdom Warrior through faith isn't a mysterious process reserved for spiritual elites. It's a daily choice available to every Kingdom Warrior.

Each morning, you have a decision: will you live by sight or by faith? Will you focus on your limitations or on God's limitless power? Will you be defined by past failures or by Jesus' victory?

"The righteous will live by faith" (Romans 1:17). Not just believe by faith or feel by faith, but live by faith—allowing it to influence every decision, every relationship, every challenge, and every opportunity.

True Kingdom Warriors aren't perfect people; they're ordinary warriors who have simply decided to take God at His word and live accordingly. They've discovered that faith isn't just the way we start with Jesus—it's the way we continue with Him, day after day, battle after battle.

So, take heart, fellow warrior. The path ahead may not be easy, but it doesn't need to be uncertain. As you cultivate this life of bold, audacious faith, you'll find yourself becoming exactly who God created you to be—a true Kingdom Warrior, advancing His purposes in an increasingly dark world.

And remember, "This is the victory that has overcome the world, even our faith" (1 John 5:4).

## Operating With a New Mind

The transformation of a believer into a Kingdom Warrior begins not with external actions but with an internal revolution—a complete renewal of the mind. As Paul urged in Romans 12:2, "Do not conform to the pattern of this world, but be transformed by the renewing of your mind." This renewing process produces what might be called a "kingdom mindset"—a fundamentally different way of perceiving reality that aligns with God's perspective rather than worldly patterns of thought.

Imagine for a moment what it would be like to see the world through God's eyes—to perceive challenges, relationships, and even your own identity the way He does. This isn't just positive thinking; it's a profound shift that changes everything.

## Breaking Free from Worldly Paradigms

The adventure toward a kingdom mindset begins with recognition of captivity. Most believers initially operate from mental frameworks shaped more by cultural conditioning than biblical truth. Kingdom Warriors actively identify and challenge these paradigms, asking uncomfortable questions about assumptions related to success, security, identity, and purpose.

Jesus consistently confronted the mental frameworks of His day, repeatedly declaring, "You have heard...but I say to you" (Matthew 5:21-48). Similarly, today's Kingdom Warriors examine prevailing cultural narratives through the lens of Scripture, allowing God's truth to dismantle false constructs. This process often creates cognitive dissonance—the uncomfortable tension that arises when deeply held beliefs are challenged—but Kingdom Warriors recognize this discomfort as essential to kingdom transformation.

In our own adventure with Jesus, we have found that the moments of greatest growth often come when we are willing to let go of comfortable but limiting ways of thinking. It's like taking off a pair of tinted glasses you didn't even know you were wearing! Suddenly, everything looks different—clearer, more vibrant, more alive with kingdom possibility.

## From Scarcity to Abundance

Perhaps the most fundamental shift in developing a Kingdom mindset involves moving from scarcity thinking to abundance thinking. The world operates from a mindset of limitation—resources are finite, opportunities scarce, and success necessarily comes at others' expense. Kingdom Warriors, however, align with Jesus' promise of life to the full (John 10:10).

This abundance mentality recognizes God as unlimited source rather than scarce resource. Kingdom Warriors approach challenges with confidence that "my God will meet all your needs according to the riches of his glory in Christ Jesus" (Philippians 4:19).

This shift manifests practically in greater generosity, creativity, and courage—Kingdom Warriors freely give, innovate, and risk because they operate from divine abundance rather than human limitation.

Can you imagine how differently you'd approach your daily challenges if you truly believed—deep in your bones—that God's resources are limitlessly available to you? Not just financial resources, but wisdom, strength, creativity, love, and power! This isn't wishful thinking; it's the reality Jesus invites us into.

> *The mark of a Kingdom Warrior isn't perfection, but persistence in pursuing Jesus' purpose.*

## Eternal Perspective in Temporal Circumstances

Kingdom Warriors develop the capacity to interpret present realities through the lens of eternity. While the world fixates on immediate results, Kingdom Warriors "fix our eyes not on what is seen, but on what is unseen, since what is seen is temporary, but what is unseen is eternal" (2 Corinthians 4:18).

This eternal perspective transforms how Kingdom Warriors navigate both success and suffering. Achievements become not ends in themselves but opportunities to advance Jesus' kingdom. Difficulties become not meaningless tragedies but potential catalysts for eternal purpose. Like Moses, warriors endure by seeing "him who is invisible" (Hebrews 11:27)—perceiving divine realities beyond material circumstances.

We are reminded of a dear friend who faced a devastating health diagnosis with remarkable peace. When we asked about her strength, she simply said, "I'm living for a different world." That's the Kingdom Warrior mindset—recognizing that what we see now is just the smallest fraction of what's real and what's coming.

## Living from Victory, Not for Victory

The world teaches us to strive for victory, but Kingdom Warriors live from a position of victory already secured through Christ. This fundamental shift—from fighting for victory to fighting from victory—transforms how warriors engage spiritual battles.

Rather than begging God for breakthrough, Kingdom Warriors declare with confidence, "Thanks be to God, who in Christ always leads us in triumphal procession" (2 Corinthians 2:14, ESV). This posture of triumphant faith doesn't deny real struggles but approaches them from a position of authority rather than anxiety.

The difference is like night and day. When you're fighting for victory, every setback feels like potential defeat. But when you're fighting *from* victory, setbacks become temporary obstacles on a journey whose glorious outcome is already determined.

## Training the Kingdom Warrior Mind

Developing this mindset requires intentional training. Just as elite athletes or special forces operators develop mental toughness through disciplined practice, Kingdom Warriors cultivate spiritual mindsets through consistent habits:

## Balanced Biblical Engagement

While we've already established Scripture as our foundation for truth, overcoming misguided ideas requires a particular approach to biblical study that emphasizes comprehensiveness and context.

Rather than selective reading that focuses only on favorite passages or themes, we need engagement with the full counsel of Scripture. This means studying entire books rather than isolated verses, understanding historical and literary context, and recognizing how individual passages fit within the broader biblical narrative.

This comprehensive approach provides protection against misguided ideas that selectively emphasize certain biblical themes while ignoring others. When we encounter a teaching that seems to elevate one scriptural theme, we can evaluate it against the whole counsel of God's Word.

## Strategic Prayer

Beyond presenting requests, warriors engage in prayer that aligns their thinking with heaven's reality. This kind of prayer doesn't just ask for things; it positions the warrior to see as heaven sees and think as heaven thinks.

## Purposeful Declaration

Warriors verbally proclaim truth to rewire neural pathways and spiritual perceptions. This isn't positive thinking; it's the intentional alignment of our speech with God's truth, recognizing the creative power of words.

## Intentional Community

Warriors surround themselves with others who reinforce kingdom thinking rather than worldly paradigms. We become like those we spend time with, and community either accelerates or hinders mental transformation.

## Lifestyle Consecration

Warriors make practical choices that strengthen rather than weaken kingdom mental frameworks. From media consumption to friendship circles, every choice either reinforces worldly thinking or kingdom mindsets.

This training isn't about perfection but progression—daily moving closer to seeing as Jesus sees, thinking as Jesus thinks, and responding as Jesus would respond.

> God doesn't give the hardest battles to His toughest soldiers; He creates the toughest soldiers out of life's hardest battles.
>
> — Unknown

Friend, the most powerful weapon you possess isn't external but internal—your transformed mind. As you cultivate this Kingdom Warrior mindset, you'll find yourself standing strong where you once faltered, advancing where you once retreated, and experiencing victory where you once knew only defeat.

The adventure begins with a simple decision: will you allow Jesus to revolutionize not just what you do, but how you think? In Chapter 13, we need to learn how to be alert to encounters with God's messengers, otherwise known as angels.

## Chapter 13

# Kingdom Warriors

## Alert to Angelic Encounters

> Are not all angels ministering spirits sent to serve those who will inherit salvation?
>
> — Hebrews 1:14

Have you ever sensed a presence that couldn't be explained? Perhaps you've experienced unlikely protection in a dangerous situation, or guidance that came at just the right moment from an unexpected source. You may have encountered more than you realized.

As Kingdom Warriors fighting in an unseen cosmic battle, we must be alert to a profound reality: angels are actively engaged in our world, serving as messengers, protectors, and allies in advancing God's kingdom purposes. While our culture often distorts angelic beings into sentimental decorations or New Age concepts, Scripture reveals them as powerful spiritual beings created by God with specific assignments in His divine plan.

> Angels are spirits, but it is not because they are spirits that they are angels. They become angels only when they are sent. For the name angel refers to their office, not their nature. You ask the

name of this nature, it is spirit; you ask its office, it is that of an Angel, which is a messenger.[1]

— St. Augustine of Hippo

Jesus Himself affirmed this reality when He said, "Very truly I tell you, you will see 'heaven open, and the angels of God ascending and descending on' the Son of Man" (John 1:51). He was declaring that His arrival had established a new connection between heaven and earth, creating pathways for increased angelic activity in human affairs.

## Heightening Your Spiritual Senses

We've learned that recognizing angelic activity requires developing spiritual sensitivity beyond our natural senses. This doesn't mean seeking supernatural experiences for their own sake, but rather cultivating awareness of how God works through all available means—including angelic messengers.

This sensitivity begins with acknowledgment. Simply recognizing the biblical reality of angels opens our spiritual eyes to their potential involvement in our lives. Many Kingdom Warriors miss angelic encounters simply because they've never seriously considered the possibility.

Prayer further heightens this awareness. As we commune with God, we attune ourselves to His movements, including those facilitated through angelic ministry. Daniel's angelic visitation came after weeks of dedicated prayer (Daniel 10:12-13). Similarly, Cornelius encountered an angel while devoted to prayer (Acts 10:30-31).

Scripture immersion calibrates our spiritual perception. By studying biblical accounts of angelic activity, we develop discernment regarding their appearance, purposes, and operations. This biblical foundation protects us from both skepticism that denies their reality and fascination that elevates them inappropriately.

## Recognizing Angelic Activity

Angels rarely announce themselves with trumpets and light shows. More often, their work happens behind the spiritual scenes or through subtle, easily-missed manifestations. We've observed certain patterns that often indicate angelic involvement:

**Supernatural provision** often signals angelic activity. Remember Elijah, exhausted and ready to die under a broom tree? "Then he lay down under the bush and fell asleep. All at once an angel touched him and said, 'Get up and eat'" (1 Kings 19:5). The food and water that sustained him for forty days came through angelic ministry.

**Unexpected guidance** frequently comes through angelic messengers. Philip experienced this when "an angel of the Lord said to [him], 'Go south to the road—the desert road—that goes down from Jerusalem to Gaza'" (Acts 8:26). This divine direction led to a divine appointment with the Ethiopian eunuch.

**Timely protection** often involves unseen guardians. Daniel testified, "My God sent his angel, and he shut the mouths of the lions" (Daniel 6:22). Similarly, Peter's miraculous prison escape came when "suddenly an angel of the Lord appeared and a light shone in the cell" (Acts 12:7).

**Extraordinary strength** can indicate angelic assistance. After Jesus' temptation in the wilderness, "angels came and attended him" (Matthew 4:11), ministering to His physical needs and strengthening Him after the spiritual battle.

*In His presence, warriors find the courage to face what seemed impossible in His absence.*

## Angels Protecting You

While popular culture often trivializes "guardian angels" into cute spiritual companions, Scripture reveals a more profound reality:

angels serve as powerful protectors of God's people, especially during kingdom advancement.

Psalm 91:11-12 declares, "For he will command his angels concerning you to guard you in all your ways; they will lift you up in their hands, so that you will not strike your foot against a stone." This isn't poetic hyperbole but a promise reflecting God's consistent pattern of angelic protection.

This protection manifests in various ways. Sometimes it prevents harm entirely—like the angel who closed the lions' mouths for Daniel. Other times it delivers from existing danger—as when angels led Lot and his family from Sodom before destruction fell. And sometimes it provides supernatural preservation through suffering—like Jesus in Gethsemane, strengthened by an angel as He faced the cross.

Throughout church history, testimonies abound of mysterious strangers appearing at critical moments, inexplicable deliverance from certain harm, and unseen forces deflecting danger. While we shouldn't attribute every fortunate circumstance to angelic intervention, we maintain awareness that many close calls may involve more than chance or coincidence.

## Angels as Messengers

The very word "angel" (angelos in Greek) means "messenger," highlighting their primary function in God's kingdom. Throughout Scripture, these heavenly messengers delivered critical information, divine instruction, and game-changing announcements.

Gabriel brought revelation to Daniel that continues to shape our understanding of prophetic timelines (Daniel 8-9). The same angel later announced the births of both John the Baptist and Jesus, forever altering human history (Luke 1). An unnamed angel instructed Philip where to go for a divine appointment (Acts 8:26) and directed Cornelius to send for Peter (Acts 10:3-6).

This messaging function continues today. Many Kingdom Warriors report sudden insights, specific guidance, or timely warnings that came through unusual means—often through what appeared to be ordinary people who delivered extraordinarily timely messages before disappearing.

While not every helpful stranger is an angel, Scripture encourages us to remain hospitable to everyone, "for by so doing some people have shown hospitality to angels without knowing it" (Hebrews 13:2). This suggests that angelic messengers sometimes operate incognito, appearing as ordinary humans while delivering divine messages.

## Angelic Assistance in Spiritual Warfare

Perhaps the most significant yet overlooked aspect of angelic ministry involves their role in spiritual warfare. Daniel 10 provides a fascinating glimpse into this reality, describing a three-week delay in answered prayer because "the prince of the Persian kingdom resisted [the angelic messenger]" (verse 13) until Michael, one of the chief princes, came to help.

This account reveals that spiritual warfare occurs not just through human prayers and actions but through angelic-demonic conflicts that directly impact earthly circumstances. When we pray, we potentially activate angelic assistance in battles beyond our perception.

The book of Revelation further illuminates this reality, describing Michael and his angels fighting against the dragon (Satan) and his angels (Revelation 12:7-9). These cosmic conflicts have direct implications for kingdom advancement on earth.

We recognize as Kingdom Warriors that we never fight alone. Beyond human allies and the Holy Spirit's power, we have angelic reinforcements deployed according to God's strategic purposes. This doesn't diminish our responsibility to engage spiritually but places our efforts within a larger cosmic campaign.

*Kingdom Warriors find their refuge not in retreat, but in the advancing presence of Christ.*

## Divine Orchestration Through Angels

Angels often function as divine stage managers, arranging circumstances for maximum kingdom impact. Consider how an angel orchestrated Peter's prison escape in Acts 12—not just freeing him but creating a powerful testimony that strengthened the early church.

Or consider the angels at Christ's resurrection, who not only rolled away the stone but strategically communicated with the women, ensuring the resurrection news spread effectively. These weren't random actions but carefully orchestrated moves in God's redemptive plan.

Similarly, angels today continue arranging divine appointments, removing obstacles to gospel advancement, and creating opportunities for kingdom breakthrough. Many "coincidences" that advance God's purposes likely involve angelic coordination behind the scenes.

We maintain awareness of this divine orchestration, recognizing that seemingly random open doors, unexpected connections, or surprising opportunities may reflect heaven's strategic arrangement through angelic ministry.

*Your effectiveness as a Kingdom Warrior is directly proportional to your intimacy with Jesus.*

## Angels and Provision

Throughout Scripture, angels frequently appear in connection with supernatural provision. Whether bringing food to Elijah in the wilderness (1 Kings 19:5-8), providing manna in the desert (Psalm 78:25 calls it "the bread of angels"), or ministering to Jesus after His wilderness fast (Matthew 4:11), angels often deliver God's provision in desperate circumstances.

This ministry of provision continues for Kingdom Warriors today. Countless testimonies describe unexpected financial gifts, timely resources, or needed supplies arriving through inexplicable means during seasons of obedient service to God's kingdom purposes.

While not all provision comes through literally angelic delivery, we recognize that angels often work behind the scenes to inspire generosity, direct resources, and ensure that those advancing God's kingdom receive what they need at exactly the right moment.

> Now to him who is able to do immeasurably more than all we ask or imagine, according to his power that is at work within us...
>
> — Ephesians 3:20

## Angelic Assistance in Breakthrough

When Kingdom Warriors face seemingly insurmountable obstacles to spiritual advancement, angelic forces often facilitate breakthrough. Consider the angel who struck down 185,000 Assyrian soldiers in a single night (2 Kings 19:35), transforming Israel's impossible situation into miraculous victory.

Or remember the angels who supernaturally opened prison doors for the apostles (Acts 5:19) and later for Peter (Acts 12:7-10), enabling the continued spread of the gospel despite opposition. These interventions weren't just displays of power but strategic operations that advanced God's kingdom in critical moments.

Today, similar breakthroughs occur when Kingdom Warriors pray persistently in alignment with God's purposes. Sudden shifts in resistant hearts, unexpected policy changes, or the falling of long-standing barriers to the gospel may involve more than human factors—they may reflect angelic operations fulfilling divine assignments.

## Discerning Counterfeit Encounters

With increased awareness of angelic reality comes increased responsibility for spiritual discernment. Scripture warns that "Satan himself masquerades as an angel of light" (2 Corinthians 11:14), highlighting the enemy's strategy to counterfeit genuine spiritual experiences.

We protect ourselves from deception through several essential practices:

- **Biblical alignment** serves as the primary filter for any claimed angelic encounter. Authentic angelic messages always harmonize perfectly with Scripture, never contradicting God's revealed Word. As Paul warned, "Even if we or an angel from heaven should preach a gospel other than the one we preached to you, let them be under God's curse!" (Galatians 1:8).
- **Christ-centeredness** characterizes genuine angelic ministry. Biblical angels consistently point toward Jesus rather than drawing attention to themselves or the recipient of their message. Any encounter that elevates human beings, angels themselves, or anything other than Christ deserves careful scrutiny.
- **Spiritual fruit** provides another key test. Authentic angelic encounters produce outcomes that align with the fruit of the Spirit—increased faith, deepened humility, stronger devotion to Jesus, greater love for others. Counterfeit experiences typically produce pride, fear, confusion, or unhealthy spiritual fascination.

- **Wise counsel** serves as a protective boundary. We submit significant spiritual experiences to mature believers for evaluation, recognizing that divine encounters withstand thoughtful examination and community discernment.

## Mel's Personal Encounter with Angels

In the beginning of this book, Mel shared a personal testimony of angelic encounter. That display of light and grace when Mel was at his lowest point was a stunning illustration of these principles in action.

We remind you of that story not to elevate experiences but to testify that angelic encounters aren't just biblical history—they continue today as part of God's ongoing work through the unseen cosmic realm. This encounter didn't make Mel special; it made him responsible—called to live in light of the reality he had glimpsed.

## Keeping the Right Focus

With all this discussion of angelic activity, we must maintain proper perspective. Angels are servants, not the focus of our worship or spiritual pursuit. Scripture consistently directs worship exclusively toward God, with angels themselves refusing adoration (Revelation 19:10, 22:9).

We appreciate angelic ministry without becoming distracted by it. Our primary focus remains on Jesus Christ—His lordship, His kingdom, and His glory. Angels serve His purposes, and our awareness of their activity should deepen our worship of the God who sends them, not divert our attention from Him.

Furthermore, while we recognize angelic involvement in kingdom advancement, we never substitute angel-consciousness for the more fundamental reliance on the Holy Spirit. Jesus promised His Spirit would be with us always, guiding, empowering, and working through us directly. Angelic assistance complements this primary relationship rather than replacing it.

Finally, we maintain healthy balance—neither dismissing the biblical reality of angels through skepticism nor becoming obsessed with supernatural experiences. We gratefully acknowledge angelic ministry when it occurs while keeping our primary focus on obeying Christ and advancing His kingdom through faithful service.

As you continue your adventure as a Kingdom Warrior, remain alert to angelic encounters—not seeking them for their own sake but recognizing them as part of God's comprehensive provision for your journey. These heavenly allies surround you more often than you realize, fulfilling divine assignments that assist your kingdom purpose.

"For he will command his angels concerning you to guard you in all your ways" (Psalm 91:11). This isn't just poetic language but practical reality for Kingdom Warriors engaged in advancing God's purposes on earth.

In the next chapter, we'll explore what it means to move beyond routine faith into a deeper awakening as a Kingdom Warrior on mission with Jesus.

PART FOUR

# THE WARRIOR'S CALL

## Chapter 14

# The Awakening

## Beyond Routine Faith

> Rejoice always, pray continually, give thanks in all circumstances; for this is God's will for you in Christ Jesus.
>
> — 1 Thessalonians 5:16-18

Have you ever felt like Dave? There he sat in his car after another Sunday morning service, the worship songs still echoing in his mind. He'd done everything right—sang the hymns, nodded at all the sermon points, faithfully dropped his tithe in the basket. Yet as he turned the key in the ignition, an unfamiliar emptiness yawned within his chest. For fifteen years, this had been his routine: arrive, worship, leave, repeat. A comfortable rhythm that demanded little and promised security.

But as he drove home, a thought pierced through his well-ordered mind like a shaft of light through a carefully maintained darkness: Was this all there was supposed to be?

## The Gentle Disruption

Friend, let us tell you something important—the Holy Spirit often works not in thunderous revelation but in gentle disruption. Those questions that unsettle your settled heart? Those whispers that disturb the silence of your spiritual complacency? That's Jesus, inviting you deeper.

> *The true strength of a Kingdom Warrior flows*
> *from time spent in the presence of the King.*

For many believers like Dave, worship has become a transaction rather than a transformation—a scheduled appointment rather than a divine encounter. As we've observed while counseling groups of long-time church members, many have substituted the rhythm of religion for Jesus' relationship of redemption. The enemy's most effective strategy isn't to pull you away from church, but to convince you that simply being present is enough.

Do you see how subtle the deception is? Regular attendance, familiar songs, consistent giving—all good things that can inadvertently become veils, obscuring the intimate communion the Holy Spirit longs to establish with you. We can master the choreography of worship while completely missing its heart.

## The Awakening Voice

For Dave, the awakening came during what should have been an ordinary Wednesday night Bible study. As the group discussed the familiar passage about the vine and the branches, the Holy Spirit suddenly illuminated what had been hidden in plain sight all along.

"I realized I'd been connected to church programs but not to Jesus Himself," Dave later shared with us. "It was as if scales fell from my eyes. I'd been doing all the right religious activities but had no actual relationship with Jesus. No conversation, no listening, no true intimacy."

This revelation often feels like waking from a dream—disorienting at first, then wonderfully liberating. The Spirit gently exposes the counterfeit comfort of routine faith, revealing it as merely a shadow of the abundant life Jesus promised you.

Has He been whispering to you? Have you felt that stirring, that divine dissatisfaction with business-as-usual Christianity? That's not a reason for guilt—it's an invitation to kingdom adventure!

> *Kingdom Warriors know that sometimes faithfulness looks like taking one more step when you can't see the end of the road.*

## THE ENEMY'S SUBTLE STRATEGY

"The adversary doesn't fear busy warriors," another friend, Lisa, explained to her small group that we were leading. "He fears surrendered ones." After twenty years of faithful service to her church, Lisa had recognized the deception that had kept her spiritually stagnant—mistaking activity for intimacy, service for surrender.

We want you to understand the enemy's strategy because it's insidiously clever: he'll let you maintain enough religious activity to feel spiritually satisfied while remaining disconnected from the transformative power of genuine communion with Jesus. Like ancient Israel, we can hold the form of godliness while denying its power, creating what Dallas Willard insightfully called "gospels of sin management"[1] rather than transformation.

Think about it—how many times have you left a worship service feeling temporarily refreshed but fundamentally unchanged, returning to a life largely unaffected by the Holy Spirit's presence, all the while unaware that what you've experienced is merely a shadow of true revival?

> *In authentic fellowship, Kingdom Warriors find both the courage to stand and the humility to kneel.*

## The Adventure to Deeper Waters

When Jesus awakens a heart, the Holy Spirit invites that heart into deeper waters—beyond the shallows of scheduled services and into the depths of supernatural relationship. This adventure requires courage to leave the familiar shore of comfortable Christianity.

For Dave, this meant completely rethinking his approach to faith. "I had to admit that I was more committed to my church identity than to Jesus Himself," he confessed to us. "My prayers were monologues, my Bible reading was academic, and my worship was performance. The Holy Spirit showed me I didn't actually know how to listen to Jesus at all."

Let us ask you some questions that might feel uncomfortable but could be the very questions the Spirit is prompting in your heart:

Are you experiencing the abundant life Jesus promised, or just a religious routine?

Do you genuinely commune with Jesus, or do you merely attend religious functions?

Has your worship become a performance rather than a relationship?

Are you allowing the Holy Spirit to develop your spiritual gifts for kingdom impact?

Could you be operating in subtle unbelief, going through motions while not expecting real transformation?

These aren't questions of condemnation but invitation—an invitation to something far more vibrant than religious routine could ever offer.

*When flesh and spirit battle within, Kingdom Warriors remember they are no longer slaves to sin but sons and daughters of the King.*

## The Mountain-Moving Faith of Kingdom Warriors

What would happen if you stepped beyond the boundaries with bold faith? You'd discover what true Kingdom Warriors already know—a faith that refuses to cower before impossibilities, recognizing that mountains exist not as permanent barriers but as divine opportunities for supernatural intervention.

This mountain-moving faith stands on the bedrock of King Jesus' character rather than favorable circumstances, enabling you to declare victory while the battle still rages. When confronting personal mountains of illness, relationship breakdown, or financial crisis, you can approach the throne with both reverent boldness and childlike trust, knowing your prayers activate kingdom resources beyond human comprehension.

We've seen this kind of faith in action—where believers understand that faith is both shield and weapon. It's defensive against doubt's corrosive whispers and offensive in advancing against entrenched obstacles that would block kingdom purposes.

The seasoned Kingdom Warriors we've mentored have learned that mountain-moving faith requires divine partnership, where human obedience meets supernatural power at the intersection of impossibility. Their faith operates with paradoxical patience and urgency—waiting on God's timing while urgently contending for breakthrough, recognizing that some mountains fall in an instant while others require persistent siege.

Unlike worldly determination built on human willpower, your faith can flow from intimate relationship with the Mountain-Maker Jesus Himself, drawing confidence not from personal strength but from experiential knowledge of God's faithfulness in previous battles. Faith grows strongest in impossibility's shadow, where human solutions have been exhausted and only divine intervention remains.

When you step into this kind of faith, what stands immovable before human strength crumbles before the authority of Jesus working through those who dare to believe His promises without reservation.

## Restoration and Revival

Do you know what true revival really is? It's not merely emotional excitement or temporary spiritual enthusiasm. It's restoration to the fullness of relationship with Jesus—the kind that transforms ordinary people into extraordinary Kingdom Warriors, comfortable believers into committed disciples, religious observers into kingdom revolutionaries.

> *Before a Kingdom Warrior faces the world,*
> *they first face their Savior.*

When you allow the Holy Spirit to awaken you from spiritual slumber, you discover that faith was never meant to be merely a component of life but its very essence. The Holy Spirit restores what was lost—intimacy with Jesus, passion for His purposes, adventure in His calling.

## From Heartbreak to Wholeness: Annie's Story

Sometimes life takes us down paths we never imagined walking. That's what happened to Annie. When her mom discovered she was pregnant as a teenager, her decision was swift and final. Annie was sent away to a home for unwed mothers, hidden from view like a family secret. She can still remember the cold walls that surrounded her and the other girls, all sharing the same fate but too wrapped in their own pain to truly connect. The day her son was born was both the most beautiful and heartbreaking day of her life. They took him away so quickly. The papers were signed, the records sealed—just like that, a piece of her heart was gone. She was told that she would never see him again. Never know if he was happy, healthy, or loved. Never hear him call anyone "Mom." Annie carried that hollow space inside her for years. Through all life's ups and downs, through raising her three beautiful daughters, there was always that quiet wondering, that whispered prayer: "Is he okay? Does he know he was loved? Will I ever see his face?"

Friends, can we share something amazing with you? Thirty-eight years. That's how long she waited. Thirty-eight birthdays she celebrated without him. Thirty-eight Christmas mornings wondering what gifts he might be opening. Thirty-eight years of prayers that seemed to echo in empty space.

And then it happened. Thirty-eight years after she gave birth to her son, she met him for the first time.

God orchestrated what she could never have planned herself —a series of "impossible coincidences" too perfect to be anything but divine. Suddenly, there he was. Her son. Standing before her for the first time in his life. Grown. Whole. Complete. We wish you could have felt what she felt in that moment. All those years of wondering, dissolved in an instant of immediate recognition and love.

The missing piece of Annie's family puzzle, finally found. He is now a part of her daughters' lives as well. They love having a brother. He is no longer a part of the distant past, but an active part of Annie's story. Her three beautiful daughters, and now her son—they're all together, a family circle that God somehow kept incomplete until His perfect timing made it whole.

If you're waiting on something that seems impossible, let this story encourage you with a powerful truth: God is so good. He restores what seems forever lost. He transforms our deepest wounds into the most beautiful testimonies. Your story isn't finished yet. And neither is His work in your life.

*The secret of Kingdom Warriors: they spend more time with their Warrior King than they do on the battlefield.*

This restoration brings vibrancy to every aspect of faith. Scripture becomes a living conversation rather than an academic exercise. Prayer transforms from obligation to opportunity. Worship shifts from performance to presence. Service flows from love rather than duty.

Can you imagine what your life would look like with that kind of vibrancy?

## Authentic Holy Spirit Transformation

Speaking of transformation, authentic Holy Spirit transformation in Jesus is characterized by a profound and genuine change that happens from the inside out. It's not about external religious behavior or mere conformity to rules, but a deep renewal of heart, mind, and character.

Some key aspects of this transformation include:

- **A growing Christlikeness**—As 2 Corinthians 3:18 describes, believers are "being transformed into his image with ever-increasing glory." This means gradually developing the character qualities of Jesus—love, joy, peace, patience, kindness, goodness, faithfulness, gentleness, and self-control (the fruit of the Spirit in Galatians 5:22-23).
- **A renewed mind**—Romans 12:2 speaks of being "transformed by the renewing of your mind." This involves a fundamental shift in thinking patterns, values, and worldview to align with Jesus' perspective rather than cultural norms.
- **A new identity**—2 Corinthians 5:17 states that "if anyone is in Christ, the new creation has come: The old has gone, the new is here!" This represents a radical change in how believers understand themselves—as God's beloved children rather than defining themselves by past failures or worldly measures.

- **A divine kingdom partnership**—As Philippians 2:13 teaches, "it is God who works in you to will and to act in order to fulfill his good purpose." This transformation isn't self-improvement but cooperation with Jesus' work within.

Authentic transformation also manifests in changed relationships, priorities, and purposes. It's marked by increasing freedom from sin's power, growing love for God and others, and alignment with Jesus' kingdom purposes. While this transformation is progressive and ongoing throughout life (not instantaneous perfection), it produces genuine, noticeable change that others can recognize.

*True warriors know that time in His presence transforms moments of weakness into demonstrations of His power.*

## Legacy of the Awakened

Those awakened by the Holy Spirit leave different kingdom legacies than those who merely maintain religious routines. They become catalysts for authentic faith, demonstrating what relationship with Jesus truly means. Their lives speak louder than their words as they carry the presence of Jesus into every sphere of influence.

Like the disciples after Pentecost, they move with purpose and power, utilizing their unique gifts not to build personal platforms but to extend the kingdom. They understand that every talent, every resource, every opportunity is meant to be surrendered to the Holy Spirit's direction.

Mark, after decades in church leadership, experienced this awakening in his sixties. "I realized I'd spent my life building a religious resume rather than eternal significance," he admitted to us. "Now I understand that my legacy isn't what I've done for Jesus, but what He's done through me."

What legacy are you building? A list of religious accomplishments or a life transformed by and used for Jesus' kingdom purposes?

As Jesus promised, you can experience abundance now—not necessarily in material prosperity, although Jesus blesses His people, but in spiritual vitality. Your faith becomes a kingdom adventure of co-creation with Jesus rather than a set of beliefs to maintain.

## The Invitation

Friend, the Holy Spirit continues to move through congregations, whispering to those caught in comfortable Christianity, inviting them to awaken to deeper communion. The invitation requires a response—a willingness to examine comfortable patterns, to question familiar routines, to risk the unknown depths of authentic relationship with Jesus.

Kingdom Warriors experience their greatest victories not through human strength but through complete surrender to the Holy Spirit's power. When facing impossible situations, they stand firmly on God's promises, refusing to be swayed by temporary circumstances that contradict eternal truths. Their faith becomes a powerful weapon as they declare God's Word over challenges, watching as mountains of opposition crumble before faith-filled proclamations.

The Holy Spirit works through their yielded hearts, accomplishing supernatural breakthroughs that human effort alone could never achieve. When Kingdom Warriors remember past faithfulness and lean not on their own understanding, they become vessels through which Jesus' mighty power flows—transforming hopeless situations into testimonies of divine intervention that inspire others to trust in Jesus' unfailing promises.

True faith in Jesus is more than intellectual agreement with a set of beliefs—it's a transformative trust that shapes your entire life. It involves surrendering to Jesus as both Savior and Lord, allowing His teachings to guide your decisions, relationships, and priorities. This faith manifests itself in loving action toward others and perseverance through life's challenges, knowing that Jesus walks alongside you. True faith isn't perfection, but rather a daily commitment to follow Jesus even when the path is difficult, trusting in His grace and finding peace in His promises as He grows you.

As the Holy Spirit awakens more hearts, the church itself awakens, becoming not just a gathering of religious observers but a movement of passionate Kingdom Warriors, committed to carrying the presence of Jesus into a world desperate for authentic faith.

*When you remain in Jesus' presence, you fight not for victory, but from victory.*

Operating in the power of the Holy Spirit means living in constant awareness of and dependence on Jesus' active presence within you. It involves yielding control of your life to the Spirit's guidance, allowing Him to produce supernatural fruit—love, joy, peace, patience, kindness, goodness, faithfulness, gentleness, and self-control—that transcends human capabilities.

When you operate in the Holy Spirit's power, you experience divine enablement for ministry, receiving spiritual gifts that edify the church and advance Jesus' kingdom. This Spirit-empowered life is characterized by boldness in sharing faith, wisdom beyond human understanding, and the ability to discern Jesus' voice amid life's complexities. Rather than relying on personal strength or wisdom, those who walk in the Spirit's power recognize that it is "'not by might nor by power, but by my Spirit,' says the LORD Almighty" (Zechariah 4:6).

Right now, Kingdom Warriors stand at the threshold of history's greatest revival, answering Jesus' clarion call to take up strategic positions in this unprecedented spiritual awakening. These devoted servants—equipped with unwavering faith and surrendered hearts—are being strategically positioned by Jesus across neighborhoods, churches, workplaces, colleges, recovery centers, prisons, among first responders, police gatherings, the physically compromised, diverse people groups, and nations to become conduits for the extraordinary outpouring of the Holy Spirit sweeping across the earth.

Unlike passive observers, these Kingdom Warriors are active participants, wielding fervent prayer, bold proclamation of truth, and compassionate service as weapons that break down strongholds of darkness. As they faithfully steward their unique spiritual gifts and callings, Kingdom Warriors become living testimonies of transformation, creating ripple effects that spread revival fire from person to person, community to community.

This new spiritual awakening transcends denominational lines, gathering those who hunger for authentic encounters with the Holy Spirit and who dare to believe that through their yielded lives, the power of Pentecost can be unleashed once again to transform our world.

*Kingdom Warriors understand that their greatest strength lies in recognizing their dependence on God.*

Will you answer the call to move beyond routine faith? Will you accept the invitation to become the Kingdom Warrior you were created to be? The choice is yours—comfortable Christianity or kingdom adventure. What will it be?

## Chapter 15

# The Divine Screening

> But do not forget this one thing, dear friends: With the Lord a day is like a thousand years, and a thousand years are like a day. The Lord is not slow in keeping his promise, as some understand slowness. Instead he is patient with you, not wanting anyone to perish, but everyone to come to repentance.
>
> But the day of the Lord will come like a thief. The heavens will disappear with a roar; the elements will be destroyed by fire, and the earth and everything done in it will be laid bare.
>
> — 2 Peter 3:8-10

Friend, have you ever wondered what it might be like when we stand before God? Let us share something profound with you that we hope will stir your heart as much as it does ours.

## A Life Reviewed

Imagine Diane standing before the great white throne, her heart pounding as she realizes that the moment of truth has finally arrived. The vast expanse of heaven stretches endlessly around her, filled with countless souls awaiting their turn. Above her, the presence of God is overwhelming—pure holiness and justice radiating with an intensity that makes her tremble.

And then it begins. A cosmic screen illuminates, and the story of her life starts to play out. But it's not just images—every thought, every motivation, every secret desire of her heart is laid bare. Nothing hidden, nothing filtered, nothing disguised.

Can you picture watching scenes from your own childhood unfold? For Diane, there's her Sunday school teacher, Mrs. Johnson, teaching about Jesus' love with such genuine warmth that even now, Diane can feel its echo across the decades.

The scenes continue into her teenage years. There's that summer camp where she felt God's presence so strongly during worship. She had almost given her life to Jesus then, but the next scene reveals her thoughts: "What will my friends think? I'll have to change too much. Maybe later..." The memory stings with fresh pain as she watches herself walk away from that pivotal moment.

Does that resonate with you? Those moments when you felt the gentle tug of God's Spirit, yet something held you back. The divine screening reveals not just our actions, but the opportunities we were given—and the responses we chose.

College years roll across Diane's divine screen. There's Professor Williams, a committed Christian who took time to answer her questions about faith with patience and wisdom. She sees herself nodding along, feeling the truth of his words—but then come the party scenes, the pursuit of popularity, the endless chase of academic success. Each time Jesus knocked on the door of her heart, she responded with the same refrain: "Not now, I'm too busy. Maybe later."

Her career years play out next. The promotion she sacrificed everything for, the relationship she prioritized over spiritual seeking, the materialistic lifestyle that consumed her attention. With perfect clarity, she now sees how God orchestrated divine appointments throughout her life—the Christian coworker who invited her to church, the street preacher whose words haunted her for days, the crisis moments when she briefly cried out to Jesus but refused to fully surrender.

> *The Kingdom Warrior's path is not about perfection, but resurrection—rising each time we fall.*

What hurts most is seeing Jesus standing there through every scene, patient and loving, extending invitation after invitation. She sees Him waiting through her young adult years as she chased relationship after relationship, seeking fulfillment in all the wrong places. She watches Him standing beside her desk during late nights at the office, offering a peace that surpassed her relentless ambition. He had been there during her moments of loneliness, offering perfect love, while she sought comfort in temporary pleasures.

We wonder, dear friend—if your life were playing on that screen right now, what would it reveal about the invitations you've received? About the gentle pursuit of a Savior who never gives up on you?

The screen shows Diane's moments of deep conviction—times when she felt the Holy Spirit's prompting so strongly that she could barely resist. Yet each time, the world's attractions proved stronger. She chose the temporary over the eternal, the shallow over the deep, the created over the Creator. All her well-crafted excuses now seem hollow in the light of divine truth.

Tears stream down Diane's face as she watches the final scenes of her life play out. She sees clearly now how the pleasures she chose instead of Jesus never truly satisfied. They were like mirages in a desert, always promising fulfillment but leaving her spiritually parched. Each worldly achievement, each material possession, each moment of fleeting happiness—they all seem so insignificant now in the light of eternity.

The screening ends, and in that moment of perfect clarity, Diane understands. It wasn't that God rejected her—she rejected Him, repeatedly, consistently, willfully. The judgment she faces is the natural conclusion of her own choices, the end result of preferring darkness to light, the world to its Creator, temporary pleasure to eternal joy.

> *The mark of a Kingdom Warrior isn't perfection, but persistence in pursuing Jesus' purpose.*

As she stands there, the weight of every missed opportunity presses upon her soul. The truth is undeniable—she loved the pleasures of the world more than Jesus. She chose the temporary over the eternal. And now, standing before the throne of judgment, she understands with painful clarity that the decision she put off throughout her life had actually been made through a thousand small choices—choices that shaped her character, determined her destiny, and led her to this moment of final revelation.

The divine court falls silent, but the verdict is already written in the story of her life—a life given every opportunity to choose Jesus but consistently choosing otherwise. The pleasure she pursued now seems like ash in her mouth, and the worldly wisdom she trusted reveals itself as supreme foolishness. For what does it profit someone to gain the whole world, yet forfeit their soul?

Scripture reminds us so clearly: "Do not love the world or anything in the world. If anyone loves the world, love for the Father is not in them. For everything in the world—the lust of the flesh, the lust of the eyes, and the pride of life—comes not from the Father but from the world" (1 John 2:15-16).

Diane's soul shatters with an anguish beyond mortal comprehension as the full weight of eternal separation crashes upon her. The darkness that awaits isn't merely the absence of light, but the absolute absence of Jesus' presence—a void so complete it would consume every memory of warmth and hope she had ever known. Every part of her being screams in protest as she realizes that this separation is permanent, irreversible, and self-chosen through all those moments she turned away from Jesus' gentle calling.

Friend, the pleasures and achievements we chase can seem so worthless in the light of eternity. What makes this reality so heart-wrenching is knowing that it doesn't have to end this way—Jesus pursues us until our final breath, offering the very relationship we were created for.

## The Wealthy Man's Judgment

Let us share another scene with you—one that might hit close to home for some of us.

Frederick stands alone now, stripped of the trappings that once defined him. The expensive suits, the luxury cars, the sprawling estate—all meaningless vapor in this holy place. This titan of industry, controller of markets, master of his domain on earth, now trembles uncontrollably before the divine screen of judgment.

The luminous display before him shows not the carefully curated narrative he spent decades constructing, but the unfiltered truth of a life lived in service to self. Each scene plays with merciless clarity, the divine perspective revealing motivations he had hidden even from himself.

> God doesn't give the hardest battles to His toughest soldiers; He creates the toughest soldiers out of life's hardest battles.
>
> — Unknown

There is young Frederick, inheriting his father's modest business, his ambitious eyes already calculating how to multiply it tenfold. The screen shows his first major acquisition—the small family company he deliberately undervalued, whose owner's desperate circumstances he exploited. Frederick watches himself shake hands with the defeated man while inwardly rejoicing at the bargain he'd secured.

"I earned everything through my own brilliance," he had often declared at charity galas where his donations were always precisely calculated for maximum tax advantage and public recognition. Yet the screen now reveals the unseen hands that supported his rise—the dedicated employees whose ideas he claimed as his own, the mentors whose guidance he later minimized, the countless strokes of fortune he had attributed solely to his superior judgment.

The scenes shift to his spiritual life—or rather, its absence. Sunday mornings spent reviewing quarterly projections while his wife attended church alone. The pastor who reached out, only to be told, "I create my own destiny. Some need the crutch of religion, but I've built my life through my own efforts." The screen zooms in on his dismissive expression, the casual arrogance with which he waved away all suggestion of divine authority.

His chest tightens as he watches his interactions with those who couldn't advance his interests—the mechanical smiles, the eyes already looking past them for someone more useful. The screen splits to reveal opportunities for compassion he never noticed: his assistant struggling with a sick child, the janitor working through cancer treatments, the homeless man he passed every day whose name he never thought to ask.

Most painful are the scenes with his family. His children's achievements reduced to reflections on his legacy. Their attempts to connect met with distracted nods as he checked messages from more important people. His wife's gradual withdrawal as she realized she had married a man who could possess everything except the capacity to be present.

> A lie doesn't become truth, wrong doesn't become right, and evil doesn't become good just because it's accepted by a majority.[1]
>
> — Booker T. Washington

"I need nothing and no one," he had proclaimed at his seventieth birthday celebration, raising a glass of champagne that cost more than his gardener earned in a month. The screen freezes on this moment, his words echoing in the vast chamber of judgment.

Now, as the final scenes of his life play out, Frederick falls to his knees. The weight of truth crushes the carefully constructed self-deception that had allowed him to build his kingdom while neglecting his soul. His wealth—the protective barrier he had erected between himself and life's uncertainties—offers no defense here.

In this moment of terrible clarity, Frederick understands at last what true poverty looks like. He had stored up treasures that could not follow him beyond the grave. He had gained the world but forfeited something far more precious.

"Lord," he whispers, the word unfamiliar on his lips, "I was wrong." The screen goes dark. In the silence that follows, Frederick awaits the verdict for a life that, despite all its material success, had missed its true eternal purpose to be with Jesus and live in eternal paradise by clinging to pride and wealth as his god.

## The Eternal Choice

In Luke 16:19-31, Jesus tells this true story about two men, the Rich Man and Lazarus.

> There was a rich man who was dressed in purple and fine linen and lived in luxury every day. At his gate was laid a beggar named Lazarus, covered with sores and longing to eat what fell from the rich man's table. Even the dogs came and licked his sores.
>
> The time came when the beggar died and the angels carried him to Abraham's side. The rich man also died and was buried. In Hades, where he was in torment, he looked up and saw Abraham far away, with Lazarus by his side. So he called to him, "Father Abraham, have pity on me and send Lazarus to dip the

tip of his finger in water and cool my tongue, because I am in agony in this fire."

But Abraham replied, "Son, remember that in your lifetime you received your good things, while Lazarus received bad things, but now he is comforted here and you are in agony. And besides all this, between us and you a great chasm has been set in place, so that those who want to go from here to you cannot, nor can anyone cross over from there to us."

He answered, "Then I beg you, father, send Lazarus to my family, for I have five brothers. Let him warn them, so that they will not also come to this place of torment."

Abraham replied, "They have Moses and the Prophets; let them listen to them."

"No, father Abraham," he said, "but if someone from the dead goes to them, they will repent."

He said to him, "If they do not listen to Moses and the Prophets, they will not be convinced even if someone rises from the dead."

## A Reflection on Divine Providence and Human Choice

In the tapestry of life, we often witness a profound irony: those blessed with abundance frequently attribute their success solely to their own efforts. The parable of the Rich Man and Lazarus stands as a stark reminder of this human tendency. The wealthy man, surrounded by comfort and luxury, failed to recognize the divine source of his blessings or his responsibility toward others. Meanwhile, Lazarus suffered in poverty, yet his faith remained intact.

The sobering reality of this true story extends beyond material circumstances to the eternal consequences of our spiritual choices. The rich man found himself separated from God's presence, while Lazarus was embraced in paradise. This stark contrast illuminates the true nature of wealth and poverty in the unseen divine economy.

Jesus Christ's sacrifice on the cross and His resurrection three days later established the path to reconciliation with God. This supreme act of love opened the way for all who believe to enter His kingdom—not through worldly achievement or moral perfection, but through faith in Him as Lord and Savior.

## The Urgency of Numbered Days

> Teach us to number our days, that we may gain a heart of wisdom.
>
> — Psalm 90:12

The ancient prayer of Moses echoes across centuries with renewed urgency for our time. It is not merely a poetic sentiment but a divine summons to sobriety and clarity about the most fundamental reality of our existence: our time on earth is finite, measured, and purposeful.

Each morning's sunrise is not guaranteed. Each breath is a gift, not a right. The beating of your heart is sustained by One who has counted its allotted rhythm before time began. The Psalmist's plea for wisdom flows from this recognition—that understanding the brevity of life transforms how we live it.

Consider the story of the rich man who built his identity upon temporal abundance while neglecting eternal treasure. His days ran out before his plans; his breath expired before his ambitions. And what awaited him? Not the continuation of comfortable ignorance, but the stark revelation of truth too late embraced.

The five brothers he sought to warn represent humanity—you and me—living in the precious interval between revelation and eternity. They had Moses and the Prophets. We have something greater: the completed Word of God and the historic reality of Jesus Christ crucified and risen. Yet how many of us, like those brothers, continue our days unmindful of their numbered nature?

Today stands as a divine appointment, a crossroads where eternal destinies are shaped by present choices. This very moment pulsates with sacred opportunity. Will you squander it on trivial pursuits? Will you invest your numbered days in what perishes, or in what endures?

The wisdom Moses sought comes only when we align our perspective with heaven's calendar—when we recognize that each day is not merely passing time but passing opportunity. Each interaction is not merely a social exchange but a spiritual encounter. Each decision is not merely about immediate consequences but eternal implications.

> *The path of least resistance often leads to the battle of most regret. Kingdom Warriors choose the narrow way.*

The sobering truth is that for some reading these words, the number is nearly complete. The final grains of sand are slipping through life's hourglass. Yet even now, at this late hour, the God who numbers our days offers redemption, purpose, and eternal significance through Jesus Christ.

Do not presume upon tomorrow. The brothers in the parable thought they had time. The rich man thought his wealth would sustain him. All were tragically mistaken. Their story is recorded not merely as history but as a serious alarm warning people to be alert spiritually.

The wise heart acknowledges that life's value is measured not by its duration but by its devotion, not by accumulation but by consecration. Number your days by their eternal impact. Count them by surrendered moments. Measure them by love expressed, truth embraced, and Jesus Christ magnified.

For when our numbered days reach their completion, the only question of consequence will be whether we recognized their purpose before they expired.

The clock is ticking. Heaven is waiting. Eternity hangs in the balance.

What will you do with this day that has been numbered for you?

The five brothers in the parable represent humanity—you and me—standing at the crossroads of belief and unbelief, with eternal implications hanging in the balance. Heaven or Hell.

The decision we face transcends all others in significance: will we spend eternity together in the presence of Jesus, or will you, through rejection or indifference, choose separation from Jesus? This question demands our honest consideration, for it not only determines our final destination but shapes how we live our remaining days on earth.

True hope in the face of mortality comes only through a relationship with Jesus Christ—a relationship that begins in this life and continues into eternity. In embracing Him, you discover not just future salvation but present kingdom purpose, not just heavenly promise but earthly meaning.

*When you align your identity with Jesus' Kingdom, your battles become stepping stones, not stumbling blocks.*

When the Holy Spirit awakens you to this kingdom reality, you gain an eternal perspective that transforms your approach to present circumstances. Difficulties become opportunities for growth rather than reasons for complaint. Blessings become resources for kingdom advancement rather than just personal comfort.

Those who embrace this spiritual awakening understand that they are not merely preparing for eternity—they are already participating in it. The line between this life and the next blurs as they recognize that eternal life isn't just a future destination but a present reality.

> So, we make it our goal to please him, whether we are at home in the body or away from it. For we must all appear before the judgment seat of Christ, so that each of us may receive what is due us for the things done while in the body, whether good or bad.
>
> — 2 Corinthians 5:9-10

The beautiful truth is that while these stories of the wealthy man, Diane, and Frederick are sobering, your story is still being written. Each day, each moment, you have opportunities to respond to Jesus' invitations.

What will your divine screening reveal? What story are you writing with your choices today?

What will your screening reveal when you look upon the story of your life? The choices you make today—each word spoken, each action taken, each thought harbored—are brushstrokes on the canvas of your existence.

## A Sincere Appeal About God's Judgment

In writing this chapter, we have shared a truth that weighs on our hearts. There's a day coming that none of us can avoid—a day when we'll each stand before God. For those who haven't developed a relationship with Him, this thought can be unsettling, but our gentle reminder of it here comes from a place of deep concern rather than fear-mongering.

> *In the battle against your flesh, surrender is the path to victory—not to your desires, but to your Deliverer.*

Think of it like this: when we ignore a relationship with someone who loves us deeply and wants the best for us, there's a natural separation that occurs. God's judgment isn't about Him wanting to punish people—it's the natural consequence of choosing to live apart from the source of all love and goodness.

The beautiful truth is that no one needs to face this judgment alone or unprepared. God has gone to extraordinary lengths to offer a way to Him through Jesus. He's not looking for perfect people, just willing hearts. The invitation to know Him is always open, regardless of your past or present circumstances.

We believe deeply that Jesus wants a genuine relationship with you—not out of obligation, but from love. He sees you completely and loves you entirely. Starting that relationship isn't about following a set of rules, but simply acknowledging your need for Him and accepting His forgiveness.

If you've felt that emptiness that comes from living without a spiritual anchor, know that it doesn't have to stay that way. The peace that comes from knowing Jesus and walking with Him daily is like nothing else this world offers.

What would it look like for you to open your heart to the possibility of knowing Him today?

## Prayer of Repentance and Surrender

*Merciful Father God,*

*We come before You today with hearts that need cleansing and minds that seek renewal. We acknowledge the ways we have wandered from Your path, clutching tightly to our own designs rather than surrendering to Your perfect will.*

*Forgive us for the pride that convinces us we know better than You. Forgive the barriers we've built in our minds against Your wisdom, choosing instead to follow the limited understanding of our own thoughts. We repent of the times we've refused Your guidance, pushing away Your gentle corrections because they did not align with our desires.*

*Lord Jesus, we surrender our minds to You. Take every thought captive that rises against Your truth. Replace our distorted thinking with Your clarity and perspective. Where anxiety has made a home, establish Your peace. Where judgment has taken root, plant Your compassion.*

*We surrender our hearts to You. Cleanse them of selfish ambition and vain pursuits. Remove the calluses formed by repeated disobedience and soften them to beat in rhythm with Yours. In the places where we've harbored unforgiveness, pour Your healing grace.*

*We surrender our wills to Yours, Jesus. Your kingdom purposes for our lives are greater than any we could imagine for ourselves. Where You lead, we will follow. What You ask, we will give. When You speak, we will listen. We lay down our plans, our timeline, our expectations at Your feet.*

*Transform us into vessels that carry Your presence into every circumstance, Jesus. Let Your will flow through us unhindered by our resistance. May our surrendered lives become a testimony of Your redeeming power.*

*We are Yours, Lord—mind, heart, and will. Complete Your work in us according to Your perfect purposes.*

*In Jesus' name, Amen.*

In the next chapter, you're invited to answer the call to become a passionate Kingdom Warrior with Jesus. Will you answer that call? Will you take your place as a Kingdom Warrior in Warrior King Jesus' unfolding kingdom story?

## Chapter 16

## A Call to Kingdom Warriors

> Then he called the crowd to him along with his disciples and said: "Whoever wants to be my disciple must deny themselves and take up their cross and follow me."
>
> — Mark 8:34

Are you feeling that stirring in your spirit? That sense that there must be more to faith than Sunday attendance and religious routine? Friend, that's not restlessness—it's a divine invitation. Jesus is calling people of all ages to rise up as Kingdom Warriors in this critical hour of history.

### The Call Across Generations

In this extraordinary moment of spiritual renewal, people from every generation are finding their unique role in God's unfolding plan. The Holy Spirit is moving powerfully across our land, and Jesus extends His invitation to all—regardless of your stage in life.

*The adventure of a Kingdom Warrior is marked not by absence of struggle, but by presence of purpose.*

**Ages 20-40: Pioneering With Passion**—You stand at a pivotal crossroads of faith—balancing energy with growing wisdom. In this season of spiritual awakening, your generation brings:

- Authentic perspective that cuts through religious formality to the heart of relationship with Jesus
- Technological fluency to spread the gospel in innovative ways previous generations couldn't imagine
- Courage to question traditions while honoring timeless truth

Go on kingdom adventure with seasoned Kingdom Warriors who have gone before you Jesus is calling you to be spiritual Kingdom Warriors—establishing new expressions of faith communities while your hearts remain flexible and your vision expansive.

**Ages 40-60: Bridging With Purpose**—You occupy a unique position as stewards of wisdom and experience yet remain adaptable to new movements of the Holy Spirit. Your generation offers:

- Seasoned leadership that provides stability during transformative times
- Professional influence in workplaces and institutions where younger warriors haven't yet reached
- Meaningful kingdom mentorship that passes spiritual legacy to the next generation

Jesus invites you to serve as interpreters between generations—translating timeless truth into contemporary relevance while preserving what matters most.

**Ages 61-86 and beyond: Blessing With Wisdom**—Your generation stands as living testimony to God's faithfulness across decades. In this awakening, you provide:

- Spiritual depth from years of walking with Jesus through life's trials and triumphs
- Prayer coverage with the perseverance and patience that only comes through experience
- Kingdom perspective that reminds us of all our earthly mission connects to eternal purposes

Jesus calls you to be spiritual elders—blessing the movement with wisdom while continuing to grow and contribute your unique gifts until your final breath.

This Holy Spirit awakening transcends age divisions, drawing us together as one unified body with Christ as the head. Your participation matters profoundly—not someday, but today. What role might Jesus be calling you to play?

## Jesus' Life Relaunch—A Kingdom Adventure for All

Jesus' Life Relaunch stands at the center of this movement, as do other churches and ministries answering the call to the unseen cosmic adventure. This isn't just another program or religious activity—it's a transformative encounter with Jesus that's igniting hearts and launching ordinary believers into extraordinary warriors with kingdom impact.

Despite how society often measures goodness—through charitable giving, church attendance, and avoiding intentional harm—the Christian faith teaches that salvation comes through something much deeper than these outward actions.

The path to heaven, according to God's word, isn't earned through our good deeds, however admirable they may be. Rather, it's through a personal relationship with Jesus Christ that begins with genuine repentance and receiving Him as Lord and Savior.

Many people believe their moral behavior and religious activities will secure their place in heaven. But the Bible specifically addresses this in Ephesians 2:8-9: "For it is by grace you have been saved, through faith—and this is not from yourselves, it is the gift of God—not by works, so that no one can boast."

This personal transformation is at the heart of the Christian message—moving beyond religious activities to experience the life-changing power of Jesus Christ's forgiveness and love. It's about acknowledging our need for a Savior and allowing that recognition to transform us from within.

The good works that follow aren't what save us—they're the natural outcome of a heart that has been changed by God's grace and forgiveness.

When you look to the cross, you see that Jesus chose not to save Himself so that He could save you. His blood, freely given, speaks of a love so profound that it willingly endured suffering to bring you redemption. In that sacred moment, when heaven touched earth through sacrifice, Jesus wasn't thinking of His own pain—He was thinking of you. The cross stands as an eternal reminder that you were worth dying for, that your freedom was purchased at the highest price, and that His love for you knows no limits.

What makes Jesus' Life Relaunch unique is its proven curriculum for heart restoration and revival, thoughtfully developed to create transformative experiences. This powerful framework seamlessly integrates with churches, prison ministries, recovery centers, first responder programs, and various other community groups, delivering consistent results across diverse settings.

It follows Jesus' proven model of intimate discipleship. Just as He gathered twelve ordinary individuals and transformed them into world-changers, Life Relaunch Experience creates a sacred space where twelve participants experience genuine spiritual renewal and profound life change.

This isn't about surface-level inspiration that fades by Monday morning. This is about deep heart restoration—the kind that redefines how you see yourself, your kingdom purpose, and your relationship with Jesus.

The true power of Jesus' Life Relaunch extends far beyond the initial two-day experience. As lives are transformed, these commissioned Kingdom Warriors carry this renewal awakening into their families, workplaces, and communities. Many go on to launch warrior teams that conduct the Life Relaunch Experience for others, creating ripple effects of spiritual awakening that touch countless lives.

We've seen marriages restored, addictions broken, purpose discovered, and spiritual gifts activated through this process. People who had been stuck in religious routines for decades suddenly find themselves alive with passion for Jesus and equipped for kingdom impact.

## Your Kingdom Warrior Invitation

Don't stand on the sidelines of what Jesus is doing in this hour. Don't settle for comfortable Christianity when kingdom adventure awaits. Don't miss the opportunity to be part of a genuine movement of God that's transforming lives and communities in the powerful name and authority of Jesus.

Life Relaunch provides a pathway to encounter Jesus in a fresh way, surrounded by others on a similar adventure of faith and transformation. Whether you're spiritually dry, hungry for more, or simply sensing God's call to deeper waters, this experience meets you exactly where you are.

The question isn't whether Jesus is moving and awakening people—He is. The question is whether you'll join Him.

Take the first step toward your spiritual awakening today. Attend a Life Relaunch Experience and discover what it means to truly live as a Kingdom Warrior in these extraordinary times!

Remember the words of Jesus from John 10:10: "The thief comes only to steal and kill and destroy; I have come that they may have life, and have it to the full." This fullness of life isn't just about eternal salvation, though that's certainly included. It's about experiencing the abundance of what it means to be a child of God right here, right now—living with purpose, power, and passion as you partner with Jesus in His redemptive work.

Throughout this book, we've explored what it means to be a Kingdom Warrior engaged in the unseen cosmic battle. We've uncovered the enemy's strategies, examined the warrior's heart, explored the warrior's arsenal, and charted the warrior's adventure. Now the question remains:

Will you answer the call?

The world doesn't need more casual Christians. It needs warriors who understand their identity in Christ, who recognize the spiritual forces at work, and who boldly advance God's kingdom in every sphere of influence. It needs men and women who refuse to be defined by fear, comfort, or cultural expectations but instead live from the unshakable truth of who they are in Jesus.

This isn't a call to religious performance or striving. It's an invitation to surrender—to yield your heart, mind, and will to Jesus in ways that allow His life to flow through you without hindrance. It's about becoming a vessel through which His power can touch a broken world.

The battle is real. The stakes are eternal. And you have been created for such a time as this.

Will you rise up as the Kingdom Warrior you were born to be?

The adventure awaits.

*Need a Life Relaunch? www.liferelaunch.org*

# Epilogue

To the One who holds all things together, to the Author and Perfecter of our faith, to Jesus Christ, King of Kings and Lord of Lords—we dedicate this work with hearts overflowing with gratitude and awe.

> *The wisdom of Kingdom Warriors: when the battle intensifies, draw closer to your fellow soldiers, not further away.*

Jesus, every word within these pages exists because of Your immeasurable grace. What began as broken fragments of our own shattered dreams, You sovereignly transformed into a message of hope for others. This book stands as a testament not to human resilience but to divine restoration—the miraculous way You take what the enemy meant for destruction and redeem it for Your glory.

*Life Relaunch Warrior* was birthed through tears, written in moments of profound surrender, and completed only by Your faithful hand guiding ours. The stories contained here—both ours and those brave souls who shared their adventure—reveal Your power to relaunch lives that seemed beyond repair.

> *Kingdom Warriors know that every person they
> encounter is either a brother or sister in Christ, or one
> who has yet to come home.*

Lord Jesus, you are the true KING WARRIOR who fought for us when we could not fight for ourselves. You entered our battlefield, bore our scars, and conquered death itself so that we might live relaunched lives. Every chapter documented in these pages points to Your victory, Jesus, not ours.

May every reader who opens this book encounter You—the Restorer of broken dreams, the Healer of wounded hearts, the Champion of the weary warrior. May they find courage to surrender their shattered pieces into Your capable hands, trusting that You create beauty from ashes and joy from mourning.

> *Kingdom Warriors understand that every temptation
> overcome becomes a testimony of God's transforming power.*

This book belongs to You, Jesus. Any wisdom it contains comes from Your heart; any comfort it provides flows from Your Spirit; any strength it imparts derives from Your power. We are just the vessels You chose to carry these words to those in need.

For every life that will be relaunched through these pages—for every Kingdom Warrior who will rise again because they encountered Your truth here—we give You all the glory, all the honor, and all the praise.

> *When darkness seems to have the final word,
> Kingdom Warriors stand firm on the promise that
> Jesus' light always breaks through.*

You alone are worthy.

With hearts bowed in worship before the King of Kings and Lord of Lords,

*Mel & Annie Goebel*

# APPENDIX A
## Bible Study Guide

This Bible study companion is designed to deepen your understanding of the spiritual warfare principles presented in this book. Each session corresponds to a chapter from the book and includes:

- **Opening Prayer:** Begin each session by inviting God's presence.
- **Scripture Focus:** Key Bible passages that illuminate the chapter's theme.
- **Discussion Questions:** Thought-provoking questions to encourage reflection and conversation.
- **Personal Application:** Practical ways to apply the teachings to your life.
- **Warrior Prayer:** A closing prayer to reinforce the spiritual principles.

This guide can be used for individual study or in a group setting. For groups, consider meeting weekly to discuss one chapter at a time.

# Study 1

## The Creation of All Things

**Opening Prayer:** "Heavenly Father, as we study Your magnificent work of creation, open our eyes to see Your glory, wisdom, and purpose in all You have made. Help us understand our place in Your grand design. In Jesus' name, Amen."

**Scripture Focus:**

- Genesis 1:1 - "In the beginning God created the heavens and the earth."
- John 1:1-3 - "In the beginning was the Word, and the Word was with God, and the Word was God. He was with God in the beginning. Through him all things were made; without him nothing was made that has been made."
- Colossians 1:16-17 - "For in him all things were created: things in heaven and on earth, visible and invisible, whether thrones or powers or rulers or authorities; all things have been created through him and for him. He is before all things, and in him all things hold together."

**Discussion Questions:**

1. How does understanding God as Creator shape your view of your own identity and purpose?
2. What aspects of creation most powerfully demonstrate God's character to you personally?
3. How does seeing creation as God's intentional design rather than random chance affect how you approach life?
4. In what ways does creation reflect the ongoing care and sustenance of God?

**Personal Application:**

- Spend time this week observing creation (perhaps in nature, or through scientific exploration) with new appreciation for God's design.
- Identify one way your understanding of yourself as God's creation challenges cultural messages about human identity and purpose.
- Create a brief personal statement about what it means to be created in God's image.

**Warrior Prayer:** "Creator God, I stand in awe of Your magnificent work. Thank You for creating me with purpose and design. Help me to see myself and all creation through Your eyes, recognizing Your authority, wisdom, and love. Draw me into deeper wonder at Your creative power, and help me to fulfill the purpose for which You created me. In Jesus' name, Amen."

# Study 2

## The Unseen Cosmic Battle

**Opening Prayer:** "Lord of Hosts, mighty in battle, open our spiritual eyes to see the conflict that rages beyond our physical sight. Equip us with wisdom and discernment as we study the reality of spiritual warfare. In Jesus' name, Amen."

**Scripture Focus:**

- Ephesians 6:12 - "For our struggle is not against flesh and blood, but against the rulers, against the authorities, against the powers of this dark world and against the spiritual forces of evil in the heavenly realms."
- Revelation 12:7-8 - "Then war broke out in heaven. Michael and his angels fought against the dragon, and the dragon and his angels fought back. But he was not strong enough, and they lost their place in heaven."
- 2 Corinthians 10:3-4 - "For though we live in the world, we do not wage war as the world does. The weapons we fight with are not the weapons of the world. On the contrary, they have divine power to demolish strongholds."

**Discussion Questions:**

1. How does understanding the cosmic battle change your perspective on everyday challenges?
2. What evidence of spiritual warfare have you witnessed in your own life or in the world around you?
3. Why might God allow this cosmic battle to continue rather than ending it immediately?
4. How can awareness of spiritual warfare empower rather than frighten believers?

**Personal Application:**

- Keep a journal this week noting situations where you sense spiritual opposition.
- Identify one area of your life where you need to recognize spiritual warfare rather than merely addressing physical or emotional symptoms.
- Practice "seeing" beyond natural circumstances to the spiritual dynamics at work.

**Warrior Prayer:** "Lord Jesus Christ, Victor over all spiritual powers, I acknowledge the reality of the unseen cosmic battle. Thank You that You have already secured the ultimate victory. Help me to recognize spiritual opposition when it comes, to stand firm in Your strength, and to fight with spiritual weapons rather than worldly ones. Empower me to live as a warrior who knows the outcome of the battle is already decided in Your favor. In Your mighty name, Amen."

# Study 3

## The Silent Guardian: Adam's Absence in Eve's Life

**Opening Prayer:** "Heavenly Father, help us understand the responsibilities You have given us to protect, guard, and speak truth into the lives of those in our care. Reveal where we have remained silent when we should have spoken. In Jesus' name, Amen."

**Scripture Focus:**

- Genesis 2:15-17 - God's command to Adam.
- Genesis 3:1-7 - The serpent's deception and Adam's silence.
- 1 Timothy 2:13-14 - "For Adam was formed first, then Eve. And Adam was not the one deceived; it was the woman who was deceived and became a sinner."
- Ezekiel 33:6 - "But if the watchman sees the sword coming and does not blow the trumpet to warn the people and the sword comes and takes someone's life, that person's life will be taken because of their sin, but I will hold the watchman accountable for their blood."

**Discussion Questions:**

1. What was Adam's responsibility as a spiritual guardian? How did he fail in this role?
2. Where in your life might you be standing silently by while those in your care face spiritual deception?
3. What makes it difficult to speak up when we see loved ones being influenced by falsehood?
4. How can we be effective spiritual guardians without becoming controlling or manipulative?

**Personal Application:**

- Identify relationships where God has called you to be a spiritual guardian.
- Ask God to reveal any situations where you have been silently watching rather than speaking truth.
- Create a specific plan to lovingly protect someone in your life from spiritual deception.

**Warrior Prayer:** "Lord Jesus, forgive me for the times I've remained silent when I should have spoken truth. Help me embrace my responsibility to guard those You've entrusted to my care. Give me courage to speak up when deception threatens, wisdom to do so with love, and discernment to know when and how to intervene. Make me a faithful guardian who reflects Your protective love. In Your name, Amen."

# Study 4

## The Origin and Nature of Demons

**Opening Prayer:** "Lord of Hosts, You have all authority over the spiritual realm. As we study the reality of demonic forces, protect our minds and hearts, keeping us focused on Your greater power and victory. Grant us wisdom without fear. In Jesus' name, Amen."

**Scripture Focus:**

- Jude 1:6 - "And the angels who did not keep their positions of authority but abandoned their proper dwelling—these he has kept in darkness, bound with everlasting chains for judgment on the great Day."
- Revelation 12:4 - "Its tail swept a third of the stars out of the sky and flung them to the earth. The dragon stood in front of the woman who was about to give birth, so that it might devour her child the moment he was born."
- Mark 5:1-20 - Jesus delivers the demon-possessed man.
- James 2:19 - "You believe that there is one God. Good! Even the demons believe that—and shudder."

**Discussion Questions:**

1. How does understanding the origin and nature of demons help us in spiritual warfare?
2. What misconceptions about demons are common in culture or even in churches?
3. How does Jesus' authority over demons give us confidence in our spiritual battles?
4. How can we maintain a balanced biblical perspective without either ignoring or obsessing over demonic activity?

**Personal Application:**

- Examine your own view of demonic activity—are you overly fearful or dismissive?
- Identify areas in your life where you may be vulnerable to demonic influence.
- Practice declaring Jesus' authority over specific situations where you sense spiritual opposition.

**Warrior Prayer:** "Lord Jesus Christ, I acknowledge Your complete victory over all demonic powers. Thank You for giving me authority in Your name. I choose to exercise that authority with wisdom and humility, keeping my focus on You rather than on the enemy. Help me recognize and resist demonic influence in my life. I declare that greater is He who is in me than he who is in the world. In Your powerful name, Amen."

# Study 5
## The Father of Lies

**Opening Prayer:** "God of Truth, expose the deceptions that have gained footholds in our lives. Give us discernment to recognize lies and the courage to embrace Your truth, even when it's uncomfortable. In Jesus' name, Amen."

**Scripture Focus:**

- John 8:44 - "You belong to your father, the devil, and you want to carry out your father's desires. He was a murderer from the beginning, not holding to the truth, for there is no truth in him. When he lies, he speaks his native language, for he is a liar and the father of lies."
- Genesis 3:1-5 - Satan's deception of Eve.
- 2 Corinthians 11:14 - "And no wonder, for Satan himself masquerades as an angel of light."
- 2 Corinthians 10:5 - "We demolish arguments and every pretension that sets itself up against the knowledge of God, and we take captive every thought to make it obedient to Christ."

**Discussion Questions:**

1. What are the most persistent lies the enemy has spoken into your life?
2. How did Satan's approach with Eve reveal his strategy of mixing truth with lies?
3. What makes certain lies particularly believable or difficult to recognize?
4. How can we become more effective at identifying and countering deception?

**Personal Application:**

- Write down specific lies you've believed about yourself, God, or others.
- Find and memorize Scripture truths that directly counter these lies.
- Practice taking thoughts captive by identifying deceptive thoughts as they arise.
- Create a "truth journal" where you record lies you've believed and God's truth that counters them.

**Warrior Prayer:** "Father of Truth, I renounce the lies I have believed about [name specific lies]. I choose to believe Your truth that [name specific truths]. Give me discernment to recognize deception when it comes, and courage to stand firmly in Your truth even when lies seem more appealing or comfortable. I take up the sword of the Spirit to cut through the enemy's deceptions. In Jesus' name, Amen."

# Study 6

## Derailing the Kingdom Adventure

**Opening Prayer:** "Lord Jesus, reveal the distractions and diversions that have pulled us away from Your kingdom purposes. Renew our focus and commitment to the adventure of following You wholeheartedly. In Your name, Amen."

**Scripture Focus:**

- Matthew 13:22 - "The seed falling among the thorns refers to someone who hears the word, but the worries of this life and the deceitfulness of wealth choke the word, making it unfruitful."
- Luke 10:38-42 - Mary sits at Jesus' feet, but Martha busies herself with worldly concerns, and Jesus responds.
- Psalm 46:10 - "He says, 'Be still, and know that I am God; I will be exalted among the nations, I will be exalted in the earth.'"
- Matthew 6:33 - "But seek first his kingdom and his righteousness, and all these things will be given to you as well."

## Study 6

**Discussion Questions:**

1. What common distractions most effectively derail your spiritual focus?
2. How does the enemy use good things to keep us from God's best things?
3. What "kingdom adventure" do you sense God inviting you into that you've hesitated to embrace?
4. How can we develop greater awareness of subtle derailments before they take us far off course?

**Personal Application:**

- Identify one specific distraction that consistently pulls you away from spiritual focus.
- Create a practical strategy to minimize this distraction.
- Schedule dedicated time this week for being still before God, away from all distractions.
- Take one step toward the kingdom adventure you sense God is calling you to.

**Warrior Prayer:** "Lord Jesus, I recognize the subtle ways I've allowed myself to be distracted from Your purposes. Forgive me for settling for less than the full adventure of following You. Sharpen my spiritual awareness to recognize distractions before they derail me. Renew my passion for Your kingdom and give me courage to say no to good things that might keep me from Your best. In Your name, Amen."

# Study 7
## Subtle Poison: Misguided Ideas

**Opening Prayer:** "Holy Spirit, reveal any misguided ideas or false beliefs that have taken root in our minds. Replace them with Your truth and wisdom. Guard us against deception that appears as wisdom. In Jesus' name, Amen."

**Scripture Focus:**

- Colossians 2:8 - "See to it that no one takes you captive through hollow and deceptive philosophy, which depends on human tradition and the elemental spiritual forces of this world rather than on Christ."
- Proverbs 14:12 - "There is a way that appears to be right, but in the end it leads to death."
- 2 Corinthians 10:5 - "We demolish arguments and every pretension that sets itself up against the knowledge of God, and we take captive every thought to make it obedient to Christ."
- 1 John 4:1 - "Dear friends, do not believe every spirit, but test the spirits to see whether they are from God, because many false prophets have gone out into the world."

**Discussion Questions:**

1. What are some common misguided ideas in today's culture that contradict biblical truth?
2. How have certain theological misunderstandings affected your view of God or your spiritual life?
3. What process do you use to evaluate whether an idea aligns with Scripture?
4. How can we help others recognize misguided ideas without becoming judgmental?

**Personal Application:**

- Identify one misguided idea you've accepted as truth without thorough examination.
- Research what Scripture actually teaches about this topic.
- Practice taking this thought "captive" and replacing it with biblical truth.
- Identify a trusted friend or mentor who can help you discern truth from error.

**Warrior Prayer:** "Father of Truth, forgive me for accepting ideas that contradict Your Word. Renew my mind according to Your truth. Give me discernment to recognize misguided ideas and the courage to reject them, even when they're popular or appealing. Help me build my life on the solid foundation of Your Word. Guide me to sources of truth and protect me from subtle poisonous ideas that would draw me away from You. In Jesus' name, Amen."

# Study 8

## Warriors Battle in the Light

**Opening Prayer:** "Father of Light, in whom there is no darkness at all, draw us out of hiding and into Your radiant presence. Expose any darkness in our lives and transform us into effective warriors who battle in Your light. In Jesus' name, Amen."

**Scripture Focus:**

- 1 John 1:7 - "But if we walk in the light, as he is in the light, we have fellowship with one another, and the blood of Jesus, his Son, purifies us from all sin."
- Ephesians 6:14-17 - The armor of God.
- Isaiah 52:7 - "How beautiful on the mountains are the feet of those who bring good news."
- John 3:19-21 - Light has come into the world, but people loved darkness instead of light.

**Discussion Questions:**

1. What does it mean practically to "walk in the light"?
2. Why do we sometimes prefer darkness to light? What makes vulnerability difficult?

3. How does walking in light affect our effectiveness in spiritual warfare?
4. How can we create communities where transparency and authenticity are valued?

**Personal Application:**

- Identify one area of your life you tend to keep hidden from God or others.
- Take a step toward transparency by sharing this area with a trusted spiritual friend.
- Practice intentional "light-walking" by immediately confessing sin rather than hiding it.
- Examine your spiritual armor—which pieces need strengthening through walking in light?

**Warrior Prayer:** "Lord of Light, I want to walk fully in Your light. Expose any darkness I've allowed to remain in my life. Give me courage to bring hidden things into the open where Your healing can reach them. Thank You that in Your light, I find cleansing, freedom, and true fellowship. Help me live transparently as a child of light, letting Your brightness shine through me to dispel darkness around me. In Jesus' name, Amen."

# Study 9

## Kingdom Warriors Stand for Truth

**Opening Prayer:** "God of Truth, anchor us firmly in Your unchanging truth in a world of shifting values and relative thinking. Give us courage to stand firm without compromise and grace to speak truth in love. In Jesus' name, Amen."

**Scripture Focus:**

- Ephesians 6:14 - "Stand firm then, with the belt of truth buckled around your waist."
- John 8:31-32 - "If you hold to my teaching, you are really my disciples. Then you will know the truth, and the truth will set you free."
- 1 Corinthians 15:31 - "I die daily" (NKJV).
- 1 Peter 2:9-10 - "But you are a chosen people, a royal priesthood, a holy nation..."

**Discussion Questions:**

1. Why is truth the first piece of spiritual armor mentioned in Ephesians 6?

2. How has cultural relativism affected the church's commitment to absolute truth?
3. What makes standing for truth particularly challenging in today's environment?
4. How can we stand for truth while still showing Christ's love to those who disagree?

**Personal Application:**

- Identify an area where cultural pressure has tempted you to compromise biblical truth.
- Strengthen your understanding of what Scripture teaches on this topic.
- Practice articulating this truth with both conviction and compassion.
- Take one specific stand for truth this week in a way that reflects Christ's character.

**Warrior Prayer:** "Lord Jesus, You are the Way, the Truth, and the Life. I choose to stand firmly on Your unchanging truth. Forgive me for times I've compromised or remained silent when I should have spoken up. Give me wisdom to discern truth from error, courage to stand for truth even when it's unpopular, and grace to speak truth in love. Help me to be a warrior who advances Your kingdom of truth. In Your name, Amen."

# Study 10
## The Power of Prayer

**Opening Prayer:** "Mighty God, teach us to pray as warriors who understand the power You've entrusted to us through prayer. Awaken us to the privilege and responsibility of intercession. Transform our prayer lives from ritual to relationship. In Jesus' name, Amen."

**Scripture Focus:**

- Ephesians 6:18 - "And pray in the Spirit on all occasions with all kinds of prayers and requests. With this in mind, be alert and always keep on praying for all the Lord's people."
- James 5:16 - "Therefore confess your sins to each other and pray for each other so that you may be healed. The prayer of a righteous person is powerful and effective."
- Matthew 18:18 - "Truly I tell you, whatever you bind on earth will be bound in heaven, and whatever you loose on earth will be loosed in heaven."
- Luke 18:1-8 - The persistent widow parable.

**Discussion Questions:**

1. How is prayer different from a spiritual warrior's perspective compared to casual, routine prayer?
2. What does it mean practically to "pray in the Spirit"?
3. How have you experienced the power of prayer in your own spiritual battles?
4. What obstacles prevent us from praying with authority and expectation?

**Personal Application:**

- Identify one area requiring fervent warrior prayer in your life or sphere of influence.
- Develop a strategic prayer plan for this situation, including Scripture promises to claim.
- Find a prayer partner to agree with you in intercession for this battle.
- Commit to praying with authority rather than uncertainty in this specific area.

**Warrior Prayer:** "Lord Jesus, I acknowledge prayer as my primary weapon in spiritual warfare. Forgive me for underestimating its power. I choose to be a warrior who prays with authority, persistence, and faith. Teach me to pray in the Spirit on all occasions. I claim Your promise that the prayer of a righteous person is powerful and effective. Strengthen me to be alert and to keep on praying without giving up. In Your mighty name, Amen."

# Study 11

## The Warrior's Deepest Secret: Presence Before Power

**Opening Prayer:** "Lord Jesus, draw us into Your presence where we find our strength, wisdom, and training for spiritual battle. Teach us to abide in You as our ultimate preparation for warfare. In Your name, Amen."

**Scripture Focus:**

- John 15:4-5 - "Remain in me, as I also remain in you. No branch can bear fruit by itself; it must remain in the vine. Neither can you bear fruit unless you remain in me."
- Psalm 27:4 - "One thing I ask from the Lord, this only do I seek: that I may dwell in the house of the Lord all the days of my life, to gaze on the beauty of the Lord and to seek him in his temple."
- Psalm 16:11 - "You make known to me the path of life; you will fill me with joy in your presence, with eternal pleasures at your right hand."
- Luke 10:38-42 - Mary choosing to sit at Jesus' feet while Martha was distracted.

**Discussion Questions:**

1. How does time in Jesus' presence prepare us for spiritual battle?
2. What distractions most commonly pull you away from focused time with Christ?
3. How do you recognize the difference between religious activity and genuine presence with God?
4. What practices have most effectively helped you experience Christ's presence?

**Personal Application:**

- Evaluate your current rhythm of time with Jesus—is it duty or delight?
- Create a specific plan to prioritize "training in His presence" this week.
- Identify and eliminate one significant distraction from your time with Christ.
- Practice being fully present with God rather than merely going through religious motions.

**Warrior Prayer:** "Lord Jesus, forgive me for trying to fight battles without first being trained in Your presence. I recognize that apart from You, I can do nothing. Draw me close to You. I choose to prioritize sitting at Your feet, learning from You, and receiving Your strength. Transform my time with You from a duty into a delight. Help me to remain in You so that I can bear much fruit. In Your precious name, Amen."

# Study 12

## Developing the Kingdom Warrior Mindset

**Opening Prayer:** "Renew our minds, O God, according to Your truth. Transform our thinking to align with Your kingdom perspective. Develop in us the mindset of spiritual warriors who see as You see and think as You think. In Jesus' name, Amen."

**Scripture Focus:**

- Romans 12:2 - "Do not conform to the pattern of this world, but be transformed by the renewing of your mind."
- Philippians 4:8 - "Finally, brothers and sisters, whatever is true, whatever is noble, whatever is right, whatever is pure, whatever is lovely, whatever is admirable—if anything is excellent or praiseworthy—think about such things."
- 2 Timothy 1:7 - "For the Spirit God gave us does not make us timid, but gives us power, love and self-discipline."
- Isaiah 26:3 - "You will keep in perfect peace those whose minds are steadfast, because they trust in you."

**Discussion Questions:**

1. What characterizes a "warrior mindset" according to Scripture?
2. How does our thinking affect our effectiveness in spiritual warfare?
3. What thought patterns from "the pattern of this world" most need transformation in your life?
4. How can we develop mental discipline in a culture of distraction?

**Personal Application:**

- Monitor your thought patterns for one day, noting negative or unbiblical thinking.
- Create "thought replacement" statements based on Scripture for common negative thoughts.
- Establish a daily practice of mind renewal through Scripture meditation.
- Identify one area where your thinking needs to shift from worldly to kingdom perspective.

**Warrior Prayer:** "Father, I surrender my mind to You for transformation. I reject thought patterns characterized by fear, doubt, defeat, or worldly values. I choose to fix my thoughts on what is true, noble, right, pure, lovely, and admirable. Develop in me the mindset of a warrior who thinks from Your kingdom perspective. By Your Spirit, give me a sound mind that recognizes Your truth and rejects the enemy's lies. In Jesus' name, Amen."

# Study 13

## Kingdom Warriors: Alert to Angelic Encounters

**Opening Prayer:** "Lord of Hosts, commander of heaven's armies, open our spiritual eyes to the reality of Your angelic servants. Increase our awareness of heavenly activity around us while keeping our focus firmly on You. In Jesus' name, Amen."

**Scripture Focus:**

- Hebrews 1:14 - "Are not all angels ministering spirits sent to serve those who will inherit salvation?"
- Psalm 91:11-12 - "For he will command his angels concerning you to guard you in all your ways."
- Daniel 10:10-14 - Daniel's encounter with an angel after twenty-one days of spiritual warfare.
- Hebrews 13:2 - "Do not forget to show hospitality to strangers, for by so doing some people have shown hospitality to angels without knowing it."

**Discussion Questions:**

1. What does Scripture teach about the role and activity of angels?

2. How have cultural misconceptions about angels affected our biblical understanding?
3. What experiences have you had that might have involved angelic activity?
4. How does awareness of angelic support affect our approach to spiritual warfare?

**Personal Application:**

- Study biblical accounts of angelic encounters, noting patterns and purposes.
- Pray for increased spiritual sensitivity to angelic activity around you.
- Thank God specifically for the unseen protection and assistance of His angels.
- Maintain a proper focus on worshipping God rather than becoming fixated on angels.

**Warrior Prayer:** "Sovereign Lord, I acknowledge the reality of Your angelic servants assigned to minister to believers. Open my spiritual eyes, like You did for Elisha's servant, to perceive the unseen realm. I thank You for the protection and assistance of angels that I may not have recognized. Increase my awareness of heavenly activity around me without falling into unhealthy fascination. Help me partner with Your purposes in both seen and unseen realms. In Jesus' name, Amen."

# Study 14

## The Awakening: Beyond Routine Faith

**Opening Prayer:** "Spirit of the Living God, awaken us from spiritual slumber and routine religion. Ignite a fresh passion for Jesus Christ that transforms every aspect of our lives. Disturb our comfortable Christianity with divine dissatisfaction. In Jesus' name, Amen."

**Scripture Focus:**

- Revelation 3:15-16, 20 - "I know your deeds, that you are neither cold nor hot. I wish you were either one or the other! So, because you are lukewarm—neither hot nor cold—I am about to spit you out of my mouth…Here I am! I stand at the door and knock."
- Romans 13:11 - "And do this, understanding the present time: The hour has already come for you to wake up from your slumber, because our salvation is nearer now than when we first believed."
- Ephesians 5:14 - "Wake up, sleeper, rise from the dead, and Christ will shine on you."
- Matthew 7:21-23 - "Not everyone who says to me, 'Lord, Lord,' will enter the kingdom of heaven."

**Discussion Questions:**

1. What are the warning signs that your faith has become routine or lukewarm?
2. How does religious activity sometimes mask spiritual deadness?
3. What awakened your faith most powerfully in the past?
4. What does Jesus' knocking on the door (Rev. 3:20) suggest about His desire for relationship even with lukewarm believers?

**Personal Application:**

- Honestly evaluate the temperature of your spiritual life—hot, cold, or lukewarm?
- Identify religious routines that have become empty of genuine connection with Jesus.
- Take one step to move beyond comfortable Christianity this week.
- Ask God to restore the joy of your salvation and rekindle passion for Him.

**Warrior Prayer:** "Lord Jesus, forgive my lukewarm heart and routine religion. I hear You knocking, seeking deeper relationship with me. Awaken me from spiritual slumber. Restore to me the joy of Your salvation and reignite my passion for You. I choose to move beyond comfortable Christianity into radical discipleship. Disturb my complacency with holy dissatisfaction until I experience the abundant life You promised. In Your name, Amen."

# Study 15
## The Divine Screening

**Opening Prayer:** "Righteous Judge, examine our hearts and reveal anything that hinders our effectiveness as warriors in Your kingdom. We invite Your searching light, knowing that Your correction leads to freedom. In Jesus' name, Amen."

**Scripture Focus:**

- Psalm 139:23-24 - "Search me, God, and know my heart; test me and know my anxious thoughts. See if there is any offensive way in me, and lead me in the way everlasting."
- 2 Corinthians 5:10 - "For we must all appear before the judgment seat of Christ, so that each of us may receive what is due us for the things done while in the body, whether good or bad."
- 1 Corinthians 3:12-15 - Works tested by fire to reveal their quality.
- Matthew 12:36 - "But I tell you that everyone will have to give account on the day of judgment for every empty word they have spoken."

**Discussion Questions:**

1. How does awareness of future accountability affect our present choices?
2. Why do we often resist self-examination and divine correction?
3. What areas of your life have you kept "off limits" to God's searching?
4. How can we maintain a healthy balance between grace and accountability?

**Personal Application:**

- Set aside extended time for divine screening, asking God to search your heart.
- Invite the Holy Spirit to reveal blind spots you cannot see on your own.
- Respond with specific confession and repentance to what God reveals.
- Create accountability with a trusted spiritual friend for ongoing transformation.

**Warrior Prayer:** "Search me, O God, and know my heart. I open myself fully to Your divine screening process. Show me anything that hinders my effectiveness as Your warrior. I will not hide or protect any area from Your searching light. Reveal any offensive way in me, any compromise, any deception I've believed. Lead me in the way everlasting. Purify me so that I can serve You with an undivided heart. In Jesus' name, Amen."

# Study 16

## A Call to Kingdom Warriors

**Opening Prayer:** "Lord of the Harvest, we hear Your call to join Your mission. Give us courage to respond wholeheartedly, overcoming fear and hesitation. Ignite in us a passion to advance Your kingdom as dedicated warriors. In Jesus' name, Amen."

**Scripture Focus:**

- Isaiah 6:8 - "Then I heard the voice of the Lord saying, 'Whom shall I send? And who will go for us?' And I said, 'Here am I. Send me!'"
- Matthew 28:18-20 - "All authority in heaven and on earth has been given to me. Therefore go and make disciples of all nations, baptizing them in the name of the Father and of the Son and of the Holy Spirit, and teaching them to obey everything I have commanded you. And surely I am with you always, to the very end of the age."
- 1 Peter 2:9 - "But you are a chosen people, a royal priesthood, a holy nation, God's special possession, that you may declare the praises of him who called you out of darkness into his wonderful light."

- 2 Timothy 2:3-4 - "Join with me in suffering, like a good soldier of Christ Jesus. No one serving as a soldier gets entangled in civilian affairs, but rather tries to please his commanding officer."

**Discussion Questions:**

1. What specific call do you sense God has placed on your life as a Kingdom Warrior?
2. What fears or obstacles have prevented you from fully answering this call?
3. How does seeing yourself as a "warrior" change your perspective on God's call?
4. What does it mean to live as part of God's "royal priesthood" in today's world?

**Personal Application:**

- Write a personal response to God's call, identifying both your commitment and your concerns.
- Take one concrete step this week toward fulfilling your calling as a Kingdom Warrior.
- Find a mentor who has responded to a similar calling who can guide you.
- Identify your specific battleground—where has God positioned you to advance His kingdom?

**Warrior Prayer:** "Lord Jesus, like Isaiah, I respond to Your call: 'Here am I. Send me!' I surrender my fears, hesitations, and excuses. I choose to step forward as a warrior in Your kingdom, embracing the specific assignment You've given me. Empower me by Your Spirit to be Your witness wherever You send me. Use me as Your instrument to extend Your kingdom and bring glory to Your name. In faith and obedience, I answer Your call. Amen."

# APPENDIX B

## Launch a Life Relaunch Experience in Your Home

### Step 1: Initial Experience

Two or more participants attend a Life Relaunch Experience at one of our official locations. Sign up online: **www.liferelaunch.org**

### Step 2: Follow-up Interview

- Following the biblical model where Jesus sent disciples in pairs
- After completion, schedule a Zoom interview at **info@liferelaunch.org**

### Step 3: Implementation & Expansion

After attending the Life Relaunch:

**Building Your First Group**

- Each original participant invites 3 more people

- This creates a group of 6 for your first home-based experience
- Format: 2-day event, 9:00am-4:00pm both days
- Meals: Lunches only (with coffee and water provided)

**Support Structure**

- An experienced Life Relaunch coach will attend your first home event
- Curriculum and materials provided for this initial experience
- Focus on inviting people with facilitator potential

**Growth Model**

- Build a team of 6 facilitators for your next Life Relaunch
- Your next event will accommodate 12 participants
- This follows the Jesus model of 12 participants
- Participants will experience heart restoration and revival

*This is a life-changing event.*

# APPENDIX C

## Scripture Reference Guide

## CHAPTER 1: THE CREATION OF ALL THINGS

**Creation and Origin**

- Genesis 1:1-31 - The complete creation narrative
- John 1:1-3 - "In the beginning was the Word..."
- Colossians 1:16-17 - "For in him all things were created..."
- Psalm 33:6-9 - "By the word of the Lord the heavens were made..."
- Job 38:4-7 - "Where were you when I laid the earth's foundation?"
- Isaiah 40:26 - "Lift up your eyes and look to the heavens..."
- Hebrews 11:3 - "By faith we understand that the universe was formed at God's command..."
- Nehemiah 9:6 - "You alone are the Lord. You made the heavens..."
- Psalm 8:3-4 - "When I consider your heavens, the work of your fingers..."

- Revelation 4:11 - "You are worthy, our Lord and God, to receive glory..."

**God's Purpose in Creation**

- Isaiah 43:7 - "Everyone who is called by my name, whom I created for my glory..."
- Psalm 19:1-6 - "The heavens declare the glory of God..."
- Romans 1:20 - "For since the creation of the world God's invisible qualities..."
- Ephesians 2:10 - "For we are God's handiwork, created in Christ Jesus..."
- Genesis 1:26-28 - Man created in God's image, given dominion
- Psalm 104:1-35 - Extensive description of God's ongoing care for creation
- Psalm 148:1-14 - All creation called to praise the Lord
- Proverbs 16:4 - "The Lord works everything to its proper end..."
- Isaiah 45:18 - "For this is what the Lord says—he who created the heavens..."
- Jeremiah 10:12 - "But God made the earth by his power; he founded the world by his wisdom..."

## CHAPTER 2: THE UNSEEN COSMIC BATTLE

**Satan's Origin and Fall**

- Ezekiel 28:12-19 - The fall of the king of Tyre (interpreted as Satan)
- Isaiah 14:12-15 - "How you have fallen from heaven, morning star..."
- Revelation 12:3-4 - The dragon's tail sweeping stars from heaven

- Luke 10:18 - "I saw Satan fall like lightning from heaven"
- Job 1:6-12 - Satan appearing before God's throne
- Jude 1:6 - Angels who abandoned their positions

## The Cosmic Conflict

- Revelation 12:7-12 - War in heaven between Michael and the dragon
- Ephesians 6:12 - "For our struggle is not against flesh and blood..."
- Daniel 10:12-14, 20-21 - Angelic messenger delayed by the prince of Persia
- Job 2:1-7 - Satan challenging God regarding Job
- 2 Corinthians 4:4 - Satan as the god of this age
- John 12:31 - Satan as the prince of this world
- 1 Peter 5:8-9 - "Your enemy the devil prowls around like a roaring lion..."
- 2 Corinthians 10:3-5 - "The weapons we fight with are not the weapons of the world..."
- 1 John 5:19 - "The whole world is under the control of the evil one"
- Colossians 1:13 - "For he has rescued us from the dominion of darkness..."

## God's Sovereignty in the Conflict

- Job 38:1-41 - God's answer to Job regarding His sovereignty
- Romans 8:38-39 - Nothing can separate us from God's love
- Colossians 2:15 - "Having disarmed the powers and authorities..."
- 1 John 4:4 - "The one who is in you is greater than the one who is in the world"

- Psalm 91:1-16 - God's protection amid spiritual dangers
- Isaiah 54:17 - "No weapon forged against you will prevail..."
- John 16:33 - "In this world you will have trouble. But take heart! I have overcome the world"
- Romans 16:20 - "The God of peace will soon crush Satan under your feet"
- 2 Thessalonians 2:8 - The Lord will overthrow with the breath of his mouth
- Revelation 20:10 - The final defeat of Satan

## CHAPTER 3: THE SILENT GUARDIAN: ADAM'S ABSENCE IN EVE'S LIFE

**Adam's Role and Responsibility**

- Genesis 2:15-17 - God's command to Adam about the tree
- Genesis 2:18-25 - The creation of Eve from Adam's side
- Genesis 3:1-6 - The serpent's temptation and Adam's silence
- Genesis 3:8-12 - Adam's attempt to shift blame
- Genesis 3:17-19 - God's judgment specifically mentions Adam's failure to heed the command
- 1 Timothy 2:13-14 - "Adam was not the one deceived; it was the woman who was deceived..."
- Hosea 6:7 - "As at Adam, they have broken the covenant..."
- 1 Corinthians 11:3 - Headship and order in relationships
- Ephesians 5:23-29 - Christ's headship as model for husbands

## The Guardian's Responsibility

- Ezekiel 33:1-9 - The watchman's responsibility to warn
- Proverbs 27:23 - "Be sure you know the condition of your flocks…"
- Hebrews 13:17 - Leaders who keep watch over souls
- Acts 20:28-31 - "Keep watch over yourselves and all the flock…"
- 1 Peter 5:2-4 - "Be shepherds of God's flock that is under your care…"
- Proverbs 31:23 - "Her husband is respected at the city gate…"
- Proverbs 4:23 - "Above all else, guard your heart…"
- Psalm 127:1 - "Unless the Lord builds the house, the builders labor in vain…"
- Ephesians 6:4 - Fathers not exasperating their children
- Joshua 24:15 - "As for me and my household, we will serve the Lord"

## Consequences of Failure

- Romans 5:12-14 - Sin entered the world through one man
- 1 Corinthians 15:21-22 - In Adam all die, in Christ all will be made alive
- Romans 8:19-22 - Creation subjected to frustration
- Genesis 3:16-19 - The consequences of the fall
- James 3:1 - "Not many of you should become teachers…we who teach will be judged more strictly"
- Matthew 18:6 - Causing little ones to stumble
- Jeremiah 23:1-2 - "Woe to the shepherds who are destroying and scattering the sheep…"
- Malachi 2:13-16 - Breaking faith with the wife of your youth

- Galatians 6:7-8 - A man reaps what he sows
- Proverbs 22:6 - "Start children off on the way they should go..."

## CHAPTER 4: THE ORIGIN AND NATURE OF DEMONS

**Origin of Demons**

- Jude 1:6 - "And the angels who did not keep their positions of authority..."
- 2 Peter 2:4 - "For if God did not spare angels when they sinned..."
- Revelation 12:4, 9 - "Its tail swept a third of the stars out of the sky..."
- Isaiah 14:12-15 - The fall of Lucifer
- Ezekiel 28:12-19 - The king of Tyre as a metaphor for Satan's fall
- Matthew 25:41 - "TThe eternal fire prepared for the devil and his angels"
- Luke 10:18 - "I saw Satan fall like lightning from heaven"
- Revelation 9:1 - The star that had fallen from the sky to the earth
- Genesis 6:1-4 - Sons of God and daughters of humans (some interpretations)
- 1 Timothy 4:1 - "Some will abandon the faith and follow deceiving spirits..."

**Nature and Characteristics of Demons**

- Mark 5:1-20 - The Gerasene demoniac possessed by "Legion"
- Matthew 8:28-34 - The demons begging to be sent into the pigs

- Luke 8:26-39 - Another account of the Gerasene demoniac
- Mark 1:23-27 - Jesus rebuking an impure spirit in the synagogue
- Acts 16:16-18 - The slave girl with a spirit of divination
- James 2:19 - "Even the demons believe that—and shudder"
- Matthew 12:43-45 - Unclean spirits seeking rest
- Luke 11:24-26 - A spirit returning with seven others more wicked
- Revelation 16:13-14 - Impure spirits that looked like frogs
- Revelation 18:2 - Babylon becoming "a dwelling for demons"

**Demonic Activity and Influence**

- 1 Samuel 16:14-23 - An evil spirit from the Lord tormenting Saul
- Job 1:6-12, 2:1-7 - Satan's activity permitted by God
- Matthew 9:32-33 - A demon-possessed man who could not speak
- Luke 13:10-17 - A woman bound by Satan for eighteen years
- 2 Corinthians 4:4 - The god of this age who blinds minds
- 1 Timothy 4:1-3 - Deceiving spirits and teachings of demons
- 1 John 4:1-3 - Testing the spirits
- Matthew 4:24 - People brought to Jesus all who were demon-possessed
- Acts 10:38 - Jesus healing all who were under the power of the devil

- Revelation 9:20 - People who did not stop worshipping demons

**Christ's Authority Over Demons**

- Matthew 8:16 - Jesus driving out spirits with a word
- Mark 3:11-12 - Impure spirits falling before Jesus
- Luke 4:33-36 - People amazed at Jesus' authority over demons
- Matthew 10:1 - Jesus giving the disciples authority over impure spirits
- Luke 10:17-20 - The seventy-two returning with joy over their authority over demons
- Mark 16:17 - Driving out demons in Jesus' name as a sign for believers
- Acts 5:16 - The apostles healing those tormented by impure spirits
- Acts 19:11-20 - Seven sons of Sceva and the evil spirit
- James 4:7 - "Submit yourselves, then, to God. Resist the devil, and he will flee from you"
- 1 John 3:8 - "The reason the Son of God appeared was to destroy the devil's work"

## CHAPTER 5: THE FATHER OF LIES

**Satan as the Source of Deception**

- John 8:44 - "You belong to your father, the devil...he is a liar and the father of lies"
- Genesis 3:1-5 - The serpent's deception of Eve
- 2 Corinthians 11:3 - "But I am afraid that just as Eve was deceived..."
- Revelation 12:9 - "The great dragon was hurled down—that ancient serpent called the devil, or Satan, who leads the whole world astray"

- 2 Thessalonians 2:9-10 - "The coming of the lawless one will be in accordance with how Satan works. He will use all sorts of displays of power through signs and wonders that serve the lie"
- 2 Corinthians 4:4 - "The god of this age has blinded the minds of unbelievers…"
- Matthew 13:19 - "When anyone hears the message about the kingdom and does not understand it, the evil one comes and snatches away what was sown in their heart"
- Acts 5:3 - "Ananias, how is it that Satan has so filled your heart that you have lied to the Holy Spirit…"
- 1 Timothy 4:1-2 - "Some will abandon the faith and follow deceiving spirits and things taught by demons. Such teachings come through hypocritical liars…"
- Revelation 20:3 - Satan, who deceives the nations, bound for a thousand years

**Deception About Identity**

- Genesis 3:4-5 - "You will not certainly die… you will be like God"
- Matthew 4:1-11 - Satan's temptation of Jesus, questioning His identity
- Luke 22:31-32 - "Satan has asked to sift all of you as wheat"
- 2 Corinthians 11:14-15 - "Satan himself masquerades as an angel of light"
- Ephesians 6:11 - "Put on the full armor of God, so that you can take your stand against the devil's schemes"
- 1 Peter 5:8-9 - "Your enemy the devil prowls around like a roaring lion…"
- Revelation 2:9 - "I know about the slander of those

who say they are Jews and are not, but are a synagogue of Satan"
- Romans 8:15-16 - "The Spirit himself testifies with our spirit that we are God's children"
- Colossians 3:3-4 - "Your life is now hidden with Christ in God"
- 1 John 3:1-3 - "See what great love the Father has lavished on us, that we should be called children of God!"

**Truth as the Weapon Against Lies**

- John 8:31-32 - "If you hold to my teaching... you will know the truth, and the truth will set you free"
- John 14:6 - "I am the way and the truth and the life"
- John 16:13 - "But when he, the Spirit of truth, comes, he will guide you into all the truth"
- Ephesians 6:14 - "Stand firm then, with the belt of truth buckled around your waist"
- Psalm 51:6 - "Yet you desired faithfulness even in the womb; you taught me wisdom in that secret place"
- Proverbs 12:22 - "The LORD detests lying lips, but he delights in people who are trustworthy"
- Zechariah 8:16 - "Speak the truth to each other..."
- 1 John 1:8 - "If we claim to be without sin, we deceive ourselves and the truth is not in us"
- 3 John 1:4 - "I have no greater joy than to hear that my children are walking in the truth"
- Psalm 119:160 - "All your words are true; all your righteous laws are eternal"

## CHAPTER 6: DERAILING THE KINGDOM ADVENTURE

**Distractions from Spiritual Focus**

- Luke 10:38-42 - Mary and Martha; "Martha, Martha, you are worried about many things"
- Matthew 13:22 - "The worries of this life and the deceitfulness of wealth choke the word"
- Mark 4:18-19 - "Still others, like seed sown among thorns, hear the word; but the worries of this life, the deceitfulness of wealth and the desires for other things come in and choke the word"
- Luke 8:14 - "The seed that fell among thorns stands for those who hear, but as they go on their way they are choked by life's worries, riches and pleasures"
- 1 John 2:15-17 - "Do not love the world or anything in the world..."
- 2 Timothy 2:4 - "No one serving as a soldier gets entangled in civilian affairs"
- Hebrews 12:1-2 - "Let us throw off everything that hinders...fixing our eyes on Jesus"
- 1 Corinthians 7:35 - "I am saying this for your own good, not to restrict you, but that you may live in a right way in undivided devotion to the Lord"
- Matthew 6:31-33 - "So do not worry, saying, 'What shall we eat?'...But seek first his kingdom"
- Ecclesiastes 1:8 - "All things are wearisome, more than one can say. The eye never has enough of seeing, nor the ear its fill of hearing"

**Worry and Anxiety**

- Matthew 6:25-34 - "Therefore I tell you, do not worry about your life..."

- Philippians 4:6-7 - "Do not be anxious about anything, but in every situation..."
- Luke 12:22-31 - "Do not worry about your life, what you will eat; or about your body, what you will wear"
- 1 Peter 5:7 - "Cast all your anxiety on him because he cares for you"
- Psalm 55:22 - "Cast your cares on the LORD and he will sustain you"
- Matthew 11:28-30 - "Come to me, all you who are weary and burdened..."
- John 14:27 - "Peace I leave with you; my peace I give you..."
- Psalm 94:19 - "When anxiety was great within me, your consolation brought me joy"
- Proverbs 12:25 - "Anxiety weighs down the heart, but a kind word cheers it up"
- Isaiah 26:3 - "You will keep in perfect peace those whose minds are steadfast, because they trust in you"

**Competing Priorities**

- Matthew 6:24 - "No one can serve two masters... You cannot serve both God and money"
- 1 Kings 18:21 - "How long will you waver between two opinions?"
- Joshua 24:15 - "But if serving the LORD seems undesirable to you, then choose for yourselves this day whom you will serve"
- Revelation 3:15-16 - "I know your deeds, that you are neither cold nor hot"
- Romans 12:2 - "Do not conform to the pattern of this world..."
- 2 Timothy 4:10 - "Demas, because he loved this world, has deserted me"

- Matthew 19:21-22 - The rich young man who went away sad
- Luke 9:57-62 - Would-be followers with competing priorities
- Genesis 13:12-13 - Lot pitching his tents near Sodom
- James 4:4 - "Don't you know that friendship with the world means enmity against God?"

**Returning to Focus**

- Psalm 46:10 - "Be still, and know that I am God"
- Lamentations 3:40 - "Let us examine our ways and test them, and let us return to the LORD"
- Psalm 119:37 - "Turn my eyes away from worthless things; preserve my life according to your word"
- 2 Chronicles 7:14 - "If my people, who are called by my name, will humble themselves and pray…"
- Joel 2:12 - "'Even now,' declares the LORD, 'return to me with all your heart…'"
- Isaiah 30:15 - "In repentance and rest is your salvation, in quietness and trust is your strength"
- Revelation 2:4-5 - "Yet I hold this against you: You have forsaken the love you had at first. Consider how far you have fallen! Repent and do the things you did at first"
- Matthew 11:28-30 - "Come to me, all you who are weary and burdened, and I will give you rest"
- James 4:8 - "Come near to God and he will come near to you"
- Jeremiah 29:13 - "You will seek me and find me when you seek me with all your heart"

## CHAPTER 7: SUBTLE POISON: MISGUIDED IDEAS

**Discerning Truth from Error**

- Colossians 2:8 - "See to it that no one takes you captive through hollow and deceptive philosophy, which depends on human tradition and the elemental spiritual forces of this world rather than on Christ"
- 1 John 4:1 - "Dear friends, do not believe every spirit, but test the spirits to see whether they are from God"
- Acts 17:11 - "Now the Berean Jews were of more noble character than those in Thessalonica, for they received the message with great eagerness and examined the Scriptures every day to see if what Paul said was true"
- 2 Timothy 3:16-17 - "All Scripture is God-breathed and is useful for teaching, rebuking, correcting and training in righteousness"
- Psalm 119:105 - "Your word is a lamp for my feet, a light on my path"
- Proverbs 14:12 - "There is a way that appears to be right, but in the end it leads to death"
- Isaiah 5:20 - "Woe to those who call evil good and good evil, who put darkness for light and light for darkness"
- Jeremiah 17:9 - "The heart is deceitful above all things and beyond cure. Who can understand it?"
- 2 Peter 1:20-21 - "Above all, you must understand that no prophecy of Scripture came about by the prophet's own interpretation of things"
- Romans 12:2 - "Do not conform to the pattern of this world, but be transformed by the renewing of your mind"

## Distortions of Biblical Truth

- Galatians 1:6-9 - "I am astonished that you are so quickly deserting the one who called you to live in the grace of Christ…"
- 2 Corinthians 11:3-4 - "But I am afraid that just as Eve was deceived by the serpent's cunning…"
- 2 Timothy 4:3-4 - "For the time will come when people will not put up with sound doctrine"
- Matthew 7:15 - "Watch out for false prophets…"
- 1 Timothy 6:3-5 - "If anyone teaches otherwise and does not agree to the sound instruction of our Lord Jesus Christ…"
- 2 Peter 2:1 - "But there were also false prophets among the people, just as there will be false teachers among you"
- 1 Timothy 4:1-2 - "The Spirit clearly says that in later times some will abandon the faith and follow deceiving spirits and things taught by demons"
- Jude 1:3-4 - "I felt compelled to write and urge you to contend for the faith that was once for all entrusted to God's holy people"
- Revelation 2:14-15 - "Nevertheless, I have a few things against you: There are some among you who hold to the teaching of Balaam…"
- 2 John 1:7-11 - "I say this because many deceivers, who do not acknowledge Jesus Christ as coming in the flesh, have gone out into the world"

## Cultural Influences vs. Biblical Truth

- Romans 12:2 - "Do not conform to the pattern of this world, but be transformed by the renewing of your mind"

- James 4:4 - "Don't you know that friendship with the world means enmity against God?"
- 1 John 2:15-17 - "Do not love the world or anything in the world"
- Colossians 2:20-23 - "Since you died with Christ to the elemental spiritual forces of this world, why, as though you still belonged to the world, do you submit to its rules"
- Ephesians 4:14 - "Then we will no longer be infants, tossed back and forth by the waves, and blown here and there by every wind of teaching"
- Matthew 16:23 - "Jesus turned and said to Peter, 'Get behind me, Satan!'"
- 1 Corinthians 1:18-25 - "For the message of the cross is foolishness to those who are perishing, but to us who are being saved it is the power of God"
- 1 Corinthians 2:12-14 - "What we have received is not the spirit of the world, but the Spirit who is from God"
- Titus 2:11-14 - "For the grace of God has appeared that offers salvation to all people. It teaches us to say 'No' to ungodliness and worldly passions"
- 1 Peter 1:14-16 - "As obedient children, do not conform to the evil desires you had when you lived in ignorance"

**Overcoming Misguided Ideas**

- Ephesians 4:22-24 - "You were taught, with regard to your former way of life, to put off your old self...to be made new in the attitude of your minds"
- Philippians 4:8 - "Finally, brothers and sisters, whatever is true, whatever is noble, whatever is right, whatever is pure..."

- 2 Corinthians 10:5 - "We take captive every thought to make it obedient to Christ"
- James 1:5 - "If any of you lacks wisdom, you should ask God, who gives generously to all without finding fault, and it will be given to you"
- Psalm 119:11 - "I have hidden your word in my heart that I might not sin against you"
- Hebrews 5:14 - "But solid food is for the mature, who by constant use have trained themselves to distinguish good from evil"
- Proverbs 9:10 - "The fear of the Lord is the beginning of wisdom, and knowledge of the Holy One is understanding"
- Psalm 1:1-2 - "Blessed is the one who does not walk in step with the wicked or stand in the way that sinners take...but whose delight is in the law of the Lord"
- Colossians 3:16 - "Let the message of Christ dwell among you richly as you teach and admonish one another with all wisdom"
- Hebrews 4:12 - "For the word of God is alive and active. Sharper than any double-edged sword, it penetrates even to dividing soul and spirit"

## CHAPTER 8: WARRIORS BATTLE IN THE LIGHT

**Walking in the Light**

- 1 John 1:5-7 - "God is light; in him there is no darkness at all..."
- Ephesians 5:8-14 - "For you were once darkness, but now you are light in the Lord. Live as children of light"
- John 8:12 - "I am the light of the world. Whoever

- follows me will never walk in darkness, but will have the light of life"
- Matthew 5:14-16 - "You are the light of the world. A town built on a hill cannot be hidden"
- Psalm 119:105 - "Your word is a lamp for my feet, a light on my path"
- John 3:19-21 - "Light has come into the world, but people loved darkness instead of light"
- 2 Corinthians 4:6 - "For God, who said, 'Let light shine out of darkness,' made his light shine in our hearts"
- Proverbs 4:18 - "The path of the righteous is like the morning sun, shining ever brighter till the full light of day"
- 1 Thessalonians 5:5 - "You are all children of the light and children of the day. We do not belong to the night or to the darkness"
- Philippians 2:15 - "Then you will shine among them like stars in the sky"

**The Armor of Light**

- Romans 13:12 - "The night is nearly over; the day is almost here. So let us put aside the deeds of darkness and put on the armor of light"
- Ephesians 6:10-18 - The full armor of God
- 1 Thessalonians 5:8 - "But since we belong to the day, let us be sober, putting on faith and love as a breastplate, and the hope of salvation as a helmet"
- Psalm 18:32-36 - "It is God who arms me with strength and keeps my way secure"
- Isaiah 59:17 - "He put on righteousness as his breastplate, and the helmet of salvation on his head"
- 2 Corinthians 6:7 - "In truthful speech and in the

power of God; with weapons of righteousness in the right hand and in the left"
- 1 John 5:4 - "For everyone born of God overcomes the world. This is the victory that has overcome the world, even our faith"
- 2 Corinthians 10:3-5 - "For though we live in the world, we do not wage war as the world does"
- Hebrews 4:12 - "For the word of God is alive and active. Sharper than any double-edged sword"
- Isaiah 54:17 - "No weapon forged against you will prevail"

**Truth and Righteousness**

- Ephesians 6:14 - "Stand firm then, with the belt of truth buckled around your waist, with the breastplate of righteousness in place"
- John 14:6 - "I am the way and the truth and the life"
- John 8:31-32 - "If you hold to my teaching, you are really my disciples. Then you will know the truth, and the truth will set you free"
- Psalm 15:1-5 - "Lord, who may dwell in your sacred tent?...The one whose walk is blameless, who does what is righteous"
- Proverbs 4:23-27 - "Above all else, guard your heart, for everything you do flows from it"
- Isaiah 11:5 - "Righteousness will be his belt and faithfulness the sash around his waist"
- Matthew 5:6 - "Blessed are those who hunger and thirst for righteousness, for they will be filled"
- Philippians 1:11 - "filled with the fruit of righteousness that comes through Jesus Christ"
- 1 Peter 2:24 - "He himself bore our sins in his body on the cross, so that we might die to sins and live for righteousness"

- Proverbs 13:6 - "Righteousness guards the person of integrity, but wickedness overthrows the sinner"

**Faith, Salvation, and the Word**

- Ephesians 6:16-17 - "In addition to all this, take up the shield of faith...Take the helmet of salvation and the sword of the Spirit, which is the word of God"
- Hebrews 11:1 - "Now faith is confidence in what we hope for and assurance about what we do not see"
- 1 John 5:4-5 - "This is the victory that has overcome the world, even our faith"
- Romans 10:17 - "Consequently, faith comes from hearing the message, and the message is heard through the word about Christ"
- Hebrews 4:12 - "For the word of God is alive and active. Sharper than any double-edged sword"
- Isaiah 59:17 - "He put on righteousness as his breastplate, and the helmet of salvation on his head"
- Psalm 119:11 - "I have hidden your word in my heart that I might not sin against you"
- 2 Timothy 3:16-17 - "All Scripture is God-breathed and is useful for teaching, rebuking, correcting and training in righteousness"
- James 1:21 - "Therefore, get rid of all moral filth and the evil that is so prevalent and humbly accept the word planted in you, which can save you"
- 2 Corinthians 10:4-5 - "The weapons we fight with are not the weapons of the world...they have divine power to demolish strongholds. We demolish arguments and every pretension that sets itself up against the knowledge of God, and we take captive every thought to make it obedient to Christ"

# CHAPTER 9: KINGDOM WARRIORS STAND FOR TRUTH

**Standing Firm in Truth**

- Ephesians 6:14 - "Stand firm then, with the belt of truth buckled around your waist"
- John 8:31-32 - "If you hold to my teaching, you are really my disciples. Then you will know the truth, and the truth will set you free"
- 1 Peter 5:9 - "Resist him, standing firm in the faith, because you know that the family of believers throughout the world is undergoing the same kind of sufferings"
- 2 Thessalonians 2:15 - "So then, brothers and sisters, stand firm and hold fast to the teachings we passed on to you"
- 1 Corinthians 16:13 - "Be on your guard; stand firm in the faith; be courageous; be strong"
- Philippians 1:27 - "Whatever happens, conduct yourselves in a manner worthy of the gospel of Christ...I will know that you stand firm in the one Spirit"
- Galatians 5:1 - "It is for freedom that Christ has set us free. Stand firm, then, and do not let yourselves be burdened again by a yoke of slavery"
- Ephesians 4:14-15 - "Then we will no longer be infants, tossed back and forth by the waves..."
- Jude 1:3 - "I felt compelled to write and urge you to contend for the faith that was once for all entrusted to God's holy people"
- Proverbs 12:19 - "Truthful lips endure forever, but a lying tongue lasts only a moment"

## Dying to Self Daily

- Luke 9:23 - "Whoever wants to be my disciple must deny themselves and take up their cross daily and follow me"
- 1 Corinthians 15:31 - "I face death every day—yes, just as surely as I boast about you in Christ Jesus our Lord"
- Galatians 2:20 - "I have been crucified with Christ and I no longer live, but Christ lives in me"
- Romans 6:11 - "In the same way, count yourselves dead to sin but alive to God in Christ Jesus"
- Philippians 3:7-8 - "But whatever were gains to me I now consider loss for the sake of Christ"
- Colossians 3:5 - "Put to death, therefore, whatever belongs to your earthly nature"
- Romans 8:13 - "For if you live according to the flesh, you will die; but if by the Spirit you put to death the misdeeds of the body, you will live"
- 2 Corinthians 4:10-11 - "We always carry around in our body the death of Jesus, so that the life of Jesus may also be revealed in our body"
- Matthew 16:24-25 - "Whoever wants to be my disciple must deny themselves and take up their cross and follow me"
- John 12:24 - "Very truly I tell you, unless a kernel of wheat falls to the ground and dies, it remains only a single seed. But if it dies, it produces many seeds"

## Enduring Persecution

- 2 Timothy 3:12 - "In fact, everyone who wants to live a godly life in Christ Jesus will be persecuted"
- Matthew 5:10-12 - "Blessed are those who are

persecuted because of righteousness, for theirs is the kingdom of heaven"
- John 15:18-20 - "If the world hates you, keep in mind that it hated me first"
- Romans 8:35-39 - "Who shall separate us from the love of Christ? Shall trouble or hardship or persecution or famine or nakedness or danger or sword?"
- Acts 5:41 - "The apostles left the Sanhedrin, rejoicing because they had been counted worthy of suffering disgrace for the Name"
- 1 Peter 4:12-14 - "Dear friends, do not be surprised at the fiery ordeal that has come on you to test you, as though something strange were happening to you"
- 2 Corinthians 4:8-9 - "We are hard pressed on every side, but not crushed..."
- Hebrews 10:32-34 - "Remember those earlier days after you had received the light, when you endured in a great conflict full of suffering"
- James 1:2-4 - "Consider it pure joy, my brothers and sisters, whenever you face trials of many kinds"
- Revelation 2:10 - "Be faithful, even to the point of death, and I will give you life as your victor's crown"

## Rejecting Worldliness

- 1 John 2:15-17 - "Do not love the world or anything in the world..."
- Romans 12:2 - "Do not conform to the pattern of this world, but be transformed by the renewing of your mind"
- James 4:4 - "Don't you know that friendship with the world means enmity against God?"
- Titus 2:11-12 - "For the grace of God has appeared

that offers salvation to all people. It teaches us to say 'No' to ungodliness and worldly passions"
- 1 Peter 1:14 - "As obedient children, do not conform to the evil desires you had when you lived in ignorance"
- Colossians 3:2 - "Set your minds on things above, not on earthly things"
- Hebrews 11:24-26 - "By faith Moses, when he had grown up, refused to be known as the son of Pharaoh's daughter..."
- Matthew 6:19-21 - "Do not store up for yourselves treasures on earth..."
- 2 Timothy 4:10 - "For Demas, because he loved this world, has deserted me and has gone to Thessalonica"
- Philippians 3:18-20 - "Their mind is set on earthly things. But our citizenship is in heaven"

## CHAPTER 10: THE POWER OF PRAYER

**Prayer as Spiritual Warfare**

- Ephesians 6:18 - "Be alert and always keep on praying for all the Lord's people"
- 2 Corinthians 10:3-5 - "We demolish arguments and every pretension that sets itself up against the knowledge of God"
- James 5:16 - "The prayer of a righteous person is powerful and effective"
- 1 Thessalonians 5:17 - "Pray continually"
- Mark 9:29 - "This kind can come out only by prayer [and fasting]"
- Daniel 10:12-13 - Daniel's prayer and spiritual warfare
- Matthew 18:18-20 - "Truly I tell you, whatever you bind on earth will be bound in heaven, and whatever you loose on earth will be loosed in heaven"

- Jude 1:20 - "But you, dear friends, by building yourselves up in your most holy faith and praying in the Holy Spirit"
- 2 Chronicles 7:14 - "If my people, who are called by my name, will humble themselves and pray...then I will hear from heaven"
- Colossians 4:2 - "Devote yourselves to prayer, being watchful and thankful"

**Types and Approaches to Prayer**

- Matthew 6:9-13 - The Lord's Prayer model
- 1 Timothy 2:1 - "I urge, then, first of all, that petitions, prayers, intercession and thanksgiving be made for all people"
- Romans 8:26-27 - "We do not know what we ought to pray for, but the Spirit himself intercedes for us through wordless groans"
- Philippians 4:6-7 - "In every situation, by prayer and petition, with thanksgiving, present your requests to God"
- Matthew 26:41 - "The spirit is willing, but the flesh is weak"
- Mark 1:35 - "Very early in the morning, while it was still dark, Jesus got up, left the house and went off to a solitary place, where he prayed"
- Luke 6:12 - "One of those days Jesus went out to a mountainside to pray, and spent the night praying to God"
- Acts 12:5 - "So Peter was kept in prison, but the church was earnestly praying to God for him"
- James 1:5-8 - "If any of you lacks wisdom, you should ask God, who gives generously to all without finding fault, and it will be given to you"

- 1 John 5:14-15 - "This is the confidence we have in approaching God: that if we ask anything according to his will, he hears us"

**Persistent and Strategic Prayer**

- Luke 18:1-8 - The parable of the persistent widow
- Matthew 7:7-8 - "Ask and it will be given to you; seek and you will find; knock and the door will be opened to you"
- Luke 11:5-13 - The friend at midnight parable
- 1 Chronicles 16:11 - "Look to the LORD and his strength; seek his face always"
- Isaiah 62:6-7 - "I have posted watchmen on your walls, Jerusalem; they will never be silent day or night..."
- Nehemiah 1:4-11 - Nehemiah's strategic prayer for Jerusalem
- Daniel 9:3-23 - Daniel's prayer of confession and petition
- Acts 4:23-31 - The believers' prayer for boldness
- Exodus 17:8-13 - Moses' hands held up in prayer during battle
- Acts 13:1-3 - Prayer and fasting before strategic ministry decisions

**Prayers and Declarations of Faith**

- Mark 11:22-24 - "Truly I tell you, if anyone says to this mountain, 'Go, throw yourself into the sea'...it will be done for them"
- Matthew 21:22 - "If you believe, you will receive whatever you ask for in prayer"
- John 14:13-14 - "And I will do whatever you ask in my name, so that the Father may be glorified in the Son"

- James 5:14-15 - "The prayer offered in faith will make the sick person well"
- Psalm 118:17 - "I will not die but live, and will proclaim what the LORD has done"
- Psalm 91:1-16 - Declarations of God's protection
- Isaiah 54:17 - "No weapon forged against you will prevail, and you will refute every tongue that accuses you"
- Joshua 1:8 - "Keep this Book of the Law always on your lips…"
- Romans 4:17 - "the God who gives life to the dead and calls into being things that were not"
- Numbers 14:28 - "What you have said in my hearing I will do to you"

## CHAPTER 11: THE WARRIOR'S DEEPEST SECRET: PRESENCE BEFORE POWER

**Abiding in Christ**

- John 15:4-5 - "Remain in me, as I also remain in you"
- Psalm 27:4 - "One thing I ask from the LORD, this only do I seek: that I may dwell in the house of the LORD all the days of my life"
- Psalm 16:11 - "You make known to me the path of life; you will fill me with joy in your presence, with eternal pleasures at your right hand"
- Psalm 91:1 - "Whoever dwells in the shelter of the Most High will rest in the shadow of the Almighty"
- Luke 10:38-42 - Mary choosing to sit at Jesus' feet while Martha was distracted
- John 14:23 - "Anyone who loves me will obey my teaching. My Father will love them, and we will come to them and make our home with them"

- 1 John 2:28 - "And now, dear children, continue in him, so that when he appears we may be confident and unashamed before him at his coming"
- Colossians 2:6-7 - "So then, just as you received Christ Jesus as Lord, continue to live your lives in him"
- Galatians 2:20 - "I have been crucified with Christ and I no longer live, but Christ lives in me"
- James 4:8 - "Come near to God and he will come near to you"

**Seeking His Presence**

- Jeremiah 29:13 - "You will seek me and find me when you seek me with all your heart"
- 2 Chronicles 16:9 - "For the eyes of the Lord range throughout the earth to strengthen those whose hearts are fully committed to him"
- Psalm 42:1-2 - "As the deer pants for streams of water, so my soul pants for you, my God"
- Exodus 33:14-15 - "If your Presence does not go with us, do not send us up from here"
- Psalm 73:25-26 - "Whom have I in heaven but you? And earth has nothing I desire besides you"
- Isaiah 55:6 - "Seek the Lord while he may be found; call on him while he is near"
- Deuteronomy 4:29 - "But if from there you seek the Lord your God, you will find him if you seek him with all your heart and with all your soul"
- Hebrews 11:6 - "And without faith it is impossible to please God..."
- 1 Chronicles 22:19 - "Now devote your heart and soul to seeking the Lord your God"
- Matthew 6:33 - "But seek first his kingdom and his righteousness, and all these things will be given to you as well"

## Spiritual Disciplines for Presence

- Matthew 6:6 - "But when you pray, go into your room, close the door and pray to your Father, who is unseen"
- Psalm 119:15 - "I meditate on your precepts and consider your ways"
- Mark 1:35 - "Very early in the morning, while it was still dark, Jesus got up, left the house and went off to a solitary place, where he prayed"
- Psalm 1:1-3 - "Blessed is the one…whose delight is in the law of the Lord, and who meditates on his law day and night"
- Luke 5:16 - "But Jesus often withdrew to lonely places and prayed"
- Joshua 1:8 - "Keep this Book of the Law always on your lips; meditate on it day and night"
- 1 Thessalonians 5:16-18 - "Rejoice always, pray continually, give thanks in all circumstances"
- Colossians 3:16 - "Let the message of Christ dwell among you richly"
- Habakkuk 2:20 - "The Lord is in his holy temple; let all the earth be silent before him"
- Psalm 46:10 - "Be still, and know that I am God"

## Transformation in His Presence

- 2 Corinthians 3:18 - "And we all, who with unveiled faces contemplate the Lord's glory, are being transformed into his image with ever-increasing glory"
- Romans 12:2 - "Do not conform to the pattern of this world, but be transformed by the renewing of your mind"
- Psalm 84:10 - "Better is one day in your courts than a thousand elsewhere"

- Exodus 34:29 - "He was not aware that his face was radiant because he had spoken with the Lord"
- Philippians 3:10 - "I want to know Christ—yes, to know the power of his resurrection and participation in his sufferings"
- Isaiah 40:31 - "But those who hope in the Lord will renew their strength. They will soar on wings like eagles"
- Acts 4:13 - "When they saw the courage of Peter and John and realized that they were unschooled, ordinary men, they were astonished and they took note that these men had been with Jesus"
- 2 Peter 1:3-4 - "His divine power has given us everything we need for a godly life through our knowledge of him"
- Psalm 34:5 - "Those who look to him are radiant; their faces are never covered with shame"
- 1 John 3:2 - "We know that when Christ appears, we shall be like him, for we shall see him as he is"

## CHAPTER 12: DEVELOPING THE KINGDOM WARRIOR MINDSET

**Renewing the Mind**

- Romans 12:2 - "Do not conform to the pattern of this world, but be transformed by the renewing of your mind"
- Philippians 4:8 - "If anything is excellent or praiseworthy—think about such things"
- 2 Corinthians 10:5 - "We take captive every thought to make it obedient to Christ"
- Ephesians 4:22-24 - "You were taught, with regard to your former way of life, to put off your old self...to be made new in the attitude of your minds"

- Colossians 3:2 - "Set your minds on things above, not on earthly things"
- Isaiah 26:3 - "You will keep in perfect peace those whose minds are steadfast, because they trust in you"
- Proverbs 4:23 - "Above all else, guard your heart, for everything you do flows from it"
- Romans 8:5-6 - "But those who live in accordance with the Spirit have their minds set on what the Spirit desires"
- 1 Corinthians 2:16 - "But we have the mind of Christ"
- Philippians 2:5 - "In your relationships with one another, have the same mindset as Christ Jesus"

## Faith and Confidence

- 2 Timothy 1:7 - "For the Spirit God gave us does not make us timid, but gives us power, love and self-discipline"
- Hebrews 11:1 - "Now faith is confidence in what we hope for and assurance about what we do not see"
- 1 John 5:4 - "For everyone born of God overcomes the world. This is the victory that has overcome the world, even our faith"
- Mark 11:22-24 - "Have faith in God...Truly I tell you, if anyone says to this mountain, 'Go, throw yourself into the sea...'"
- 2 Corinthians 5:7 - "For we live by faith, not by sight"
- Romans 4:18-21 - "Against all hope, Abraham in hope believed...being fully persuaded that God had power to do what he had promised"
- Ephesians 6:16 - "In addition to all this, take up the shield of faith, with which you can extinguish all the flaming arrows of the evil one"

- James 1:6 - "But when you ask, you must believe and not doubt, because the one who doubts is like a wave of the sea"
- Matthew 17:20 - "If you have faith as small as a mustard seed, you can say to this mountain, 'Move from here to there,' and it will move"
- Romans 10:17 - "Consequently, faith comes from hearing the message, and the message is heard through the word about Christ"

**Perseverance and Endurance**

- Hebrews 12:1-3 - "Let us run with perseverance the race marked out for us, fixing our eyes on Jesus"
- James 1:2-4 - "Consider it pure joy, my brothers and sisters, whenever you face trials of many kinds...so that you may be mature and complete"
- Romans 5:3-5 - "Not only so, but we also glory in our sufferings, because we know that suffering produces perseverance"
- 2 Timothy 2:3 - "Join with me in suffering, like a good soldier of Christ Jesus"
- Galatians 6:9 - "Let us not become weary in doing good, for at the proper time we will reap a harvest if we do not give up"
- 1 Corinthians 9:24-27 - "Everyone who competes in the games goes into strict training...to get a crown that will last forever"
- Philippians 3:13-14 - "Forgetting what is behind and straining toward what is ahead, I press on toward the goal"
- 2 Timothy 4:7-8 - "I have fought the good fight, I have finished the race, I have kept the faith"
- Hebrews 10:36 - "You need to persevere so that when

you have done the will of God, you will receive what he has promised"
- Revelation 2:10 - "Be faithful, even to the point of death, and I will give you life as your victor's crown"

**Kingdom Perspective**

- Matthew 6:33 - "But seek first his kingdom and his righteousness, and all these things will be given to you as well"
- 2 Corinthians 4:16-18 - "For our light and momentary troubles are achieving for us an eternal glory that far outweighs them all"
- Colossians 3:1-2 - "Since, then, you have been raised with Christ, set your hearts on things above, where Christ is..."
- Philippians 3:20 - "But our citizenship is in heaven. And we eagerly await a Savior from there, the Lord Jesus Christ"
- Matthew 6:19-21 - "Do not store up for yourselves treasures on earth...But store up for yourselves treasures in heaven"
- Romans 14:17 - "For the kingdom of God is not a matter of eating and drinking, but of righteousness, peace and joy in the Holy Spirit"
- Luke 17:20-21 - "The kingdom of God is in your midst"
- 1 John 2:15-17 - "The world and its desires pass away, but whoever does the will of God lives forever"
- Hebrews 11:13-16 - "They were longing for a better country—a heavenly one"
- Revelation 21:1-5 - "Then I saw 'a new heaven and a new earth'...He will wipe every tear from their eyes"

# CHAPTER 13: KINGDOM WARRIORS: ALERT TO ANGELIC ENCOUNTERS

**Ministering Angels**

- Hebrews 1:14 - "Are not all angels ministering spirits sent to serve those who will inherit salvation?"
- John 1:51 - "You will see 'heaven open, and the angels of God ascending and descending on' the Son of Man"
- Daniel 10:12-13 - The angel's message that Daniel's prayers were heard from the first day
- Acts 10:30-31 - Cornelius' angelic visitation during prayer
- 1 Kings 19:5-8 - "Then he lay down under the bush and fell asleep. All at once an angel touched him and said, 'Get up and eat'"
- Acts 8:26 - "An angel of the Lord said to Philip, 'Go south to the road—the desert road—that goes down from Jerusalem to Gaza'"
- Daniel 6:22 - "My God sent his angel, and he shut the mouths of the lions"
- Acts 12:7 - "Suddenly an angel of the Lord appeared and a light shone in the cell"
- Matthew 4:11 - "Angels came and attended him"

**Angels as Warriors and Guides**

- Psalm 91:11-12 - "For he will command his angels concerning you to guard you in all your ways"
- Genesis 19 - Angels leading Lot and his family from Sodom
- Luke 22:43 - "An angel from heaven appeared to [Jesus] and strengthened him"
- Daniel 8-9 - Gabriel bringing revelation to Daniel

- Luke 1 - Gabriel announcing the births of John the Baptist and Jesus
- Acts 8:26 - Angel instructing Philip where to go
- Acts 10:3-6 - Angel directing Cornelius to send for Peter
- Hebrews 13:2 - "For by so doing some people have shown hospitality to angels without knowing it"
- Daniel 10 - Three-week delay in answered prayer due to spiritual warfare
- Revelation 12:7-9 - Michael and his angels fighting against Satan and his angels

**Angels as Servants**

- Acts 12 - Angel orchestrating Peter's prison escape
- Matthew 28 - Angels at Christ's resurrection communicating with the women
- 1 Kings 19:5-8 - Angels bringing food to Elijah in the wilderness
- Psalm 78:25 - Reference to manna as "the bread of angels"
- 2 Kings 19:35 - Angel striking down 185,000 Assyrian soldiers
- Acts 5:19 - Angels supernaturally opening prison doors for the apostles
- 2 Corinthians 11:14 - "Satan himself masquerades as an angel of light"
- Galatians 1:8 - "Even if we or an angel from heaven should preach a gospel other than the one we preached to you, let them be under God's curse!"
- Revelation 19:10 and 22:9 - Angels refusing worship
- Psalm 91:11 - "For he will command his angels concerning you to guard you in all your ways"

# CHAPTER 14: THE AWAKENING: BEYOND ROUTINE FAITH

**Authentic Holy Spirit Transformation**

- 1 Thessalonians 5:16-18 - "Rejoice always, pray continually, give thanks in all circumstances; for this is God's will for you in Christ Jesus"
- John 15 - The vine and the branches
- 2 Timothy 3:2-5 - "Having a form of godliness but denying its power"
- John 10:10 - "I have come that they may have life, and have it to the full"
- Matthew 17:20 - Description of mountain-moving faith
- 2 Corinthians 3:18 - "Being transformed into his image with ever-increasing glory"
- Galatians 5:22-23 - Fruit of the Spirit
- Romans 12:2 - "Transformed by the renewing of your mind"
- 2 Corinthians 5:17 - "If anyone is in Christ, the new creation has come: The old has gone, the new is here!"
- Philippians 2:13 - "It is God who works in you to will and to act in order to fulfill his good purpose"
- Zechariah 4:6 - "'Not by might nor by power, but by my Spirit'"
- Acts 2 - The power of Pentecost

# CHAPTER 15: THE DIVINE SCREENING

**Divine Providence and Human Choice**

- 2 Peter 3:8-10 - "The day of the Lord will come like a thief...and the earth and everything done in it will be laid bare"

- Revelation 20:11 - Description of the great white throne of judgment
- Mark 8:36 - "What good is it for someone to gain the whole world, yet forfeit their soul?"
- 1 John 2:15-16 - "If anyone loves the world, love for the Father is not in them"
- Luke 16:19-31 - The story of the rich man and Lazarus
- Psalm 90:12 - "Teach us to number our days, that we may gain a heart of wisdom."
- 2 Corinthians 5:9-10 - "So we make it our goal to please him...For we must all appear before the judgment seat of Christ..."
- Ephesians 2:8-9 - "For it is by grace you have been saved, through faith..."

## CHAPTER 16: A CALL TO KINGDOM WARRIORS

### Jesus' Life Relaunch

- Mark 8:34 - "Whoever wants to be my disciple must deny themselves and take up their cross and follow me"
- John 10:10 - "The thief comes only to steal and kill and destroy; I have come that they may have life, and have it to the full"
- Hebrews 12:2 - "Jesus, the pioneer and perfecter of faith"
- Matthew 28:19-20 - The Great Commission
- 2 Corinthians 5:17-21 - "God made him who had no sin to be sin for us, so that in him we might become the righteousness of God"
- Ephesians 6:10-18 - Spiritual warfare and the armor of God

## Epilogue

- Hebrews 12:2 - "The pioneer and perfecter of faith"
- Revelation 19:16 - "King of Kings and Lord of Lords"
- Genesis 50:20 - "You intended to harm me, but God intended it for good"
- Isaiah 61:3 - "Beauty instead of ashes, the oil of joy instead of mourning"

# Notes

## Introduction
1. Charles H. Spurgeon, "The Church of Christ," Sermon delivered at the Metropolitan Tabernacle, Newington, 1861.

## 1. The Creation of All Things
1. Abraham Lincoln, letter to Thurlow Weed, March 15, 1865.

## 2. The Unseen Cosmic Battle
1. C.S. Lewis, *The Screwtape Letters*, HarperOne, 2001 (Originally published 1942).
2. Warren Wiersbe, *The Bumps Are What You Climb On: Encouragement for Difficult Days*, Baker Books, 1980.

## 4. The Origin and Nature of Demons
1. Remy de Gourmont, *The Angels of Perversity*, Dedalus/Hippocrene, 1992.

## 5. The Father of Lies
1. Charles Baudelaire, "The Generous Gambler *[Le Joueur généreux]*," *Le Spleen de Paris (Petits Poèmes en Prose)*, No. 29, (1869) [tr. Edward K. Kaplan (1989)].
2. William Cowper, "God Moves in a Mysterious Way," *Olney Hymns*, 1779.

## 6. Derailing the Kingdom Adventure
1. This quote has been attributed to Billy Graham in many sources. However, the original work in which Billy Graham first used the phrase is currently unknown.

## 7. Subtle Poison
1. This quote has been attributed to Booker T. Washington in many sources.

However, the original work in which Booker T. Washington first used the phrase is currently unknown.

## 9. Kingdom Warriors Stand for Truth

1. Jackie Hill Perry, *Gay Girl, Good God*, B&H Books, 2018.
2. Nabeel Qureshi, *Seeking Allah, Finding Jesus*, Zondervan, 2014.
3. Oswald Chambers, *My Utmost for His Highest: Updated Edition*, Discovery House Publishers, 1992 (Originally published 1935).

## 10. The Power of Prayer

1. E.M. Bounds, *Power Through Prayer*, Baker Books, 2007 (Originally published 1907).
2. Oswald Chambers, *My Utmost for His Highest: Updated Edition*, Discovery House Publishers, 1992 (Originally published 1935).
3. Anne Lamott, *Traveling Mercies: Some Thoughts on Faith*, Knopf Doubleday Publishing Group, 2000.
4. Oswald Chambers, *My Utmost for His Highest*, Discovery House Publishers, 1992 (Originally published 1935).

## 11. The Warrior's Deepest Secret

1. Rick Warren, *The Purpose Driven Life*, Zondervan, 2002.
2. Brother Lawrence and Joseph de Beaufort, *The Practice of the Presence of God*, Whitaker House, 1982.

## 12. Developing the Kingdom Warrior Mindset

1. This quote is popularly attributed to Marcus Aurelius and is probably an inexact, modernized translation of his ideas in Book IV, Section 3 of his *Meditations*.

## 13. Kingdom Warriors

1. St. Augustine of Hippo, *Enarrationes in Psalmos [Exposition on the Book of Psalms]*, 103, 1, 15: PL 37, 1348.

## 14. The Awakening

1. Willard, Dallas, *The Divine Conspiracy*, HarperOne, 1998.

## 15. The Divine Screening

1. This quote has been attributed to Booker T. Washington in many sources. However, the original work in which Booker T. Washington first used the phrase is currently unknown.

# Bibliography

## Biblical References

All biblical references are from the New International Version (NIV) unless otherwise noted.

## Literary Works and Quotations

Aurelius, Marcus. *Meditations.* Translated by Gregory Hays, Modern Library, 2002.
Baudelaire, Charles. "The Generous Gambler *[Le Joueur généreux]*." *Le Spleen de Paris (Petits Poèmes en Prose),* No. 29, 1869. Translated by Edward K. Kaplan, 1989.
Bounds, E.M. *Power Through Prayer.* Baker Books, 2007 (Originally published 1907).
Chambers, Oswald. *My Utmost for His Highest.* Discovery House Publishers, 1992 (Originally published 1935).
Cowper, William. "God Moves in a Mysterious Way." *Olney Hymns,* 1779.
de Gourmont, Remy. *The Angels of Perversity.* Dedalus/Hippocrene, 1992.
Hippo, St. Augustine of. *Enarrationes in Psalmos [Exposition on the Book of Psalms].* written between the years 392–422.
Lawrence, Brother and Joseph de Beaufort, *The Practice of the Presence of God.* Whitaker House, 1982 (Originally published 1692).
Lewis, C.S. *The Screwtape Letters.* HarperOne, 2001 (Originally published 1942).
Lincoln, Abraham. Letter to Thurlow Weed, March 15, 1865.
Spurgeon, Charles H. "The Church of Christ," Sermon delivered at the Metropolitan Tabernacle. Newington, 1861.
Wiersbe, Warren. *The Bumps Are What You Climb On: Encouragement for Difficult Days.* Baker Books, 1980.
Willard, Dallas. *The Divine Conspiracy.* HarperOne, 1998.

## Modern References and Influences

Hill Perry, Jackie. *Gay Girl, Good God.* B&H Books, 2018.
Lamott, Anne. *Traveling Mercies: Some Thoughts on Faith.* Knopf Doubleday Publishing Group, 2000.
Qureshi, Nabeel. *Seeking Allah, Finding Jesus.* Zondervan, 2014.
Warren, Rick. *The Purpose Driven Life.* Zondervan, 2002.

## Additional Resources

Life Relaunch Ministry. *Life Relaunch Experience Curriculum and Resources.* www.liferelaunch.org

## Note on Personal Testimonies

Many of the narratives and testimonies included in this book are based on personal experiences of the authors, Mel and Annie Goebel, as well as individuals they have encountered through their ministry work. Names and certain details may have been changed to protect privacy while preserving the essential truth of these experiences.

# About the Authors

**MEL GOEBEL** Mel Goebel's journey from prison inmate to ministry leader demonstrates the transformative power of God's grace. After a troubled youth marked by poor choices and addiction that led to two prison terms, Mel experienced a supernatural encounter with an angel in his prison cell that forever changed the trajectory of his life.

Upon his release, Mel dedicated himself to studying God's Word and serving others. He founded The Library of Hope, which has placed thousands of inspirational books in prisons across America. His firsthand understanding of spiritual captivity and freedom gives him unique insight into the unseen cosmic battle that shapes our lives.

Mel's testimony has inspired audiences across the country, from churches to corporate settings. His straightforward, authentic teaching style breaks down complex spiritual principles into practical applications that resonate with people from all walks of life.

**ANNIE GOEBEL** Annie Goebel's path to ministry began in a turbulent childhood within a military family. The instability of frequent moves combined with her father's struggles with alcohol created an environment where Annie learned early to fend for herself. After running away from home as a teenager and experiencing the consequences of her own destructive choices, Annie found herself at a breaking point in the Black Hills of South Dakota.

It was there, under the stars, that Annie surrendered her life to Jesus and began the journey of restoration that would eventually lead her to ministry. With a heart particularly attuned to those trapped in addiction and despair, Annie brings compassion and wisdom born from her own painful experiences.

Annie's gift for communicating complex spiritual truths with clarity and warmth complements Mel's teaching style. Together, they lead Life Relaunch, a ministry dedicated to helping individuals break free from spiritual captivity and step into their God-given purpose as Kingdom Warriors.

**TOGETHER IN MINISTRY** Mel and Annie's unique ministry partnership began after God miraculously brought them together in their shared passion for setting captives free. Married since 2015, they travel extensively, conducting Life Relaunch Experiences that have transformed thousands of lives.

Their approach combines solid biblical teaching with practical application and spiritual activation. Having both experienced dramatic life transformations through Jesus Christ, they bring authenticity and authority to their message of spiritual warfare and kingdom advancement.

The Goebels currently reside in Florida, where they continue to develop resources and train leaders for the Life Relaunch movement while remaining actively involved in their church, prison ministry, addiction recovery programs, homes where Life Relaunch is being conducted, and other people groups.

For more information about Life Relaunch or to contact Mel and Annie, visit **www.liferelaunch.org**.

Made in the USA
Las Vegas, NV
03 July 2025

24365998R00174